Bravo, Stanley!

The Racing History of Stanley
and the
1906 Stanley Land Speed Record

H. James Merrick

Published by the Stanley Museum, Inc.

© 2006 Stanley Museum, Inc.

Bravo, Stanley!
by H. James Merrick

For further information, contact
The Stanley Museum, PO Box 77, Kingfield, Maine 04947
Telephone: 207-265-2729 Facsimile: 207-265-4700
E-mail: maine@stanleymuseum.org

First Edition (limited to 1,000 copies)

Library of Congress Cataloguing-in-Publication Data

Merrick, H. James
  Bravo, Stanley! : the racing history of Stanley and the 1906 Stanley land speed record / H. James Merrick.
    p. cm.
  Includes bibliographical references and index.
  ISBN 1-886727-11-2
  1. Stanley Steamer automobile–History. 2. Automobiles, steam–History. 3. Automobile racing–United States. I. Title.

TL200.M47 2006
629.222'2–dc22

2005057573

Acknowledgements

The author wishes to express his gratitude for assistance received from all the research facilities and libraries he consulted during the research phase of this work. I particularly wish to thank Henry Scannell, Uma Murthy, David Petersante and the research staff of the Boston Public Library, Boston, Mass.; Charles Lakin and the reference staff of the Miller Library, Colby College, Waterville, Me.; and the microfilm department at the Maine State Library in Augusta, Me. Access to historic newspaper databases and microfilm provided by these libraries was of great assistance to the research for this book.

I am also indebted to the automotive historians who graciously read the hastily written draft of this book and made a number of helpful comments and suggestions, particularly Dick and Yvonne Punnett, and Kit Foster. I was privileged to work with Mr. Foster for several years during which time he was conducting research for his book, *The Stanley Steamer: America's Legendary Steam Car* (Kingfield, Me.: Stanley Museum, c2004), and a large portion of the research and the new discoveries found during that effort have found their way into this expanded work on the Ormond Beach events. I wish to thank ophthalmologist James R. Putnam, MD, of Waterville, Me., for sharing his special knowledge of eye trauma in clarifying the mystery of Marriott's Eye.

We all owe a great deal of debt to Raymond W. Stanley, who amassed a fascinating and important collection of newspaper clippings, photographs, and other archival resources relating to the speed contests at Ormond/Daytona, and to his son, Francis Stanley, who had the foresight to preserve his father's collection and donate the Raymond W. Stanley Archive to the Stanley Museum. I also wish to thank my colleagues on the Staff of the Stanley Museum, past and present, without whose assistance this work would not have been possible.

We also wish to express our gratitude for the support of Stanley Museum trustee D. Howard Randall, Jr., and the Randall Family for their generous contribution to the publication of this book in honor of their father, Donald H. Randall. Randall, a noted Stanley collector and historian, first proposed and pressed for the commemoration of the Stanley Land Speed Record some fifty years ago at the semicentenary of the event. Howard remembers vividly going to Fred Marriott in 1955 with his father Donald to enlist Fred's support in celebrating this historic event.

Without question I could not have endured and produced this work without the support of my family, my wife, Sandra, and my two young daughters who are convinced that there is (or was) no finer car in existence than the Stanley steamer. We should all be blessed with smart children.

H. J. Merrick
Mount Vernon, Maine

Dedication

In memory of my grandfather, Hubert J. Merrick (1875-1961), of Waterville, Maine. An independent Maine Yankee, a lover of poetry and mathematics, the first in his generation to leave the farm, attend college, and set up shop on his own as a merchant. One of the first in the family to learn to drive a car (he grew up just a few blocks away from Newton Stanley's garage and Stanley dealership in Waterville), it is not known for certain whether he learned to drive on Stanleys but later on he was never fond of driving gasoline-explosive cars.

Table of Contents

Preface

Few automotive marques enjoy the iconic stature of the Stanley. Visitors to the Stanley Museum marvel. Stanleys on the road elicit gasps of recognition. The response, "That's a STANLEY!?" is common. Add the eponymy of the words, Stanley Steamer—even Stanley steam car—to a history that borders on mythological, and the picture takes shape.

For the Stanley's 25 years of presence in the marketplace, it would be hard to identify any one event responsible for this stature. But one above all others pushes the Stanley to that mark: the 1906 land speed record of 127.659 mph. In an era when records fell by the day, if not the hour, this one lasted four years, and even then was only beaten by four miles an hour. It was also the only American automobile to successfully challenge the European juggernaut of Napiers, Darracqs, Mercedes, and Fiats.

As if that record wasn't enough, the crash of the Stanley the following year, trying to break its own record in 1907, generated more legend. "The Stanley brothers would give a steam car to anyone who dared to open up the throttle." (You run out of steam if you do.) "No one ever found out how fast the Stanley would go because no one ever dared to open the throttle." (Same.) "The Stanley flew through the air farther than the Wright Brothers at Kitty Hawk." (Only the front end of the Stanley came off the ground when it crashed.) Perhaps you know some stories yourself.

For nearly ten years, the Stanley Museum has been celebrating centennials of the iconic Stanley. In 1997, it was the centennial of its first steam car in Newton, Mass. In 1999, it was the centennial of F.O. and Flora Stanley driving the first automobile, a Stanley-designed Locomobile steam car, to the top of the Mt. Washington Carriage Road in the White Mountains of New Hampshire, still today the world's most challenging mountain road. In 2004, it was the centennial of the Stanleys, with its $750 6 hp Stanley, defeating all but an $18,000 60 hp Mercedes up that same mountain road in the first Climb to the Clouds race.

Without question, the 2006 centennial of the Stanley land speed record is the granddaddy of all centennials. Author and Stanley Museum archivist Jim Merrrick tells us more here than any book to date. It also straightens out a few myths, and gives us details and background never before revealed. My favorite is the length to which the American and European automotive industry went to deny the Stanley its place in competition and in history. This book, timed to this centennial, intends to write back into history, once and for all, one of the most astonishing automotive records of all time.

Susan S. Davis
Stanley Museum, Publisher.

Foreword

Very good things can come from very small places. My wife and I found this out when a chance acquaintance (a true museum-going fanatic) told us of the existence of a Stanley Museum located in tiny Kingfield, Maine. This was in the days before the omniscient and googled internet, when serendipity was almost a necessity for successful research. At that time we were searching for information about the noted Stanley twins, progenitors of the unique Stanley Steamers of early automotive fame, and it had never occurred to us that a museum might exist to celebrate their innovative cars.

Celebrate is an apt word. The Stanley Museum is also a publishing house, and in these last several years it has produced two important and definitive books about Stanley Steamers that cast new light on pioneer automotive history. This book, *Bravo, Stanley*, is the second one and touches on that bizarre venue, the long wide Ormond/Daytona Beach, once an auto racecourse of international fame.

The Stanley Steamers raced on this beach from 1903 to 1907, and author H. James Merrick traces their triumphs and tragedies in fascinating detail. Jim is surely a devotee of the old canard that truth is stranger than fiction, because *Bravo, Stanley* adds new insight and well documented stories to beach racing lore. Just as one example, I had tried for some time to run down more extensive information on the two Stanley "Vanderbilt" Specials, so called because they were originally built to race in the Vanderbilt race of 1906. They were brought to the beach in 1907 but remained vaguely in the background until Jim Merrick's intensive research brought them to life in this book.

One last note about the Stanley Museum. If at all possible, make a pilgrimage to Kingfield. Our trek there was adventurous and surprising, and the main surprise remains that the president of the technically oriented Stanley Museum, Susan S. Davis, is a lady of uncommon energy and versatility. She belongs in that category of successful modern lady executives, and one of her best decisions was the recruitment of researcher and author, H. James Merrick.

Dick Punnett
Ormond Beach, Florida

Introduction

by H. James Merrick

Imagine, if you will, that you are driving down a highway at about 70-75 mph with a wooden canoe strapped to the top of your car. Something goes wrong – a knot slips, a strap breaks, something – and you lose the canoe. It goes sailing off the car and makes a tumbling, un-canoe-like dance across the pavement, finally coming to rest smashed and broken. To any admirer or collector of vintage canoes a true nightmare, but one which most people can at least visualize.

Now imagine the same scenario only you are traveling twice as fast – 140-150 mph – and once again, the canoe goes flying off out of control, only this time, imagine that you are sitting inside the canoe when this happens. A true nightmare for anyone, to be sure, but perhaps as close as anyone can come to appreciating the situation Fred Marriott found himself in at the time of his spectacular crash at Ormond Beach, Florida, on January 25, 1907.

Marriott first ventured to Florida in 1906, 100 years ago, as a crew member on the Stanley Motor Carriage Company's racing team. The company was founded by the Stanley Brothers, identical twins and a fascinating pair of Maine Yankees who had, late in life, tossed their hats into the ring of early automobile manufacturers. The brothers had designed a practical vehicle using steam power in 1897, and had focused their own personal efforts into making fast cars. In 1906 the company was making its first official entry into the speed tournaments on the Florida beach. The Stanleys had built a special aerodynamic steam-powered racer,

designed to break the existing mile record, and Marriott, the foreman of the company's repair department, had been tapped to drive the car. On Friday, January 26, 1906, Marriott exceeded even the Stanley Brothers' most optimistic projections, setting a new World's Land Speed Record of 127.66 mph, the first time any motor car had traveled more than two miles a minute.

This book is devoted to the history of the record-breaking exploits of Fred Marriott and the Stanley team at the Ormond/Daytona Beach races in 1906 and 1907. First-hand accounts based on diaries, letters, early newspaper clippings and other sources have been used to present the story, supplemented by later recollections and analysis of photographs and reconstructed racing sequences and results. Background history on both the Ormond Beach races and biographical information on the Stanleys and other participants have been added to fill out the story. Technical data on the Stanley racer and its unique, canoe-derived body have been included when found in the literature of the period; a full-bore engineering reconstruction and analysis of the capabilities of the Stanley racer, without actual records to go on, is beyond the scope of this book.

The triumphs and tribulations of Fred Marriott and the Stanley team at the Ormond/Daytona Beach races have become as much legend as history over the years, presenting historians with some fascinating quandaries. Some of the principle characters in this book, it turns out, were great storytellers; still others were those with great stories to tell. With so many colorful and compelling stories, it is often difficult to tell which is which, and when to focus on strictly documented events at the risk of shortchanging the reader.

A case in point: Raymond Stanley, the son of F.E. Stanley, tells a wonderful story of an impromptu race on the beach during which he sat at his father's side, at age eleven certainly one of the youngest "mechanicians" in Ormond history. Raymond had been left at home in Newton, Massachusetts, at the onset of the 1906 races, as it was deemed more important for him to continue his schooling uninterrupted. His father, apparently realizing that he was about to make racing history and that it might be worthwhile for his son to experience it first-hand, relented and sent for his son who arrived two days before the races began. Raymond later recalled this story when discussing the history of the Stanleys' special Vanderbilt racers:

"About this same time two special Stanleys were built to compete in the Vanderbilt Cup Race. Though they never competed in that event, they both established great records as racers. It was in one of these cars that I rode with my father at Daytona Beach in 1906 when we struck up a race with Walter Christie, who was driving one of his famous front-wheeled racers. We were traveling along faster than I had ever ridden before and rapidly overtaking Christie, who was quite a bit ahead. There was no windshield on the car and I had no goggles on. Each grain of sand thrown up by the tires of the Christie car seemed to hit me right in the face. I covered my face with both hands, but even so it looked like a raw beet when we finished. We beat the Christie soundly, but I never saw much of the race. I was quite cool to offers to ride in a racing car after that." (R. W. Stanley, 1945: p.20).

Such is the lot of the historian to ponder the discrepancies of intriguing first-hand stories which do not quite fit the facts. The Vanderbilt cars, of which Raymond speaks, were not built until May 1906, four months after the end of the 1906 Ormond races, and did not see action on the beach until the 1907 tournament. Raymond Stanley did not accompany his parents to Ormond in 1907, and could not have raced in one of the Vanderbilt cars at that time. Neither could J. Walter Christie have been involved, for he, too, did not attend the 1907 Ormond races. If the event took place as Raymond recalled, it could only have happened in 1906, and could not have involved the Vanderbilt cars. It may be that F.E. and his son got involved in an impromptu race with Christie while driving the Stanley Model H "Gentlemen's Speedy Roadster" which was one of the cars available, and capable, of making such a race on the beach in 1906. Raymond, however, continued to refer to the car as one of the Vanderbilt racers some 40 years later, in oral history interviews recorded not long before his death. (R. W. Stanley 1984). The discrepancy remains unresolved.

Not so is the overall story of Fred Marriott and the Stanley Land Speed Record. Auto racing history is rich with tales of victories and failures, but Marriott's story is particularly fascinating as he lived to experience spectacular examples of both. As for Marriott's celebrated accident, it is a peculiarity of motor racing that failure, in the guise of an horrific crash, can itself be achievement, in the event of a miraculous survival. Marriott is one of the fortunate ones for whom failure became achievement and disaster became victory – especially for the historians, who revel in the unexpected circumstance that he lived to tell the tale.

Bravo, Stanley!

Ormond/Daytona Beach, Florida, January 1906. *The beach is shown here at low tide, wide, smooth and virtually flat - near perfect conditions for racing. Auto racing here from 1903 to 1910 established this course as the fastest in the world, giving weight to its later claim as the "Birthplace of Speed."*

Larz Anderson Auto Museum.

CHAPTER ONE

"Stanley Will Win."

AS THE YEAR 1905 drew to a close, the American public's fascination with speed and automobiles was naturally drawn to the upcoming Ormond/Daytona Beach races in Florida, where world record times were in the offering. The previous year's tournament had seen earlier records shattered on the smooth, hard-packed sands of the beach, and there was a real possibility that the unheard-of speed of two-miles-a-minute might even be reached.

Fueling the intense interest were reports that many of the fastest cars and daredevil drivers from Europe were planning to come to Florida to compete for the speed prizes for the first time. There were even rumors of a special steam-powered racer in the works at the Stanley factory in Massachusetts, built only for speed and only for Ormond. Could the fantastic speeds be reached without tearing the machines apart? No one knew for sure, but there was only one way to find out...

SUNDAY, OCTOBER 29, 1905
(NEW YORK):

FLORIDA AUTO RACES CALL FOR HIGH SPEED.

Winning Car in Two-Mile Event Must Equal 120 Miles an Hour.

CONTESTS FOR ALL CLASSES.

Sport Will Begin Jan. 22 at Ormond Beach, and Continue One Week.

Nineteen events for the Florida coast races on the Ormond beach have been arranged by the officials of the Florida East Coast Automobile Association. The racing will begin Jan. 22 and will be continued through the week. The contests include five one-mile events, one for kilometer records, one at two miles, four at five miles, four at ten miles, two at fifteen miles, one, a free-for-all championship for American cars, at thirty miles, and a one-hundred-mile event for all cars for the big free-for-all championship cup. The Dewar Cup for the world's one-mile championship will be competed for a second time and a new trophy has been added known as the Minneapolis Cup, donated by the Minneapolis Automobile Club which is the home club of Asa Paine, the new President of the Florida East Coast Automobile Association.

The events provide for all weights and powers. The two-mile race is a decided novelty in that it stipulates that the winning car must equal or exceed *[120]* miles an hour. This will be at the rate of a mile in half a minute, a feat that has never been accomplished, even under the excep-

tional racing conditions that the Florida beach affords. The best time ever made there is 32 4-5 seconds for the mile by H. L. Bowden's 120 horse power Mercedes. Some fast racing cars, however, are being prepared to win the two-mile record cup, and it will be a decided triumph in automobile racing speed if the excessive rate demanded to take the cup is maintained.

(*New York Times, 10/29/1905, p.12.*)

SUNDAY, NOVEMBER 19, 1905
(NEW YORK):

The revised programme of events for the fourth annual Ormond-Daytona automobile races to be held on the Florida beach during the week beginning Jan. 22 has just been issued by W. J. Morgan. In all twenty-seven events are scheduled. There will be two special championships for steam cars, at one and five miles respectively, and events have been arranged for steam cars in the mile and kilometer trials. No entries have yet been made for the two-mile a minute race, but Mr. Morgan has been assured that more than one car will be prepared to try for that unusual record. The entries will close Jan. 8, with Mr. Morgan at 116 Nassau Street.

(*New York Times, 11/19/1905, p.13.*)

SUNDAY, JANUARY 7, 1906
(NEWTON, MASS.):

Frank took out his racer, & I scolded him unmercifully for doing it on Sunday.

(*Augusta Stanley, Diary 1906.*)

WEDNESDAY, JANUARY 10, 1906
(NEW YORK):

WORLD'S FASTEST AUTOS
TO RACE AT ORMOND.

Ten Cars Ready to Try
for Two Miles in One Minute.

FOUR NATIONS REPRESENTED.

America Has Ten of the Twenty-two Machines Entered
for Florida Contests – Few Amateurs.

Twenty-two racing automobiles, representing four nations – France, Italy, England, and America – have been entered for the speed contests on the Ormond-Daytona beach, Florida, beginning on Jan. 22. These cars include some of the fastest and most celebrated racing machines in the world, and for the first time in automobile racing two cars of phenomenal power will be seen – the 250 horse power American-built car entered by Alfred G. Vanderbilt and the 200 horse power French Darracq car, which will be driven by Hemery, the winner of the Vanderbilt Cup last October.

These cars will take part in twenty-seven different events, a number being entered in ten or a dozen contests. One of the Darracq cars, the 100 horse power machine entered by Arthur L. Guinness of London, heads the list, being placed in fourteen events. Guinness is a young amateur driver of London, a nephew of Lord Cecil, and besides the big championship events, in which he will meet the best professional drivers of the world, he is entered in the two Corinthian contests at ten miles each.

The amateur events have not filled readily, the only competitors besides Guinness being J. R. Harding of Brooklyn and E. N. Harding of this city, who have entered English Daimler cars. Lancia, Cedrino, and Fletcher, driving the Italian Fiats; Sartori, driving Vanderbilt's powerful new machine; Louis Ross or F.E. Stanley, driving the new Stanley steam car, and Hemery will be seen in a dozen events, including all the championships, the Dewar one-mile international championship, the 100-mile international race, and the great two-mile-a-minute trophy race.

Fletcher, who will drive the Fiat car used by Lancia in the late Vanderbilt race, and now owned by the banker, George W. Young of this city, and Cedrino are already on the beach. Lancia will leave this week, and Hemery, with the other French drivers, will arrive here next week. Plans have been made to ship a number of the American cars to Ormond this week.

(New York Times, 1/10/1906, p.6.)

SATURDAY, JANUARY 13, 1906
(NEW YORK):

En Route to Ormond. Southern Railway...
Have a fine state room - & a good luncheon on
the train. Spent the afternoon & evening easily
with Frank reading & talking as we rode along.

(Augusta Stanley, *Diary 1906.*)

SUNDAY, JANUARY 14, 1906
(BOSTON):

TO ORMOND NEXT.
ORMOND AFTER NEW YORK SHOWS.

Grand Exodus from the Metropolis to Florida Will
Follow the Closing of the Exhibitions This Week.

RACES IN SOUTH BETTER THAN EVER.

List of Entries in the Various Events, and the Men Who Are Relied
Upon to Win the Honors for America.

With the closing of the automobile shows in New York city on Saturday evening next will come a great exodus to Ormond, where the recognized champions of the world, the most famous of motor operators and their machines will compete for the promised honors.

Ormond has, since the first meet there, four (sic) years ago, gained a name in motoring annals

Map of Ormond and vicinity on the East coast of Florida, 1904. Ormond and parts of Volusia County were still thinly settled in the early part of the Twentieth Century and occasionally escaped the attention of map makers. This early map was produced by the prominent German cartographic firm of Wagner & Debes, Leipzig, and was published in Baedeker's The United States with an Excursion into Mexico in 1904.
Courtesy of the Roy Winkelman Collection, Florida Center for Instructional Technology, College of Education, University of South Florida.

second to none in the world. Its course and the speed developed has surpassed even the famous Dourdan course, where heretofore the world's records have established in large numbers, but which has taken second place since the world's kilometre and the world's mile marks were established on the east coast of Florida a year ago.

The experiences and successes of a year ago are to be repeated at Ormond next week if the expressed views of the knowing ones are anywhere near right. Certain it is that the famous manufacturers have displayed an unexampled amount of interest in the various events, and men celebrated for their successes in the international events of the past half-dozen years have gone to Florida to secure, if possible, the honors there.

Ormond, a meet in herself, and one which the real enthusiast will not miss for considerable, will open up the southern circuit of racing, including the big events at Palm Beach, Miami, and, last but not least, the great Cuban road race, for which most of the foreigners are entered.

There is reason to believe that the number of spectators at Ormond will be greater than ever, and in more ways than one the week at that place will be a record one.

Twenty-two individual entries have been made for the meet. The total entry list for all events is 166. The touring cars which figured so prominently in last year's races are not prominent this year, and the great Derby includes only the fastest cars in the world in two classes. The races will not drag, but will go off with a snap, and every race will be interesting.

The cars entered this year show an increase of over 25 per cent., and for the first time in automobile history two cars of 200-horsepower or over are on the list. None but the best of drivers, with the latest of cars, are on the list. Over 20 who figured as probable entries failed to come to the scratch. Perhaps a few of these may try to make late entries, and perhaps the receiving board, to whom matters will now be referred, will consent to the accepting of these late entries.

The foreign cars again predominate in the entry list. The American makers have not come forward liberally to defend the stars and stripes. America must again take a back seat unless Alfred Gwynne Vanderbilt, with his 250-horsepower car, made in America by himself, saves the day. Americans are hoping he will do so.

F.N. (sic) Stanley of Newton, with his great steamer, the only steamer entered, will also fly the stars and the stripes. The other makers of steam cars did not make entry.

Europe sends her greatest drivers for the meet, including Lancia, who was here in the Vanderbilt race last October, and who had the race won when he lost through an accident. Cedrino, also of Italy, is on the ground. France sends Hemery, winner of the Vanderbilt race, and England sends Walter Clifford Earp and Guinness, a young amateur sportsman.

Italy is reinforced by George W. Young, an American sportsman, for whom H. W. Fletcher, winner of the Vanderbilt [*qualifying*] race at Ormond last year, will drive, and England is reinforced by William Hilliard, who will drive a Napier. Guinness, the Englishman, drives a French Darracq.

American sportsmen will look to Walter Christie to carry away a lot of honors, for he has constructed a new car for the meet.

(Boston Herald, 1/14/1906.)

SUNDAY, JANUARY 14, 1906 (ORMOND):

Later – marched through Georgia into Florida – reaching Ormond at about 8-30. Very uninteresting trip. Was nearly two hours late into St. Augustine. Found Mr. & Mrs. Hathaway at the train to meet us – right at the door of the hotel.

(Augusta Stanley, *Diary 1906.*)

MONDAY, JANUARY 15, 1906 (ORMOND):

Ormond Florida – It is so warm I am almost melted. I sit by the open windows and the soft air comes in like an August day at home…Frank took us up to Mr. Price's orange grove and we picked oranges and tangerines – they were lovely. Went out in the touring car in the afternoon on the beach and saw them work out the racers – ours went well. Spent all afternoon on the beach.

(Augusta Stanley, *Diary 1906.*)

MONDAY, JANUARY 15, 1906 (ORMOND):

NEW RACER IS FASTER THAN THE "TEA KETTLE."

Hundreds of people were scattered along the Ormond-Daytona beach this afternoon to watch the first trial of the steam car which arrived yesterday. No watch was held today on any of the quarter or half-mile sprints, but all the chauffeurs and car owners who saw the new racer go, agreed that it is much faster than the Stanley "tea-kettle" with which Louis Ross scooped so many prizes in last year's races. Two slight drawbacks developed in a little tank leak and poor packing in the piston. The new car, which has previously been tried only on two hills near Boston, can develop almost twice the power of the Ross tea-kettle, having but one engine, against two in the old steamer. The machine runs with extraordinary ease and seems sure to prove a star entry.

(*New York Journal, 1/15/1906.*)

TUESDAY, JANUARY 16, 1906 (ORMOND):

Ormond. 70 degrees – but so much dampness makes it very disagreeable... Today our Racer went a mile, timed strictly correct in 30 3/5 seconds – the fastest a car ever went a mile in the world. Frank is in transports of delight over it, as it is better than he thought it would do against the wind. Reporters are interviewing him all the time.

(Augusta Stanley, *Diary 1906.*)

WEDNESDAY, JANUARY 17, 1906 (ORMOND):

Ormond – a little cooler today... In the afternoon went with Mr. and Mrs. Hathaway over to Daytona after seeing the fizzle of the flying machine.

Found Daytona a very pretty residential town.

Frank broke the engine in the Racer this afternoon - & Frank telephoned for another to be sent from home. Prescott to bring it.

(Augusta Stanley, *Diary 1906.*)

THURSDAY, JANUARY 18, 1906 (ORMOND):

The boys got the car fixed up & the men were all out on the beach.

(Augusta Stanley, *Diary 1906.*)

THURSDAY, JANUARY 18, 1906 (ORMOND):

TRYING THE RACERS ON DAYTONA BEACH.
STANLEY'S LITTLE RACER BEAT THE FLYING DUTCHMAN.
Lancia Has His Big Machine Out for Its First Trial Run, but Time Was Not Taken.

Lancia, with his 110-horsepower Fiat, appeared on the course here today for the first time, and a large crowd watched the trial spins of the famous machine, of which much is expected. No time

The Stanley race team at Ormond Beach, January 1906. *A number of the Stanley cars entered in the races assemble on the beach (a close-up view of the beach scene in the photo on p. xvi). A Stanley Model H, the "Gentlemen's Speedy Roadster," bearing number 15 stands to the left, the Stanley racer, or "Rocket," sits off to the right. Team members and interested spectators mingle about the "pit area."*

Larz Anderson Auto Museum.

Spectators and contestants gather on the beach for the 1906 races.

Photo Era, Stanley Museum Archives.

was taken, but estimates put the rate as close to that needed to win the two-mile-a-minute contest.

Both Stanley cars were out this afternoon. Once during the trials the new steamer, with Marriott driving, overtook and passed the car *[Lancia's Fiat]* ahead of it. Though the relative merits are not shown, as no race was on, the incident stirred up interest among spectators.

Stanley's gentlemen racer was also out, and the little car, for the time, was the center of interest. Both steam cars are attracting much interest here, and admirers predict much, especially for the steamer racer.

Four trial races were run today between Stanley's gentleman's small racing car and Bowden's Flying Dutchman. Basle drove the Flying Dutchman and Frank Durbin piloted them (sic). The little Stanley racer, one race, went for two miles, and in others a mile stretch was used. Stanley's car took all the races. These trials furnished unusual excitement for hundreds of spectators, and from start to finish interest was at a fever heat.

Trial runs over the famous beach here, made almost daily by the drivers whose names have become familiar in all sections of the world, are serving to keep interest on the qui vive, and confidence is daily increasing that the record of two miles a minute will be made this year.

The unofficial time made by Fred Marriott in Stanley's freak racer, has started all guessing. This machine made the mile here in 30 3-5 seconds, and though the time is, of course, unofficial, the fact that the four watches which caught him during the test agree to within a fraction of a second, regarding the time made, there is an almost absolute confidence that the time is correct.

Mr. Stanley is confident that with the proper conditions prevailing on the beach, he can clip off this 3-5 of a second and make the mile in half

a minute flat. Daily runs over the course are being made by this machine, which is entered as 30-horsepower.

Stanley has another car here of smaller horsepower, known as the gentleman's racer, and much is expected of this. It is a new car, built for speed, and yet differing greatly from the other racing machines. It is entered for several events next week and its driver is confident that it will at least let the others know they have had a race.

(*Florida Times-Union, 1/18/1906.*)

FRIDAY, JANUARY 19, 1906 (ORMOND):

Ormond – warm and lovely. Am feeling more like myself today. Frank telegraphed last night for Prescott taking Raymond with him – and we had a dispatch saying that they should be here Saturday night.

Went over to the beach today to see the flying machine go up, but it failed to make the trial. The weather is glorious.

(Augusta Stanley, *Diary 1906.*)

SATURDAY, JANUARY 20, 1906
(NEW YORK):

AUTO MILE IN 31 SECONDS.

Earp Beats Gasoline Car Records at Ormond – Faster Time Expected.

Word was received at Madison Square Garden yesterday from Florida that the

Englishman H. Clifford Earp, driving the new high-powered six-cylinder Napier car, had made a mile in 0:31. This is the fastest time ever made over a measured mile track by a gasoline-propelled car. The best time hitherto was 0:32 4-5, done last year by H. L. Bowden's 120-horse power Mercedes, but his car was considerably over the standard weight, and the record was not accepted by the American Automobile Association. The accepted mile record is 0:34 2-5, made by Arthur Macdonald in the Ormond races last year, driving an 80-horse power Napier car.

That the long-talked-of achievement of two miles in one minute will be accomplished next week is now accepted as a certainty by automobilists who are judges of the speed possibilities of the fast cars that are entered for the coming contests. F.E. Stanley (sic), driving his freak steam car, did even better than Earp two days ago, when, in a trial, he was reported to have gone a mile in 0:30 4-5.

(New York Times, 1/20/1906, p. 7.)

SATURDAY, JANUARY 20, 1906 (ORMOND):

Ormond - the warmest day since I came to Florida. Rode over to Daytona in the morning with Mr. & Mrs. Hathaway. It was slightly foggy on the beach when we first started. But it lifted and was gorgeous. Like Daytona very much.

Went to Mr. Anderson's orange grove with Mr. & Mrs. H[athaway] & Mrs. Wood & Frank and got all we wanted.

Waiting for the races to start. *A young woman works on a sand sculpture of a race car on the sands of Ormond Beach. January conditions in Florida could range from cold and damp to hot and humid, but full dress was considered socially proper on the beach at this time, temperature notwithstanding. Photo by Nathan Lazarnick.*

Courtesy George Eastman House.

Raymond, Prescott & the engine got here at 9-30 - all right.

(Augusta Stanley, Diary 1906.)

SUNDAY, JANUARY 21, 1906 (ORMOND):

Colder - and rain in the morning. A great many came last night - the Bowdens, Mr. Morgan, etc. The house is filling fast but there are not as many as was looked for.

Went over on the beach and saw the flyer go up - and come down and throw out the pilot right close to us. We heard him strike and thought he was badly hurt. But he came out all right after all. Was frightened almost to death - for I thought he was going to fall on us - and jumped out of the car - but the telegraph pole saved us from the flyer.

(Augusta Stanley, Diary 1906.)

SUNDAY, JANUARY 21, 1906 (NEW YORK):

AUTOISTS OFF FOR FLORIDA.

Speed Enthusiasts Leave in Special Cars for Ormond Races.

Several hundred automobilists left the city last night immediately after the close of the two automobile shows for Ormond, Fla., where the speed contests on the beach track will be held this week, beginning Tuesday. All of the trains that left the city for the South during the midnight hours were crowded. Many of the travelers had engaged private cars. Alfred G. Vanderbilt had a special car for his party. The new 250 horse power car just completed for Vanderbilt is expected to make fast time, but the experts are skeptical regarding its possibilities, owing to the fact that the car has had no opportunity for a trying-out test. The big 200 horse power Darracq racer that arrived from France last week is considered as one of the most promising cars to establish new motor records. Hemery, the Vanderbilt Cup holder, came out to drive the car. He will meet his old foe of the Vanderbilt Cup race, Lancia, who has been on the Ormond Beach for a week trying out his new 110 horse power Fiat.

Henry Ford, whose new racing car is looked upon as one of the dark horses of the meet, left last night with an enthusiastic party. With him was Frank Kulick, who will drive the car. Frank Kull, who will drive the new Wallace car, also left last night in the special car carrying about twenty Wayne representatives.

Hamilton's glider carried out to the beach. *Part of the pre-race attractions of the 1906 Ormond meet was to be an aerial exhibition of a glider piloted by aeronaut Charles Hamilton. After several aborted attempts the glider was towed aloft on January 21 by a 60 hp touring car, but stalled out at 300 feet when the underpowered car faltered shifting gears. Hamilton crashed into a telegraph pole by a bungalow on the side of the beach, right in front of a Stanley touring car holding F.E. and Augusta Stanley. Hamilton was shaken up but uninjured. F.E., an early member of the Aero Club of New England, was interested in aeronautics, but after this incident Mrs. Stanley wanted no part of air travel.*

Harper's Weekly.

For the week's races twenty-two cars have been entered, but it is believed one or two will be withdrawn. The greatest interest centres in the two-mile-a-minute race, and it is confidently expected that probably two or three of the fast cars will succeed in making a mile in thirty seconds.

(*New York Times, 1/21/1906, p.9.*)

MONDAY, JANUARY 22, 1906
(ORMOND):

Warm and beautiful. I should say HOT. The big racer went out on the beach and [ran] a very fast mile that was not timed. Then a timed kilo. in 19 1/5 worlds unofficial record. But cracked his cylinder and coasted the last half. The men put in the other engine and will be ready for the race tomorrow. A great many came tonight – all the officials.

(Augusta Stanley, *Diary 1906.*)

MONDAY, JANUARY 22, 1906 (DAYTONA):

STANLEY THE FAVORITE FOR SPEED CROWN.

Inventor Confident His Freak Car Will Beat
Two Miles a Minute.

RACING ENTHUSISTS ARRIVE AT ORMOND.

Great Things Are Expected of Earp and His Napier.

Glorious Florida weather, balmy, but bracing, gave hundreds of auto racing enthusiasts who thronged the clubhouse balconies and lined the beach to-day hope for a brilliant week of sport. The Stanley steamer, the new Christie wonder, the Dinsmore Mercedes and the Reo Bird were out for practice. The others were at the garages, having the finishing touches put on them in preparation for the opening of the tournament to-morrow.

The marvelous running of the Stanley steamer in practice has made the Yankee flyer the prime favorite for the gold two-mile-a-minute crown, the Dewar Mile Cup and all the races up to five miles. It has been clocked reliably for a mile in 30 3-5 seconds, but Stanley, and Marion (sic), his driver, are confident that it can go away below the half minute for the mile.

"I'll show a mile under favorable conditions as fast as a kilometer was ever run, which is 20 3-5 seconds, by Hemery and his Darracq," said Stanley to-day.

Stanley's car made a kilometer to-day in 19 1-5 seconds, which is equivalent to about 30 4-5 seconds to the mile.

"Stanley Will Win," says Lancia.

The good opinion of the speed qualities of the Stanley is shared by all the rival drivers here. Lancia says the Stanley will win the sprints and that the only show for the big gasoline cars will be in the Minneapolis cup, and the other long-distance events.

The advance guard of the circuit chasers now here is smaller than last year at this time, but the main crowd is expected from shows by the night trains.

The race committee decided to-day that to-morrow shall be devoted to mile contests, the trial heats of the Dewar cup and heavyweight championships and the middleweight and steam championships complete. No fear is felt that with competent officials running the races this year the programme will not be finished in time. Alden McMurtry was at work all day installing his timing apparatus.

All times so far made have been taken by the drop of flag and cannot be too seriously regarded. No one doubts the Stanley time, though, as it has easily run away from all the flyers in practice.

(*The Evening Mail [New York], 1-22-1906.*)

TUESDAY, JANUARY 23, 1906 (ORMOND):

AUTO RACES AT ORMOND START THIS MORNING.

Hundreds Arrive – Hotels All Crowded.

MACHINES IN PRACTICE SPINS.

Christie Racer Cracks Two Cylinders In Practice Trial on the Florida Beach Course.

(Jan. 22.) – Hundreds of automobile enthusiasts from the North arrived here this evening. The railroad travel has been so heavy that all trains are from five to ten hours late. Every hotel

Picnicking on the beach, January 1906. *A group of fashionably dressed spectators sit down on the dunes with box lunches. One commonly reported complaint among Ormond spectators was that the concessionaires on the beach over-charged for these lunches and other services. Poor viewing areas, long delays between events, and lack of communications added to spectators' woes, but many came anyway hoping to catch a glimpse of the "speed demons" in action. Photo by Penfield.*
New York Times,
Stanley Museum Archives.

in Ormond and Daytona is packed, and accommodations are at a premium. Early this afternoon during the few hours of low tide all of the racing cars were out for a final practice spin, and the best performance is credited to the Stanley steamer, which was unofficially timed a kilometer in twenty seconds. This beats the world's kilometer record of 0:20 3-5, made last month by Hemery with the new two-hundred horse-power Darracq car. By some of the watches the time was caught at 0:19 1-5, and the enthusiasts claim the car will equal this time in the regular races.

Walter Christie had the misfortune to crack two of his cylinders of his car. This car was to have been driven in some of the important championships by Chevrolet, and considerable disappointment is felt over the accident.

All of the contesting cars were weighed in during the day, and as far as known every one was able to get beneath the limit in its respective class.

The beach course is in excellent condition, and as no storms are predicted the chances of its remaining in good condition throughout the week are excellent. It is certain that all the records from one kilometer to one hundred miles which were made last year will be lowered before the close of this week's tournament.

The officials announced to-night that the first races to-morrow will be started at 9:30 o'clock in the morning. The first events to be run off will be the one-mile races, including the preliminary heats of the mile championship for the Sir Thomas Dewar trophy. Among the competitors who will start are:

Hemery, 200-horse power Darracq; Clifford Earp, 100-horse power Napier; Lancia, Cedrino, and Fletcher, in 110-horse power Fiats; Frank Kulick, 105-horse power Ford; Marriotte (sic), Stanley steamer; Joe Downey, 110-horse power Mercedes; and A. L. Guiness (sic), the young English amateur, in his 100-horse power Darracq.

It is estimated that several thousand people have journeyed here from north of Mason and Dixon's line, while as many more have come from Washington, Richmond, Atlanta, and other Southern cities. The sole topic of conversation in the hotel lobbies is upon the events of the week. Eager anticipation and excitement prevail, and every one is positive that a phenomenal record-breaking week is in store. Positive expressions are heard on every hand that the mile record will be placed at 30 seconds, thus accomplishing the long-wished-for goal of automobilists.

(*New York Times, 1/23/1906, p.6.*)

"One of the finest automobile courses in the world." Encaptioned so by The Horseless Age, this publicity photo was commissioned in early 1903 by J. F. Hathaway, who sits in his Stanley Runabout, center left, opposite a three-wheeled "sand sailer" built by Daytona resident Ernest J. Mills. Another Stanley and two steam Locomobiles mingle with a number of curved-dash Oldsmobiles, pedal rickshaws, a bicycle and a motorcycle, and a heavily-loaded Chicago Omnibus (left). Rounding out the modes of transport is a solitary horse and wagon to the distant rear. Photo by Edward G. Harris.

The Horseless Age, courtesy Leroy Cole.

CHAPTER TWO

"An Ideal Race Course."

"It was a man by the name of Hathaway that really started that whole thing of racing and he was a very close friend of my father's. And he kept at him, trying to get my father to come down and he didn't want to do it. 'No, I'm not gonna go down - way down there - no point in that, you know...' Finally, he weakened him. That's the fella that I told you that kept his eye on the judges' stand. But he was the one who really got the thing started down there in Ormond or Daytona or whatever you wish to call it."

Raymond W. Stanley. (R. W. Stanley 1984.)

IN THE WINTER OF 1876 a young man from Portland, Maine, set off on a journey south from New York City, hoping to start a new life and restore his health in the more favorable climate to be found on Florida's east coast. The young man, John Anderson (1853-1911), purchased a seaside plantation along the Halifax River near a small retirement colony founded by some prominent families from New Britain, Conn. - all former employees of the Corbin Lock Company - who rather unimaginatively had named their community "New Britain." Although a fellow New Englander himself, Anderson harbored a particular conviction that localities should have local names, and used his influence once he rose to prominence to rename the Florida community after one of the first settlers of the area, and the town came to be known as Ormond.

John Anderson was neither a pioneer nor a retiree but a newcomer of wealth and privilege. Born into one of the most prominent

John Anderson (1853-1911). Born in Portland, Maine, the son of a railroad magnate, Anderson moved to Florida for health reasons and invested in citrus groves. He went into partnership with Joseph D. Price, building and managing the Hotel Ormond and other seasonal resorts, including the Bretton Woods, NH, hotels. The team of Anderson and Price became tireless promoters of their resorts, their communities, Good Roads and automobile tourism. Together they helped to organize, promote and sponsor the Ormond Beach races and the Climb to the Clouds on Mt. Washington.
Courtesy Ormond Beach Historical Trust.

Portland families, the son of "General" Samuel J. Anderson, the president of the Portland and Ogdensburg Railroad (now the Maine Central), Anderson had been employed at the banking house of Jay Cooke & Company in New York City. As a member of the leisure class, Anderson was accustomed to spending his summers at the Crawford House, an early seasonal resort in the White Mountains of New Hampshire (his father had built the railway through Crawford Notch), and was quick to see the potential of a winter resort on the waterfront at Ormond Beach, and how such a resort would spur development of the area.

Ormond, however, was still a 24-hour stage-coach ride from St. Augustine, or an equally unappealing 40-mile stage ride from the near-est steamboat port at Volusia on the St. John's River. Anderson, aware of the impact of his father's railroad on tourism in the White Mountains, set out to change that by promoting a local rail connection, and by the mid-1880s the St. John's and Halifax River Railroad connected Ormond to the main east coast trunk line at Palatka, a one-hour journey by rail. Anderson had found a partner and soul-mate in another newcomer, Joseph Downing Price (1853-1911), a civil engineer from Covington, Kentucky, who shared Anderson's vision for an Ormond Beach resort. Together Anderson and Price planned and built the Hotel Ormond, which opened its doors in 1888. Two years later the pair sold the hotel to railroad magnate Henry Flagler, but were retained as managers.

Wealthy vacationers from the north began

Joseph D. Price (1853-1911). A native of Kentucky, Price came to Ormond, Fla., and like-wise invested in citrus groves. In partnership with John Anderson he managed the Hotel Ormond and the Bretton Inn in Florida during the winter, and the Mt. Pleasant Hotel in Bretton Woods, NH, and the Bretton Hall in New York City during the rest of the year. Like Anderson, Price became a prominent member of his community, serving on the local town council and as Mayor of Ormond.
Courtesy Ormond Beach Historical Trust.

Hotel Ormond. *This view is from the opposite side of the bridge over the Halifax River. The beach lies about a half mile behind the hotel.*
Stanley Museum Archives.

to flock to Ormond Beach in the winter, attracted by sun and surf, the area's rural tranquility, excellent sport fishing, and the hospitality of its grand seaside resorts – the Hotel Ormond and the nearby Coquina Hotel. In addition to all of the area's amenities, word, too, began to spread of Ormond's remarkable beach. "Ormond beach is firm, hard sand, absolutely without a pebble, and out two hundred yards is a bar which precludes any possibility of a treacherous current," wrote one visitor in early 1898. "The beaches," the visitor marveled, "are like wide concourses of two hundred and fifty feet, hard as a snarl roadbed, and long enough for a day's ride. The hoofs of the horses resound as if on asphalt, leaving never a trace of a wagon track, and hardly a mark of a hoof. The bicyclists find the greatest degree of satisfaction here, for a cinder path is a sand pit in comparison to the hard and level beach, which requires but the slightest push to speed the wheel." (Jerome 1898.)

Ormond's unusual beach owes its characteristics to its geological composition and configuration. The hard surface of the beach is largely made up of tight-grained effluvial quartzite sands, and the broad, shallow slope of the shore land formation insures that the beach remains largely unaffected by ocean currents under normal conditions. The result is a wide,

almost flat, smooth, hard-packed surface extending for more than 25 miles. (Beeman 2000; Punnett 2004: p.14.) The nature of the beach gave rise to some specialized sand-sailing sports at Ormond, where turn-of-the-century visitors would attach small sails to bicycles and larger tricycle sand-sailers, taking advantage of prevailing winds and a seemingly endless beach. (Punnett 2004: pp.3, 13.)

Sand Sailer versus Stanley. *Ernest J. Mills pits his wind-powered sand sailer against Hathaway's steam-powered Stanley. Mills later built a larger version of beach sailer using lightweight racing wheels and pneumatic tires supplied by the Stanley Brothers by arrangement through their mutual friend, J. F. Hathaway, seen here in his Stanley Runabout.*
The Horseless Age, courtesy Leroy Cole.

Anderson and Price became highly regarded as managers in the resort hotel industry, and in 1895 the pair were hired as managers of the Mount Pleasant Hotel in Anderson's old stomping grounds in the White Mountains, alternating the summer seasons there with winters at the Hotel Ormond. When the grand Mount Washington Hotel, sister to the Mount Pleasant, was finished in 1902, Anderson and Price divided their summer management duties between both hotels respectively. Anderson, it is said, was chagrined that they had missed an opportunity to name the new hotel after the original name given to the locality, Bretton Woods, but made up for it by seeing that the local post office and train depot were established under that name (McAvoy 1988: pp.224-225.) The following year Anderson and Price purchased the Coquina Hotel in Ormond Beach, eventually renaming it the Bretton Inn. Another hotel, Bretton Hall, situated in New York City, would also be run by the partnership under Price's management.

At the turn of the century hoteliers like Anderson and Price were becoming aware of a new phenomenon – some of their guests were bypassing the railways, steamboats and stagecoaches leading to their resorts, and were arriving directly by horseless carriage. The new motor cars were becoming increasingly popular among wealthy tourists and their families, the class of clientele the hoteliers wished to attract, so many resorts began to provide special accommodations to "stable" the new motor carriages during their guests' stay. Motoring in the day was considered something of an adventure sport – if the cars were primitive the roads were even more so. The Good Roads movement, which sought to focus attention on improving the nation's deplorable roads infrastructure, was initially organized by the national cyclists' organization, the League of American Wheelmen, and was quickly adopted by the newly formed American Automobile Association. Anderson and Price, already convinced of the necessity of reliable transport to bring guests to their hotels, needed no special suasion to see the value of good roads, of which the beach at Ormond was attracting attention as a natural example, and they began to host good roads meetings at their hotels.

In 1902 one of the early automobilists to

bring his car to the Hotel Ormond was James F. Hathaway (1847-1913) of West Somerville, Mass. A partner in the firm of Sprague and Hathaway, dealers in photographs, frames, photographic equipment and supplies, Hathaway was a longtime business associate and friend of the Stanley Brothers of Newton, Mass., who had recently branched out from their photographic dry plate business to manufacture the Stanley steam car. Hathaway was an enthusiastic early customer, and had even driven his Stanley over a timed mile at the Narragansett Park track in Cranston, RI, one of the fastest tracks in the country *[also considered the earliest circular automotive racetrack in the country – see Foster 2004: p.182]*. Hathaway was not the first motorist to see Ormond Beach as a potential race course, nor the first to publicly advocate its use as such (see Birchwood 1902: pp. 985-987), but he was the first to put the beach to an actual feasibility test for that purpose. As an experiment, Hathaway carefully measured out a mile straightaway on the beach in late 1902, and reportedly drove his Stanley over the distance nearly 15 seconds faster than his earlier time at Narragansett, using the exact same car. (Ryan 1934: p.AA2.)

Impressed, Hathaway embarked on a personal letter-writing campaign to major newspapers and automotive media to promote Ormond Beach as a motor racing venue. "The beach is probably the finest in the world," wrote Hathaway. "It extends along the coast for more than 30 miles in a straight line and it is from 400 to 600 feet wide at low water. The average rise of the tide is about two feet. There is always a good beach for riding several hours every day. The sand is nearly as hard as asphalt and very smooth. There are no stones. No road or street was ever built that is so smooth to ride upon as this beach," he declared, echoing the

Hathaway promoting the automobile in Florida. *J. F. Hathaway introduces automobiling to some Massachusetts guests in front of "The Studio," an Ormond Beach cottage in 1904. Hathaway is seated on the left front seat of his Stanley surrey; beside him (with derby hat) is Boston businessman, A. Shuman. John Shepard, another prominent Boston merchant, sits in the rear seat beside Mrs. Hathaway; Mrs. Shepard and Mrs. Shuman stand to the rear. Photo by Walter R. Merryman.*

Stanley Museum Archives.

sentiments of the previous enthusiast five years earlier. "It is an ideal race course and a place where records will be made in the future." (*Motor Age*, February 5, 1903.)

The promotion of Ormond Beach by Hathaway and others soon attracted the attention of "Senator" William J. Morgan (1861-1941), an automotive correspondent with *The Automobile Magazine*, a New York-based journal. Morgan, a Welsh immigrant, had been an early cycling champion (he was nicknamed "The Senator" as a pro rider, in deference to his oratorical skills), and was later a prominent cycle racing promoter with a controlling interest in a number of major velodromes on the east coast. Morgan was also an established journalist, with credentials established at several early cycling and automotive journals. Although he had never been to Florida, Morgan had ear-

lier heard of the east coast beaches proposed as a potential racecourse, and was intrigued by the auto-racing possibilities of Ormond explored by Hathaway. As luck would have it, *The Automobile Magazine* had been seeking a southern-based winter racing event to round out the annual motor racing schedule, and Morgan was dispatched to investigate. (Morgan 1903: pp. 425-426.)

Morgan arrived in Ormond sometime in February 1903 to find the beach, the accommodations, the rail connections, and the weather beyond all expectations for a successful winter race meet. The winter season was rapidly on the wane, however, and it is doubtful that Morgan alone could have organized a last-minute auto race without the enthusiastic support of Anderson and Price. The two hoteliers offered to roll out the red carpet for the event, providing accommodations and financial support, if Morgan would organize the meet and utilize their hotel as headquarters.

Anderson and Price's offer to cover expenses eliminated the first of two obstacles facing Morgan - funding an event for which one could not charge spectators for admission. As Morgan would recall later, "there were no gate receipts charged on the beach simply because you could not charge unless you fenced the entire beach in," a logistical impossibility, and "besides," Morgan went on, "it was Federal property." (*New York Times*, October 12, 1913, p.S5.) The second obstacle was obtaining official sanction for the races from the American Automobile Association, which required that the event be sponsored by a local auto club. Without an organized auto club already in place, Morgan essentially had to create one.

Morgan opted to draw on what he per-

ceived to be the larger concentration of Florida motorists to be found in the municipal environs of Jacksonville, and was able to attract a sufficient number to an organizational meeting to form the Florida Automobile Association (FAA). Believing he had his sponsoring organization in place, Morgan set off to entice racing enthusiasts to come to Florida and fill the entrant slots on the rapidly approaching Ormond tournament, scheduled for March 26-28. In hindsight, Morgan may have picked the wrong horse, as a rival group local to Ormond formed the Daytona and Seabreeze Automobile Association and independently commenced on some groundwork on the upcoming races, even guaranteeing prizes for some events. Left unconsulted in Morgan's absence, the FAA group grew suspicious and came to believe that they had been duped by Morgan, withdrawing their sponsorship and in effect declar-

Olds and Hathaway with "Senator" Morgan, Ormond 1903.
Ransom Olds, left, and J. F. Hathaway pose in a curved-dash Oldsmobile with "Senator" William J. Morgan standing to the right. Morgan, nicknamed during his earlier career as a bicycle racer and promoter, became one of the most active early auto race organizers, taking charge of all the Ormond Beach races through 1910 and numerous other events, including the 1904 and 1905 Climb to the Clouds contests at Mt. Washington. Photo by Walter R. Merryman.
Ormond Beach Library,
courtesy Dick and Yvonne Punnett.

ing the event off. Upon his return Morgan had to scramble to salvage the meet, eventually working with the Daytona and Seabreeze group to sponsor the races with a reduced field. (Morgan 1903: pp.426-430.)

The last-minute sponsorship problems may have significantly reduced participation in the 1903 event; still, a number of prominent early auto manufacturers showed up. Among them was Alexander Winton in his Winton Bullet No. 1, with which the builder had high hopes of setting a world record. Despite expectations and numerous attempts, Winton could only manage a mile straightaway in 52 1-5 seconds, 3-5 of a second shy of

Winton "Bullet" versus the Olds "Pirate." *Alexander Winton edges out a victory over the Olds "Pirate" driven by Horace T. Thomas in this artist's depiction of the one-mile Hotel Ormond Cup Challenge race in 1903.*

Painting by Buz McKim.

the standing US record and further still off the world's record. In a separate trial, Winton did manage to set a new American kilometer record of 32 4-5. Slower yet more successful was Ransom E. Olds's entry, nicknamed the "Pirate" by Senator Morgan, and driven by Horace T. Thomas to a new mile record for cars under 1,000 pounds in 1:06:1-5. Olds also watched with some pride as several of his company's early curved-dash Oldsmobiles ran off perhaps the first stock car race at an official meet. Motorcycle pioneer Oscar Hedstrom established a new mile record of 1:03:1-5 on his Indian, the first world's record set on the beach. J. F. Hathaway, who might well have been astounded that his letter-writing campaign of two months' previous could have led so quickly to organized racing at Ormond, drove his stock Stanley runabout to a new steam record on the beach in 1:28:2-5.

On the last day Winton's Bullet No. 1 and the Olds Pirate faced off in the one-mile Hotel Ormond Cup Challenge race, often referred to as the first "drag race" on the beach. The race certainly lived up to its expectations as Thomas, driving the lighter Pirate, cracked off an early lead at the start, only to be caught at the end by the Bullet, which snatched the victory away by 1-5 of a second, finishing in 1:15. (Punnett 2004: pp.8-14.) The races were deemed a success and plans were made to make them an annual event. The Daytona and Seabreeze club was disbanded and reconstituted as the Florida East Coast Automobile Association, with John Anderson named as first vice-president – the new group would sponsor the Ormond races to follow.

For the 1904 Ormond races Senator Morgan had the benefit of a nine month leeway to organize and promote the event, although

"The Auto Race at Ormond." Anderson and Price helped promote the 1904 races with this elegant pamphlet published by the Hotel Ormond and the Florida East Coast Hotel Company.
Stanley Museum Archives.

ironically, the most significant promotion of the beach came but a few weeks before the start of the races, just as it had in 1903. In the face of allegations by Alexander Winton that the beach was not as fast as advertised, Morgan devised a plan to arrange for some pre-race time trials on the beach to put the question to rest. He invited the Packard Motor Car Company to send down their new racer, the 22 hp "Gray Wolf," for a pre-race tune-up under the guise of testing the new timing apparatus on the beach. The Stevens-Duryea Company also sent down a skeletal racer called the "Spider," and both cars proceeded to break many of the course records set the year before.

Morgan's gambit paid off, and when the races commenced in earnest there were more than 15 powerful racing machines, mostly expensive imports, in attendance. With the cars came their wealthy, aristocratic owners, creating a decidedly new social dimension to the

proceedings. Leading the parade of blue bloods was William K. Vanderbilt, Jr., of New York, one of the heirs to the Vanderbilt fortune. "Willie K," as he came to be known, was a motorcar enthusiast, having driven everything from early Stanley-designed steam Locomobiles to the powerful 90 hp Mercedes he had brought with him to Ormond, and had personally established the premier motor racing prize in the US – the Vanderbilt Cup. Joining Vanderbilt were fellow Mercedes owners, H.L. Bowden, S.B. Stevens, and James L. Breese; other gentlemen owner/drivers taking part in the races were B.M. Shanley (Decauville), William Wallace (De Dietrich), F.A. La Roche (Darracq), J. Insley Blair (Panhard), and W. Gould Brokaw (Renault).

American manufacturers and their advocates were not left out. In addition to the previously mentioned Packard and Stevens-Duryea, other US makers likewise sent innovative cars to the contest, among them J. Walter Christie who entered his first front-wheel-drive

William K. Vanderbilt, Jr. in his 90 hp Mercedes racer, Ormond 1904. Although this imported Mercedes was designed for road racing and not straightaway beach trials, Vanderbilt, at the wheel, successfully drove it to set a land speed record of 92.3 mph in the mile on January 27, 1904. He then went on to set six more world records at longer distances before the end of the 1904 Ormond tournament.
Scientific American, Stanley Museum Archives.

Barney Oldfield in Winton Bullet No. 2, Ormond 1904. *Oldfield scored an upset win over Vanderbilt's Mercedes in the one-mile free-for-all, a race pitting the hardscrabble bicycle racer, Oldfield, in an American car against the wealthy aristocrat, Vanderbilt, in an imported foreign car. A broken crankshaft put Oldfield and his car out of commission for the remainder of the tournament.*
Scientific American, Stanley Museum Archives.

racer, and Walter Baker, who sent a radical streamlined electric-powered car, the "Torpedo Kid." Other domestic racecars included a 70 hp Peerless driven by Joseph Tracy, and two new Winton Bullets entered by Alexander Winton, the larger of the two, the 120 hp Bullet No. 2, to be driven by professional driver Barney Oldfield. Oldfield, already a racecar celebrity, was perhaps the antithesis of the millionaire owner-drivers at the meet. A former hardscrabble bicycle racer who had gone directly into high speed auto racing (legend has it that Henry Ford gave him but a few hours of behind-the-wheel instruction before sending him out onto the track for his first race), Oldfield was poised to give the aristocrats a run for their money, a situation that did not sit well in the stratified class structure that had materialized on the beach.

Missing from the list of US manufacturers entered were F.E. and F.O. Stanley of the Stanley Motor Carriage Company of Newton, Mass. Seven months earlier, F.E. Stanley had driven a special streamlined steam car in a one-mile

match race to a world steam track record, 1:02:4-5, as part of the Decoration Day races at the Readville track in Boston, and two weeks later it was reported that Stanley had submitted an entry fee for the 1904 Ormond races. (*The Horseless Age*, June 10, 1903, p.694.) Also racing his stock Stanley at the Readville meet was Louis S. Ross of Newtonville, Mass., the son of a prominent local contractor hired to construct the new Stanley factory in Watertown, Mass. Despite reports that Stanley was at work on an even more powerful racer for the mile record – "especially to go against Winton for sport or money to any figure…to show the world that the light, ball bearing, steam-driven car is…the quickest of all automobiles that can be built" (Dolnar 1903b: p.181) – and despite the urging of long-time Stanley friend J.F. Hathaway, F.E. opted to forgo the Ormond races. Last minute negotiations with the Eastman Kodak Company over the sale of the Stanley Dry Plate business, combined with his twin brother's absence due to illness (F.O. Stanley was forced to relocate to Colorado with a serious prognosis of tuberculosis), left Stanley little choice. To represent the interests of steam, Louis Ross took his stock Stanley runabout to Ormond instead.

Vanderbilt began the 1904 record breaking

Louis S. Ross at Readville, 1903. *Ross, right, lines his stock Stanley Runabout up at the starting line against a White steamer during the Decoration Day races at the Readville track, May 30, 1903.*
The Horseless Age, courtesy Leroy Cole.

with a request, quickly granted, for a preliminary one-mile time trial on January 27, in which his Mercedes promptly dispatched the world record in a single run of 39 seconds flat. Vanderbilt entered the one-mile free-for-all on the second day as a clear favorite, but after the qualifying heats there emerged a distinct challenger – Oldfield in the Winton Bullet No. 2. The final shaped up to be a classic confrontation between a homegrown US car versus a foreign import, and between an establishment millionaire versus a working class upstart. Oldfield triumphed in this contest, but a broken crankshaft on his car the following day precluded any further head-to-head match ups, and Vanderbilt proceeded to clean up, establishing new world records at five, ten, twenty, thirty, forty, and fifty mile distances.

Louis Ross took up where J. F. Hathaway had left off the year before and entered his stock 8 hp Stanley runabout (either a Model BX or CX – the exact model is undetermined, as photos of the car show it stripped of its seats and other diagnostics) in the individual time trials. Ross not only eclipsed Hathaway's steam

Hugh Willoughby in his 11 hp Autocar, Ormond 1904. *Early bicycle, automobile and aviation pioneer Hugh de Laussat Willoughby competed at Ormond in 1904, finishing second to Louis Ross in the five-mile race for two-passenger runabouts. Willoughby was one of the first Americans to own and ride a "boneshaker," an early velocipede, and later became one of the first Americans to own and race a motor carriage. After his appearance at Ormond he became an early aviator of note.*
Stanley Museum Archives.

beach record, he set a world record for steam cars at 55 2/5 seconds in the mile, and followed up with a new steam kilometer record in 34 2/5. Ross also entered a five-mile race for two-passenger runabouts, defeating his only competition, an 11 hp gas-powered Autocar driven by Hugh L. Willoughby, by a wide margin. (Punnett 2004: pp.18-47.)

By the end of the 1904 tournament nearly every world speed record of note had been set on the Ormond-Daytona beach, and Senator Morgan set out to entice the European drivers to venture overseas the next winter and take part in the record breaking that their cars had begun without them in 1904. At the urging of Anderson and Price, hotel owner Henry Flagler began expanding the Hotel Ormond's facilities for accommodating larger numbers of motorcars by building the Ormond Garage. And to just about everyone it seemed that the true kings of speed were the powerful internal combustion vehicles that had been anointed on the sands of Ormond. That conviction was about to be challenged.

Louis S. Ross at Ormond, 1904. *Ross took his stock Stanley Model B or C (indistinguishable because the seats have been removed) to Ormond and set steam records on the beach in the mile and the kilometer.*
Ormond Beach Library, courtesy Dick and Yvonne Punnett.

CHAPTER THREE

"The Hydrocarbon Branch."

"The gasoline explosive engine carriage seems to have its greatest popularity across the water. Judging from reports it appears that many thousand of these vehicles are now in use in France and that the makers are unable to fill their orders. Although America is generally in the front rank when it comes to mechanical improvements we have to take our hats off to France this time. While the number of tricycles done sold in France reaches up in the thousands it is doubtful if a hundred all told has been sold here. What are the advantages and disadvantages of this form of power?

"They are cheaper than the electric carriage… With gasoline at 10¢ per gal[lon] they can be run for about 1/2¢ per mile. As gasoline is obtainable in any country village their range of action is practically unlimited. But they emit a bad odor and the engine has either to be kept running all the time when the carriage is at rest or if stopped a few turns must be made by hand in order to start it, and they do not have the latitude of speed a carriage should possess. The engine is quite apt to run out of time and requires the attention of more than an ordinary mechanic to repair it.

"But with all these faults the number now in use exceed all other types."

F.O. Stanley. (F.O. Stanley 1899.)

FROM THEIR INITIAL experiments with their first steam carriage in the fall of 1897 to the manufacture of their refined direct-drive model of 1903 [*also referred to as "gear drive"*], the Stanley Brothers worked to perfect the nimble, lightweight, amply-powered, swift-and-sure steam carriage that would be their hallmark. While doing so they realized that their principal competition in the overall automotive world would neither come from the numerous other steam car manufacturers nor from the intriguing but still impractical electrics, but from the "gasoline explosive engine" side of the industry – what the early automotive journal *The Horseless Age* had dubbed "the hydrocarbon branch." (*The Horseless Age*, January 29, 1902, p.130.)

The early internal combustion motor carriages were indeed dominant in France, where prominent makers such as A. Darracq et Cie.,

Decauville, DeDion et Bouton, Léon Bollée, Mors, Panhard, Renault, and others emerged, many eventually focusing on producing large, expensive, high-powered racing machines. Other European manufacturers – Mercedes in Germany, Napier in Britain, Fiat in Italy, among others – would struggle to catch up. With the new motorcars came a lexicon of new automotive terminology, with a distinctly French influence. Words such as *chauffeur* and *garage*, even the word *automobile* itself were early Gallic constructions, soon to enter into universal usage.

F.E. Stanley had an opportunity to view the early French auto industry first-hand in July 1899, during a business trip to Paris aimed at exploring the European market for the Stanley steam car, the manufacturing and marketing rights to which had recently been acquired by the Locomobile Company of America. Stanley

Léon Serpollet and Frank L. Gardner. *French steam pioneer Léon Serpollet (left) mans the tiller of a 1900 Gardner-Serpollet steamer. Frank L. Gardner of Philadelphia, was Serpollet's partner and financial backer. Gardner, a wealthy American expatriate, led an adventurous rags-to-riches life on three continents, speculating in gold and diamond mines with several fortunes won and lost, before settling in Paris and investing in Serpollet's steam automobile enterprise. Serpollet's premature death from tuberculosis in 1907 brought a close to European manufacture of steam cars.*

Courtesy Jean-Michel Horvat.

also met with his French counterpart, the steam car pioneer Léon Serpollet (1858-1907), who with the wealthy American mining magnate, Frank L. Gardner (1853-1930), was producing the Gardner-Serpollet steamer in a market otherwise dominated by internal combustion. (Foster 2004: pp.63, 65-69.) Some of Stanley's initial observations on the French auto market have survived in a series of letters to his twin brother, F.O. Stanley, back home in Newton, Mass.:

"This forenoon I went out to the parks where the motor carriages are most numerous and saw hundreds of them. The three wheeled ones like the De Deon (sic) are most numerous… I find that they go just as fast as they can at times, excepting when down near the business part of the city."

"This afternoon I went to the automobile show, and I must say I was surprised. There are no less than 98 different manufacturers having exhibits and they will average at least 6 machines each or a total of more than 600 machines. The machines for carrying two [*passengers*] are started at from $1000 to $2000 and weigh from 1200 to 1800 lbs. There are many of them guaranteed to run 20 miles an hour and some faster. But I am satisfied from what I see on the road that our machine geared two to one (2 to 1) would down them easily, the best of them."

"Steam," Stanley continued, "is conspicuous on account of its absence. There are several larger machines for carrying from 4 to 6 tons propelled by steam and that is all. Nothing light for pleasure of that kind. So our machine will be a type all by itself & I am sure will cause a sensation." (F.E. Stanley, letter to F.O. Stanley, July 7, 1899; Stanley Museum Archives.)

Shortly afterwards, Stanley was able to view the start of the Tour de France, a 1,350-mile auto endurance run undertaken by 43 powerful French racecars and sponsored by the Automobile Club of France. His remarks and insights border on wonder: "We went out on the road two miles from the starting point and stationed ourselves at a slight bend in the road where we could see each way at least 1/2 mile. The road was about level as the machines approached us but slightly up grade as they went by. The first to pass was M. Charron… His machine [*a Panhard*]…weighed about 2000 pounds and [*was*] propelled by a motor of about 20 H.P. The speed as he passed was terrific, and as soon as he was past us he was completely hid from our view by a cloud of dust. I was surprised by the tremendous speed…"

"We were stationed at a street crossing and just in front of us was a slight elevation. This machine [*a Panhard*] managed by R. de Knyff came at a rate of speed that I never saw excelled by an express train. When it went over the elevation in the road in front of us it jumped clear off the ground and reminded me of the experience we used to have sliding down John Lane hill." [*A steep hill in Kingfield, Maine, popular for winter sledding during the twins' childhood.*]

Stanley noted that the first-place Panhard covered the 191-mile first stage of the race in an average speed of nearly 36 mph, while the last-place car averaged more than 27 mph. "So you see they have got speed if nothing else, and that up to the present time seems to be the only object." The days' experience fresh in his mind, Stanley concluded, "I am more confident every day that a machine like ours will have a large sale here both on account of price and quiet running. But as far as speed is concerned especially for long distances the steam carriage will not be the machine of the future." (F.E. Stanley letter to F.O. Stanley, July 17, 1899; Stanley Museum Archives.)

Stanley's last remark has been interpreted by some as an early realization that steam would not be a viable competitor to the "gasoline explosive engine" cars in the long run, but that is not necessarily the case. Stanley was a pragmatic manufacturer whose immediate concerns involved the present, where steam cars were still highly competitive. The future was another matter, and even there the prospects for touring and utility steamers seemed favorable. For the present, Stanley could see possibilities of designing a steam racer that could out-sprint the most powerful gas cars over short distances. And there was another aspect of auto racing where steamers could demonstrate their superiority over the hydrocarbon branch – the hill climb.

Hill climbing, once considered the true mark of a reliable touring car, was at this time also becoming a popular competitive event. At some early automobile shows and exhibitions, such as the Charles River Park contest held outside of Boston in November 1898 and the first New York Auto Show in Madison Square Garden in November 1900, artificial wooden ramps were constructed to test and demonstrate the hill climbing abilities of manufacturers' cars. The Stanley Brothers participated, unofficially, at the Charles River Park exhibition, when F.E. Stanley drove one of their first steam carriages to a mile in 2:11, the fastest time of the day, and followed with a decisive ascent of the 90-foot hill-climbing ramp, far outperforming the other participating cars with a single trial. The resulting wave of interested customers convinced the Stanleys to actively enter the automotive market. (F.O. Stanley 1930: pp.2-3; Foster 2004: pp.49-52.)

The following year, after the sale of their fledgling auto business to the short-lived partnership of John Brisben Walker of the Mobile Company and Amzi L. Barber of the Locomobile Company, the Stanleys had an opportunity to carry their steamer's hill climbing exploits to new heights. Walker's flair for publicity and showmanship and Barber's insistence on rigorous reliability trials to prove the mettle of all his new cars and yachts, gave F.O. Stanley free rein to tackle the most challenging (and by car, unclimbed) mountain road in the northeast, the Mt. Washington Carriage Road in New Hampshire. F.O. and his wife, Flora, set out from their Newton home on August 26, 1899, in one of the first of the Stanley Brothers' new model steamers, now marketed as a Locomobile. On August 31st, they made the first successful ascent of the treacherous eight-mile carriage road up Mount Washington by motorcar, in two

F.O. and Flora Stanley on Mt. Washington, August 31, 1899. *F.O. and Flora Stanley made the first successful ascent of the Mt. Washington Carriage Road by motor car on August 31, 1899. The two hour and ten minute journey (delayed several times by necessary stops for water pumping and tank filling) was part reliability test and part promotional tour for the Locomobile Company which had earlier acquired manufacturing and marketing rights to the Stanley motor carriage.*

Stanley Museum Archives.

The Start of the 1903 Commonwealth Avenue Hill Climb. *The course followed the carriage road up the 13 percent grade in the background, still much the same today only more densely developed.*

The Horseless Age, courtesy Leroy Cole.

hours, ten minutes running time (the steep terrain requiring a number of stops to replenish water to the boiler and the tanks). (*Among the Clouds* September 1, 1899, p.1; Flora Stanley 1899: pp.14-16; F.O. Stanley 1930: pp.7-8.) The intrepid Mrs. Stanley accompanied her husband, partly to serve as "brakeman" by chocking the wheels at each stop if needed (the car's band brakes did not work in reverse motion), and partly to lend a sense of normalcy to the undertaking and to reassure the carriage road authorities that her husband was not attempting a reckless stunt – not with his wife along (a trend continued at two subsequent Carriage Road ascents by early steamers which were driven by young men accompanied by their mothers). F.O. followed this motoring accomplishment with a similar mountaineering first,

Frank Durbin and Raymond Stanley in the winning Stanley at the 1903 Commonwealth Avenue Hill Climb. Durbin was foreman of the Stanley Motor Carriage Company's Testing Department, and became the factory's chief competition driver with his victory in this event. The car is a stock 1903 Stanley Runabout equipped with a special larger-sized boiler and burner for more power. Cars were required to carry passengers for the climb and many participants filled their seats with small boys – F.E. did likewise by adding his nine-year-old son, Raymond, as a last-minute passenger.
The Horseless Age, courtesy of Leroy Cole.

ascending Surprise Mountain, in nearby Intervale, NH, by steam car on July 14, 1900. (*Boston Globe* July 15, 1900, p.9.)

One of the first organized hill climbing contests in the United States was held on April 20, 1903, on the outskirts of Boston on a steep, recently constructed carriage road. Sponsored

A Stanley on the Mt. Washington Carriage Road above tree-line, 1903. This is believed to be Austin Y. Hoy of Chicago making the first ascent of the mountain by a Stanley on September 2, 1903. Hoy was accompanied by his mother, Mrs. Albert H. Hoy, who may have taken this photograph. The Hoys reached the summit in 1 hour 39 minutes running time, unofficially a new record, their ascent delayed almost three and a half hours due to descending teams of horses with the right of way.
The Automobile Magazine,
Stanley Museum Archives.

by the Massachusetts Automobile Club, the Commonwealth Avenue Hill Climb took place on a fifth-of-a-mile course that climbed a smooth grade averaging 13 per cent. Nearly 50 vehicles made the climb, all successfully, but the steam cars virtually owned the course – the slowest steamer finishing a full ten seconds ahead of the fastest gasoline car, a Stevens-Duryea. The Stanley entry, a 1903 six horse power runabout (all stock except for a somewhat larger boiler) driven by Frank Durbin with F.E. Stanley's nine-year-old son Raymond as the required passenger, turned in the fastest time of the day with a remarkable run of 16 3-5 seconds. (Dolnar 1903a: p.601; Foster 2004: pp.161-165.) "It was a beautiful spectacle," declared one reporter of the Stanley's trial, "and to many the performance was really wonderful." (*Boston Herald* April 21, 1903, p.1) "It was a great day for steam," recalled Raymond Stanley, "and this performance laid a solid foundation to the Stanley's reputation as a hill climber." (R.W. Stanley 1945: p.19.)

The hill climbing predominance of steamers was coming under increasing pressure, however, as the hydrocarbon branch strove to catch up. On August 1, 1902, the first gasoline-powered car, a 12 hp Model C

AUTOMOBILE GALA WEEK IN THE WHITE MOUNTAINS.
JULY 11 TO 16, 1904.
Rendezvous at Crawfords, Fabyan and Bretton Woods the 9th and 10th.
Grand Contest by the Titans of the Road in their Climb to the Clouds on Mt. Washington.

BIRD'S-EYE VIEW OF THE WHITE MOUNTAINS NEW HAMPSHIRE.

The Climb to the Clouds, 1904. The 1904 map of the planned routes for the first Climb to the Clouds at Mt. Washington, including the reliability tours and Good Roads promotional runs sponsored by Anderson and Price at the Bretton Woods hotels, and laid out with the assistance of J. F. Hathaway.
Splash Pan, courtesy of Douglas A Philbrook.

Packard, finally made it to the summit of Mount Washington (in over three hours running time), three years after F.O. and Flora Stanley first steamed their way up the carriage road. The following year on August 26, 1903, the steam record was surpassed by a Phelps touring car in the first officially timed ascent of one hour and 46 minutes. The gas car's record on the mountain only lasted a week when it was trimmed to one hour and 39 minutes by a Stanley steam runabout driven by Austin Y. Hoy of Chicago on September 2. The disparity between the hill climbing abilities of the steamers and the best gas cars was narrowing. (*The Bulb Horn* XII:4, pp.2-3, October 1951.)

Head-to-head climbing competition returned to the Commonwealth Avenue Hill Climb on April 19, 1904, and this time the hydrocarbon branch was determined to avenge their complete shutout of the year before. For the steamers this event featured the hill climbing debut

of two remarkable Stanley drivers: Fred Marriott of Needham and Louis S. Ross of Newtonville. Marriott, the foreman of the Stanley factory repair department, drove his stock, 6 hp Stanley to a first place finish in its class, equaling the hill record of 16 3-5 seconds established by Frank Durbin the year before. Ross, the son of the Stanleys' building contractor, drove his heavier Stanley over the course to victory in its class in 18 3-5. The steam camp's best effort, turned in by Marriott, proved to be only good enough for third place overall by the end of the day. Two powerful gas cars, a 40 hp Georges Richard-Brasier driven by H. B. Hills and a 60 hp Mercedes driven by H. L. Bowden, covered the course in 15 2-5, winning their respective classes. (*The Horseless Age* April, 27, 1904, pp.451-453.) Although they knew by now that hill climbing victories were no longer a steam certainty, the Stanleys would never settle for third place again.

With gas cars becoming more competitive at hill climbs, the events themselves began to attract more interest, a trend which did not pass unnoticed in the mountainside resorts. Messrs. Anderson and Price, already rewarded for their support of racing at Ormond Beach by the annual influx of numerous race officials, drivers, owners, reporters, spectators, and fans to the Hotel Ormond and other nearby resorts, now began to promote their summer hotels in the White Mountains, the Mount Pleasant and the Mount Washington at Bretton Woods, as ideal headquarters for an international hill climbing contest up Mount Washington. Race organizer par excellence, Senator William Morgan quickly signed on to reprise his successful role as at Ormond, and the Climb to the

Clouds was born. Sponsored by the White Mountains Road Improvement Association, the event was scheduled for July 11-15, 1904, and included a two-day post climb reliability tour through the White Mountains, advocated by none other than motoring enthusiast J. F. Hathaway and embraced by the sponsors as an opportunity for good roads (and area resorts) promotion. Hathaway and his Stanley would not only take part in the tour, he apparently was instrumental in the route planning, preparing some of the earliest auto touring maps of the White Mountains, later made into a promotional brochure distributed by Anderson and Price. (Morgan 1904: pp.740-741.) Morgan secured permission from the Mount Washington Road Company for use of the

F.E. Stanley at Readville, 1903. *F.E., his head barely visible above the cockpit of the Stanley "Torpedo" (or "Turtle") racer, steams across the finish line with a new steam track record in the mile, 1:02 4-5, during a special match race with George C. Cannon at the Readville track on May 30, 1903. Unlike race car events today, the organizers required the manufacturers' logos on the cars to be covered while competing, hence the Stanley logo on the side of the car is covered by a blank sheet of paper.*
Stanley Museum Archives.

course (cars at this time were only allowed on the road by special permission), and race sanction by the Automobile Association of America. The event benefited from strong local support, excellent accommodations and rail connections necessary for the event's success, although the limited access for spectators and the unpredictable mountain weather were causes for concern.

The steamer's defeat at Commonwealth Avenue in 1904 and the advent of the Climb to the Clouds may have caused a shift in the racing focus of the Stanley Motor Carriage Company. The previous summer saw F.E. Stanley roll out a special streamlined racer at the Readville track in Boston for the Decoration Day races on May 30, 1903. Stanley matched his machine in a hard-fought series of mile trials against an equally radical steam racer designed and driven by George C. Cannon, a student at Harvard University. The match lived up to its billing as both drivers and their machines pressed each other hard, eclipsing the world steam track record, Stanley triumphing with a new record of 1:02 4-5. (*Boston Globe* May 31, 1903, p. 10; Foster 2004: pp.165, 167.) Both Stanley and Cannon made independent plans to go to Ormond for the 1904 tournament, but neither would take part, Louis Ross taking his first venture into international competition with his stock Stanley instead.

Stanley apparently intended to build a faster, more powerful steam track racer for short distances, his eye on the mile record, but the call of Mount Washington and the opportunity to reclaim the hill climbing honors first established by his twin brother in 1899 and the need to reassert the steamer's ascendancy in hill climbing may have taken precedence in Stanley's view. This may have been as much a strategic marketing decision as a competitive

one – at the risk of losing ground to gas car sales within its customer base, the Stanley had to maintain a performance edge over its competition, and at this stage the Stanley Brothers must have realized their best tack lay in hill climbing – the mile record could wait. In any case, Stanley did not prepare a new track racer for the 1904 Readville races as he did the year before. Instead he prepared a lightweight 1903 Stanley runabout with a larger-than-stock burner and boiler, just as he had for the first Commonwealth Avenue climb in 1903, and set out for Mount Washington.

F.E. and Augusta Stanley arrived at the Climb to the Clouds to find an impressive entry list of powerful cars and experienced drivers – "the great guns in the automobile world," Mrs. Stanley observed – many of them veterans of track and beach racing, including Ormond. (A. Stanley 1904: p.13.) Three weeks before an unofficial course record of 48 minutes 39 seconds had been established in a trial ascent by

F.E. Stanley beside the Cog Railway, Mt. Washington, 1904. *Stanley and his mechanician, Joseph Crowell, maneuvered their Stanley Runabout up onto the railway platform at the summit of Mt. Washington to be photographed next to the Cog Railway after establishing a new hill climbing record on the mountain on July 12, 1904. Photo by Walter R. Merryman.*
Courtesy John Burnham, Stanley Museum Archives.

Auto parade in the White Mountains. *F.E. and Augusta Stanley in their 1903 6 hp Stanley Runabout, left, follow closely behind first-place finisher Harry Harkness in his 60 hp Mercedes while on parade through the White Mountains following the Climb to the Clouds, July 13, 1904. The mountain resort in the background is the Crawford House in Crawford Notch, NH, which served as the summer residence for John Anderson for several years before he went into the hotel business with Joseph D. Price at Ormond Beach and Bretton Woods.*

Lewiston Journal, Stanley Museum Archives.

Otto Nestman in a seven hp Stevens-Duryea. This record would fall six times in the first day of racing alone. First H. Ernest Rogers in a 24 hp Peerless, then Harry Fosdick in a 20 hp Winton, followed by Percy P. Pierce in a 28 hp Pierce, and then A.E. Morrison in another 24 hp Peerless, all in turn succeeded in lowering each others' time. In the afternoon James L. Breese, driving the same 40 hp Mercedes he raced at Ormond earlier in the year, lowered the record even further to 34 minutes 9 4-5 seconds. Finally F.E. Stanley, representing the only chance for steam (Webb Jay's White steamer having bowed out with a flat), set off after all the heavyweight gas cars and completed the day's record-breaking with a startling run of

31:41 2-5, his little red Stanley winning its class (over a second-place Olds) by more than 35 minutes. (*Among the Clouds* July 12, 1904, p.1; *The Automobile* July 16, 1904, p. 51.)

For the free-for-all on the second day of climbing, Stanley and his mechanician, Joseph Crowell of Newton, lightened their little stick-seat runabout of its front seat and all expendable gear, and scorched up the mountain in an early morning run of 28:19 2-5. An enthusiastic crowd including renowned automobile tourist Charles J. Glidden cheered the US-made Stanley on its record-braking effort, and during a lull in the action Stanley was persuaded to run his car up some skids to the mountain-top railway platform, as far as a vehicle could go unaided and where photographers could best record it. Car after car attempted, and failed, to surpass the pinnacle the Stanley had achieved, and it appeared that the steamer had reclaimed its mastery in hill climbing. The day and the record would ultimately fall to an $18,000 gas-powered import, however – a 60 hp Mercedes driven by Harry Harkness in a white-knuckle run of 24:37 3-5. Harkness, it was reported, was so shaken by his ordeal that he let his mechanician bring his car down off the mountain while he descended by the cog railway. Stanley drove the little red steamer down himself, even though he no longer owned it – he had reluctantly sold it at the summit to a local spectator, Kendrick Kendall of Goffstown, NH, for its stock price of $650, as obligated by the event rules. (*The Automobile* July 16, 1904, pp. 54, 58; A. Stanley 1904: p.13; Merrick 2004: p.20.)

Heavy rains washed out the carriage road and the third day of climbing, so the contestants settled for an impromptu parade around the Bretton Woods area, joined by New Hampshire Governor Bachelder who was attending a Good Roads conference organized by the hill climb sponsors, the White Mountains Road Improvement Association. For the auto parade the Stanleys continued to make use of their record-setting Stanley, as it would be some time before the new owner would take delivery. For the two-day post-climb tour that followed, the Stanleys would use their new black 1904 Model CX as they joined J. F. Hathaway and the other participants on a scenic, hotel-hopping mountain rally. "These runs were very enjoyable," wrote Augusta Stanley, "as every hotel on the route kept open house and fairly urged us to partake of their hospitality. Our party was composed of such men as Glidden, Whipple, Fosdick, Breese, Winton, Phelps, and their ladies, and many known to automobile

Louis Ross in his steam racer, 1904. *This early photo of Ross and his car was published in the Boston Globe on May 21, 1904, prior to the racer's debut on the Readville track on May 30. The Globe reported that Ross's car was equipped with two 3 x 4-inch Stanley engines and a 24-inch copper-shelled Stanley boiler which would have had to have been specially supplied by the Stanley factory at this date. The photo shows the car before its exhaust vent or "smokestack" was added just behind the driver's cockpit. Perhaps in keeping with its homebuilt construction, Ross reportedly drove the racer over public roads from his Newtonville home to the racetrack at Readville.*

Stanley Museum Archives.

fame." As might be expected in a field of such competitive drivers, the hospitable and leisurely side of the tour was quickly transformed by the opportunities for "scorching" *[i.e.: speeding and impromptu racing, usually in excess of social propriety and prudence].* "The first day the 'brushes' on the road were numerous," reported Mrs. Stanley, "but the 'Stanley' was well up to the front, as you can perhaps imagine." (A. Stanley 1904: p.13.) In fact the Stanleys' "dark horse" brushed past every car on the narrow road, including the lead car containing "Number One" (thought to be Charles Glidden) who is said to have declared: "Mr. Stanley, you have a marvelous machine. You can beat us up hill or on the level. You are King of the Road of this contest!" Having christened the Stanley with a lasting moniker, the tour's "Number

The Ross "Wogglebug," rear view. *Ross's car was photographed on a white sheet with its outer carapace removed outside his Newtonville home in 1904. The two 8 to 10 hp Stanley engines (especially the right engine) can be seen in the rear where they are connected to the axle, driving each rear wheel. The 24-inch Stanley boiler, wrapped in asbestos, sits amidships with a rectangular water tank alongside, right.*

Courtesy Buz McKim,
International Speedway Corporation.

One" firmly requested that F.E. Stanley "not pass our car for the rest of our journey." (*Lewiston Evening Journal* September 1, 1904.)

While the Stanleys did not prepare another special racer for the 1904 Decoration Day races at Readville as they had the year before, the track did witness the debut of another remarkable steamer which emerged from the Newtonville basement of Stanley aficionado Louis Ross (1877-1927). Ross's streamlined racer, nicknamed the "Airship" by the *Boston Post*, bore a graceful body of aluminum or "tinplate," somewhat reminiscent of early French airship designs but probably owing its shape more to other radical racers such as the electric Baker "Torpedo Kid" which Ross had seen at Ormond five months earlier. Underneath its tapered body, the Airship rode on a steel chassis built by Frank Worcester of the Watch City Automobile Company of Waltham, Mass., suspended on four semi-elliptic springs. (Edmands

1952: p.2.) The rest of the car, its power plant and controls, were initially made up of stock Stanley components, although in a rather unique configuration, with two 2 1/2 x 3 1/2 inch Stanley engines mated with two 16-inch Stanley boilers, providing an estimated 15 to 18 hp. (F.O. Stanley 1930: p.8.)

Ross's home-built racer was almost certainly his own design, although apparently carried out under the watchful eye of F.E. Stanley. "Almost every Sunday my father would go up to Rosses house in Newtonville, Mass., and look over what Ross was doing," recalled Raymond Stanley, who often tagged along. (R.W. Stanley MS notes, Stanley Museum Archives.) Stanley may have provided some technical advice or input, but the Airship's chassis, suspension, metal body, and dual engines and boilers were

The Ross "Wogglebug," front and side view. *The conical nose cone, left, contained a second water tank; the cylindrical tanks visible likely contained pressurized pilot and burner fuels. The driver sat in the simple seat, center, with the steering lever on his left and the throttle on his right. The driver's seat and the boiler were positioned off-center on the left-hand side of the car to better distribute weight during racing through turns on counter-clockwise tracks.*

Courtesy Buz McKim,
International Speedway Corporation.

completely different from any other Stanley vehicle (an early 1900 version of the Stanley pacing tandem, produced by Locomobile in limited numbers, had two boilers mated to one engine). Stanley almost certainly contributed to Ross's efforts by providing Ross with the latest

Ross in action at Narragansett Park, 1904. *Ross took his racer to Narragansett Park in Cranston, R.I., on September 10, 1904, setting new steam track records at five and ten miles and several distances in between, including a new mile record of 57 4-5. He defeated Frank Durbin, driving the 1903 Stanley "Torpedo" racer, in a five-mile steam race, but was not so fortunate in the match race against H. L. Bowden's Mercedes driven by Charles Basle, shown here, even though Ross had the rail. The "Wogglebug" threw a tire and suffered a blow-out, and Ross later worked on refining the smoothness of his racer's operation prior to the Ormond races.*

Cranston Historical Society.

Stanley components not yet on the market, for it was reported that when Ross's racer finally emerged from his basement it was equipped with two 3 x 4-inch Stanley engines, and a single, large 24-inch copper-shelled boiler, boosting its power rating to 20 hp. (*Boston Globe* May 21, 1904, p.2.) It has been suggested that the two engines, each driving a rear wheel, would have been difficult if not impossible to synchronize, leading to a perceptible wobble in the rear end of the car. Another source noted that "both engines are controlled by one throttle, and any difference in speed of either engine…is taken care of by the elasticity of the steam." (*The Automobile* February 4, 1905, p.214.) When later observed in action at Ormond, a *Boston Herald* journalist was

inspired to nickname the car after a popular comic strip character spun off from the Oz stories of L. Frank Baum, and the "Teakettle" (as it was called then) came to be known in its afterlife as the "Wogglebug." (Foster 2004: pp.171, 183.)

Woggle or not, Ross's innovative car had a lackluster debut at Readville, as it only managed a second-place finish behind H.L. Bowden's Mercedes in an early heat for the ten-mile open before rain and muddy conditions postponed the races. When competition resumed on June 11, Ross entered his racer in the five-mile steam race but lost a tire and again finished second, this time to Frank Durbin driving a stock 8 hp Stanley. (Barrett 1998: 20; *Boston Globe* June 12, 1904, p.1.) Ross managed a far more impres-

The Wogglebug at Weigh-in, Ormond 1905. *The Wogglebug easily passed its weigh-in, tipping the scales at 1,250 lbs, almost 1,000 lbs under the 2,204 lb limit. The car has been equipped with aluminum disk wheel covers and a lowered smokestack to improve its aerodynamics. J. Wiley Edmands, Ross's chief mechanic and assistant, stands behind the racer just ahead of the cockpit.*
Stanley Museum Archives.

sive performance at Narragansett Park in Cranston, RI, on September 10, setting new world's steam track records at five miles in 4:37 2-5, and at ten miles in 10:26 2-5. During these speed trials Ross was also clocked in record time at the two, three, and four mile distances, and drove his final mile in 57 4-5, a new steam track record for the mile. Ross also went head-to-head with H.L. Bowden's Mercedes in a

Ross and competitors at the Ormond Garage, 1905. *Louis Ross poses in his "Wogglebug" (No. 4, left foreground) with a number of other competitors including H. L. Bowden's "Flying Dutchman" (No. 2, right) in front of the Ormond Garage. The garage was built in 1904 for the Hotel Ormond to accommodate the cars and chauffeurs of its motoring guests, and it expanded the hotel's ability to house the influx of race cars and crews during the annual Ormond Beach Tournaments.*
Stanley Museum Archives.

match race, leading for two miles before blowing two tires, and receiving plaudits for making "a plucky effort to finish the race." (*The Car* October 19, 1904, p.278.)

At some point before the end of the year and the start of the 1905 Ormond races, Ross

Newton F. Stanley (1868-1947). *Newton, the oldest nephew of the Stanley Twins, worked for his uncles as a chief emulsion-maker at their Dry Plate factory and later served as a Stanley automobile agent in Waterville, Me., and as a factory inspector. Newton accompanied the Ross team to Ormond in 1905 – whether informally on the Stanley company's behalf, or on his own initiative, is unknown.*
Stanley Museum Archives.

"feverishly worked day and night in order to get it ready for the race of the year" (*Boston Herald* June 11, 1927, p.5), apparently to correct the tire problems that had plagued his efforts earlier at Readville and Narragansett Park. Ross's car weighed in at 1,250 lbs with full tanks, easily meeting the 2,204 lb weight limit set by the racing board for competition in its class. To enhance the aerodynamics of the car Ross lowered the height of the "smoke stack" behind the driver and added aluminum disk covers on the wire-spoke wheels. (*The Automobile* February 4, 1905, p.214; Edmands 1952: p.2.)

Frank Croker in his Smith & Mabley Simplex, Ormond 1905. *Croker, the son of a prominent New York City politician, sits at the wheel of his 75 hp S&M Simplex alongside his mechanician, Alexander Raoul, as they prepare to set out on a pre-race trial on the beach. The two would be involved in a high-speed collision with F.E. Stanley's nephew, Newton Stanley, who was riding along the water's edge on a motorcycle. In the accident the Simplex went out of control and overturned, fatally injuring both Croker and Raoul.*
Automobile Topics, Stanley Museum Archives.

Ross arrived in Florida for the 1905 races with his newly configured racer and a stock 8 hp Stanley, and was accompanied by his assistant, J. Wiley Edmands of Newton Highlands, Mass. Another stock Stanley, a 10 hp machine driven by R.R. Kimball, also took part in the tournament, but it is not clear if any of these cars had direct factory support. There are no contemporary accounts placing F.E. Stanley or his twin brother F.O. (still in illness-enforced exile in Colorado) at Ormond Beach in 1905, but their nephew, Newton Stanley, was apparently part of the Ross team as he was reported to be staying near the beach at the Ross cottage. (*New York Times* January 22, 1905, p.1.)

Newton Stanley (1868-1947) had worked

for his uncles at the Stanley Dry Plate Company as one of their chief emulsion makers until the sale of the firm to Eastman Kodak in early 1904. Newton, an avid motorist despite a serious accident three years earlier, had returned to his father Isaac's farm in Kingfield, Maine, looking for land for himself and his fiancée, and had plans to open a Stanley agency in the area. In January the local Franklin County newspaper reported that Newton was visiting friends in Waban (part of Newton, Mass.) and planned to go to Florida for a few weeks. (*Franklin Chronicle* January 11, 1905, p.2.) It was to be a very long visit.

Late on Saturday afternoon, January 21, Newton was riding a motorcycle along the water's edge at Ormond Beach, perhaps to check on the pre-race condition of the course, when he was rapidly overtaken from behind by a 75 hp Smith & Mabley Simplex driven by amateur driver Frank Croker. Newton apparently swerved left, out away from the water, either to avoid a crashing wave or to clear out of the path of Croker's car. Alas, Croker attempted to do the same, striking Stanley on his left side and losing control of his car, which flipped and rolled at high speed. Alexander Raoul, Croker's mechanician, was killed almost instantly; Croker was transported to a hospital in Daytona where he died the next morning. It was the first fatal accident recorded on the beach. (*Automobile Topics* January 28, 1905, pp.1245-1247; Punnett 2004: pp.28-30.)

Newton Stanley, his leg badly shattered, was taken to a hospital in St. Augustine where he was later reunited with his parents and his fiancée. Sympathies in the racing fraternity and

H.L. Bowden's "Flying Dutchman," Ormond 1905. *Herbert L. Bowden of Waltham, Massachusetts, constructed this special 120 hp Mercedes by linking two 60 hp Mercedes engines together (the second engine came from his speedboat, Mercedes U.S.A.) and elongating the frame of his Mercedes to accommodate them. Driven by Charles Basle (standing behind car to the left), the "Flying Dutchman" set a new record in the mile trials at 34 1-5, and later in the meet trimmed that to 32 1-5. Both records were unofficial as Bowden's car was determined to be overweight. Photo by Richard H. LeSesne.*

Stanley Museum Archives.

William K. Vanderbilt, Jr., in his Mercedes, Ormond 1905. *"Willie K" returned to Ormond in 1905 with a 90 hp Mercedes specially set up for straightaway beach racing, but gear trouble kept him from improving on his record-setting performance of 1904. Relegated to the sidelines for most of the meet, Vanderbilt was gracious to his fellow competitors but not to the inept organizers who took over the tournament, and he never competed at Ormond again. Photo by Richard H. LeSesne.*

Stanley Museum Archives.

in the press tended to side with the deceased, but this view was not shared in the Stanley family where they felt that the blame for the accident had been unfairly shifted onto their injured son. Isaac wrote to friends back in Kingfield that his son was "riding a motor bicycle out of the way of the race track but the man with the big auto racer came down the track at a 40 second clip, and lost control of his carriage and ran into Newton." Indignant, the elder Stanley wrote: "Newton wanted me to tell you that the big son of a gun did not show up in the races." (Isaac N. Stanley letter to "Albert," February 8, 1905, Stanley Museum Archives.) Newton Stanley eventually underwent a partial amputation of his injured leg and a lengthy convalescence, finally returning home to Kingfield five months after he left for Ormond. (*Franklin Chronicle* July 5, 1905, p.2 and August 9, 1905, p.2.)

It was unseasonably cold when the races

finally began on January 24, but the weather was only a minor inconvenience compared to the inept local meet organizers put in place by the Florida East Coast Automobile Association, which had dismissed the able Senator Morgan and his experienced staff at the eleventh hour and had replaced the event managers with amateurs and volunteers. Logistical problems and scheduling snafus, including some absurd misreading of tide tables, lead to exasperating delays, disruptions, and hostile reactions from contestants and spectators alike. The tournament got off slowly, with the first day's contests focusing solely on mundane stock car events. Louis Ross entered his stock 8 hp Stanley in the five mile race for stock cars valued between $651-$1,000, taking the event in 6:42 3-5, more than a minute and a half ahead of second-place finisher W.E. Evans and his 10 hp Autocar. (Foster 2004: pp.183, 479; Punnett 2004: pp.28, 30-31.)

Day Two featured many of the marquee events and brought out the real heavyweights: a bevy of 90 hp Mercedes, one driven by the returning William K. Vanderbilt and two others by E.E. Hawley and S.B. Stevens; a 90 hp Napier driven by Arthur MacDonald; a 90 hp Fiat driven by William Wallace; a 90 hp De Dietrich driven by H.W. Fletcher; an 80 hp Mercedes driven by B.M. Shanley; M.G. Bernin's 60 hp Renault; and the 60 hp Peerless "Green Dragon" driven by Barney Oldfield. H.L. Bowden was also in attendance with a special 120 hp Mercedes, the "Flying Dutchman," powered by two 60 hp Mercedes engines linked together. Against this formidable array of internal combustion cars stood Louis Ross and his 20 hp, home-built Wogglebug, which lead off the mile speed trials with a new World record of 38 seconds, eclipsing Vanderbilt's record set the year before. Five minutes later MacDonald's 90 hp Napier lowered the record further to 34 2-5 with a speed of 104.65 mph, breaking the 100 mph barrier on US turf for the first time. MacDonald's speed was trimmed by 1-5 of a second some 15 minutes later by Bowden's Flying Dutchman. Bowden's time was later decreed "unofficial" as his car was determined to be overweight;

Ross winning the first heat for the Dewar Trophy. *Ross, on the water side, sprints off the line, followed (right to left) by Arthur MacDonald in a 90 hp Napier, William K. Vanderbilt and E. E. Hawley in 90 hp Mercedes. Ross's homebuilt racer triumphed over the powerful European production race cars with a competition record of 41 3-5. Photo by Walter R. Merryman.*

Ormond Beach Library, courtesy Dick and Yvonne Punnett.

MacDonald held the beach record (the World record status of his run wound up in dispute betwixt French and British racing authorities); Ross and the Wogglebug were recognized with the undisputed World steam record.

The premier event of the day was the one-mile international challenge for the Sir Thomas R. Dewar Trophy, one of many sporting awards newly established by the heir to the Scottish distillery firm. This prestigious, independent award was to be given to the winner of a one-mile, rolling start, straightaway race to be held for the first time at Ormond Beach in 1905. Ross, through an exchange of numbers with Willie K. followed by some last-minute withdrawals, was by chance awarded the "pole" position on the ocean side for the first heat, lining up next to MacDonald's Napier and the two big Mercedes driven by Vanderbilt and Hawley. Ross's position allowed him to use the steamer's "latitude of speed" to best advantage, approaching the line as slowly as possible to keep the gas cars in low gear, and then opening the throttle wide for a jump start as soon as the line was crossed. Ross had found that the new Stanley burner on the Wogglebug had to be lowered to maximize combustion, leaving only 2 1-3 inches of ground clearance and potential pilot problems. "He took no chances on the possibility that the pilot might go out when he started to move up to the line, but on a pre-arranged signal he turned on the main burner and his assistant running along beside him reached his arm into the 'smoke stack' and dropped a 'hurricane match' down a boiler tube igniting the vapor in the burner chamber." (Edmands 1952: p.3.) It is not known if Ross employed this crude, but effective method in the Dewar trials, but he was first across the finish line in the first heat with a competition record of 41 3-5, followed by MacDonald,

Ross at steam, Ormond 1905. *Louis Ross puts his steam racer through its paces on the beach during the 1905 races.*

Courtesy Frank Lee,
via Dick and Yvonne Punnett.

Hawley and Vanderbilt (the latter two men eliminated).

In the final heat Ross went "wheel to wheel" with MacDonald's Napier, nipping the Englishman by 1-5 of a second, with William Wallace's 90 hp Fiat third, and Barney Oldfield's Peerless "Green Dragon" a distant fourth. (*Automobile Topics* January 28, 1905, pp.1256-1257.) It was almost unthinkable – Louis Ross had taken on some of the world's most powerful cars from the hydrocarbon branch with his little home-built steamer and had snatched away one of the most prestigious speed prizes in the world. The Wogglebug proved equally unmatched among the steamers, winning the one mile steam car race for the R.C. Clowry Trophy in 57 2-5, with Webb Jay's 20 hp White steamer second in 58 1-5, Ross's 8 hp stock Stanley driven by J. Wiley Edmands, third, and R.R. Kimball's 10 hp Stanley fourth. The Wogglebug finished the day with a victory in the one-mile race for the Corinthian Cup for amateur drivers, outracing a 90 hp Mercedes driven by S.B. Steven with a winning time of 41 3-5 – the driver was identified by *Automobile Topics* as A.W. Walker "for Louis Ross."

The Wogglebug and crew, Ormond 1905. *Louis Ross, right, and his assistant J. Wiley Edmands, pose with the Wogglebug on the beach. In the eight events in which it was entered, Ross's car won seven and finished second in the other, setting two world records and one competition record on the beach.*

Stanley Museum Archives.

Thursday, January 26, was marked by subfreezing temperatures and gale force winds, but several of the remaining sprint events were held, the Wogglebug continuing its winning streak with a first place finish in the mile race for Class A cars (in 42 seconds), followed by S.B. Stevens' Mercedes, second. The results were exactly the same in the one-kilometer race for cars weighing 1,432-2,204 lbs: Louis Ross, Ross Steamer, first (in 29 2-5), and S.B. Stevens, Mercedes, second. In the one-kilometer race for the Bowden Trophy, Ross had to settle for second place (in 28 1/5) behind MacDonald in the Napier, which took the cup with a time of 27 3-5. Ross finished off his record breaking at Ormond with a World steam record of 24 1-5 in the kilometer trials. (Foster 2004: pp. 183-187.) By the close of the 1905 Ormond tournament Ross had entered his Wogglebug in eight events, scoring seven firsts and one second place finish, and setting two World steam records and one competition record – a performance unmatched by any other home-built race car. Before returning home to Massachu-

setts, Ross sold his racer to Charles Heineman, a wealthy sportsman from New York, because, it was reported, "he did not care to pursue a racing career." (*New York Times* January 29, 1905, p.10.) Other sources indicate that Ross sold his machine at this time because he knew the little car would not have the speed to defend the Dewar Cup or compete in speed trials in the future. (*Boston Globe* May 30, 1905, p.11.) The Wogglebug was later entered in an exhibition mile at the Brighton Beach track near Coney Island, NY, on May 6, 1905, when Joe Nelson crashed it through a rail fence in an attempt to break Ross's steam track record set at Narragansett Park eight months earlier. (*New York Times* May 7, 1905, p.11.) With Ross pursuing other interests and the Wogglebug history, the 1906 Ormond races and the land speed record were now wide open to all comers. Ross's car was already being acclaimed in automotive circles as a "Stanley." In Watertown, Mass., they must have certainly been wondering what a real Stanley could do.

CHAPTER 4

Mr. Stanley, His Foreman, and His Flying Canoe.

"That evening [November 18, 1899] before dusk Mr. Stanley took me out alone in the front seat of the two-seater and we drove out toward Natick [a suburb west of Boston].

"As we returned there was a piece of reasonably smooth road. Mr. Stanley 'let her out'. We whizzed. It took my breath away. No windshield, no headlights except kerosene lanterns.

"As we slowed down Mr. Stanley said 'Arthur, I believe the time will come when one of these cars will go a mile in two minutes.' And probably at that moment we were concluding a sprint of at least a mile a minute – but we had no speedometer. The reason for fixing a mile in 'two minutes' was to be traced in the great dispute among horsemen as to the ultimate speed of a horse in harness.

"Mr. Stanley was a horse-fancier. Among his disputants the leader was Dr. George Bailey, of Portland, horseman and 'Vet.' He showed by figures that it would forever be impossible for any trotter or pacer to beat two minutes. That's why Mr. Stanley set that as the limit for the automobile."

Arthur Gray Staples. (*Lewiston Evening Journal.*)

ON JUNE 1, 1849, the population of the western Maine town of Kingfield (662 souls in the 1850 census) was increased by two, with the birth of a pair of identical twin boys in the homestead of Solomon and Apphia Stanley. The arrival of twins in a small rural town in the mid-nine-teenth Century might have been seen as remarkable, even though, as one of the twins would later characteristically relate, the town experienced an "epidemic of twins" that year, the Stanley Twins being but one of three sets born to families in the community. (F.O. Stanley circa 1940.)

The Stanley Twins would soon come to be seen as remarkable beyond the simple circum-stance of their arrival. Born into a nurturing family marked by a passion for literary, musical and cultural interests – their father was the local schoolmaster and their mother conveyed a love of reading, music and drama – the Twins were christened Francis Edgar and Freelan

Oscar, their names said to be taken from char-acters in the novels of Sir Walter Scott. Known to friends and family as Frank and Freel, upon maturity and in partnership they were com-monly referred to as "F.E." and "F.O." Their five siblings' names also reflected the family's cul-tural and scholarly leanings: their older brother, Isaac Newton Stanley, their younger brothers, John Calvin French (named as well for a mater-nal uncle), Solomon Liberty (the namesake of his father and grandfather), Bayard Taylor (named for a prominent contemporary poet and author), and their solitary sister Chansonetta (literally "little song" – a notation for a short choral composition).

One of the earliest anecdotes of the Twins as youngsters involves their passion and skill in whittling, even in the family kitchen under the encouragement of their mother, whereby they made their own toys, puzzles and playthings. (F.O. Stanley circa 1940; R.W. Stanley 1932:

Stanley Homestead, Kingfield, Maine. *The Stanley Twins and their siblings were born in this 19th Century rural farmhouse overlooking the east bank of the Carrabassett River. Beyond the house is a small brook, Stanley Stream, where the boys built water wheels and worked out the mechanics of their water-powered lathes and other wood-working equipment. The house still stands today. Photo by Chansonetta Stanley Emmons.*

Stanley Museum Archives.

p.10.) At about nine years of age their handicraft expanded to producing water-wheels in a small brook behind their farmhouse, and thence to powering wood-working lathes and saws, and their first attempts at manufacturing. Their first foray into entrepreneurship, the production of one-cent toy tops for local youths, was too successful – "we quickly exhausted the market," F.O. recalled, "and the business was soon at a standstill." There was however, as the Twins soon discovered, a ready market for wooden spools to replace the oft-broken ones on warping-bars on hand looms found in every weaver's home, and they found they could produce the much sought-after replacements for two cents apiece. "So you see," wrote F.O., we were rapidly becoming wealthy, even at that early age." (F.O. Stanley circa 1930.)

Historians recognize this focus on whittling as a standard element in biographies of early American inventors, dubbed by some as the "myth of the Yankee Whittling Boy" (Cooper 2003: pp.85-86), in which inventive creativity is charmingly attributed to talents developed in adolescence through the use of a pocket knife. While there is much to be said for the analogy of whittling and creativity, and its reality and myth, in the Stanley Brothers we have a case of two gifted inventors who were also skilled carvers – "Yankee Whittling Boys" in fact. Examples abound, in artifacts and oral history, of the Twins' whittling skills: a set of chessmen intricately carved by F.E. from an old broom handle at his summer home on Squirrel Island, Maine; wooden puzzles and crossbows carved by F.O. at his convalescence home at Estes Park, Colorado; and the well-crafted violins produced by both men as a life-long hobby.

The Stanleys' whittling skills were so renowned that stories persist that the early machinists' patterns for Stanley cars were hand-carved by the brothers. The actual patterns for automotive parts were no doubt professionally

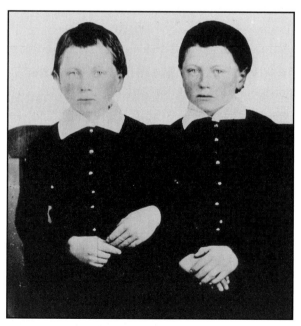

Francis Edgar and Freelan Oscar Stanley. *This early tintype from the mid-1850s shows Frank and Freel together as young boys; family identification places Frank on the left. Freel, according to family lore, was the first born.*

Stanley Museum Archives.

machined, but the legend, like so many other Stanley stories, may have some validity. As a visitor to the Stanley Works in 1903 disdainfully noted: "There is not one single intelligible drawing in the Stanley factory. When anything new is required, pencil sketches are sometimes made, and more times Stanley tells the men what he wants, or makes it with his own hands... the completed thing itself... being simply repeated from the model..." – the "Yankee Whittling Boys" in action. (Dolnar 1903b: p.211.)

The Twins' father, Solomon Stanley 2nd (1813-1889), was a man of principle, an abolitionist and an early advocate of the Temperance Movement, although he was not always a sound judge of the same qualities in others. While he tended to his duties as schoolmaster he entrusted the operation of his dry goods store to an unscrupulous partner, a drinker and a gambler, who subsequently abandoned the business leaving Solomon heavily in debt. Solomon felt honor-bound to repay his creditors and struggled for years to redeem his reputation, efforts for which he was revered in his hometown. His ordeal impressed upon his children the rewards of staying true to one's ideals and of making good on one's commitments, as well as the need for honesty and caution in partnerships and business dealings, the avoidance of debt, and adherence to the principles of temperance. (Emmons 1916: pp.6-7.)

This period of family adversity brought another life lesson to the young Twins: that they could cope with hard luck without abandoning their pride. This principle manifested itself, at age ten, in their earnest desire to attend their father's school in clothing made of store-bought fabric instead of homespun. To this end the youngsters embarked on their most ambitious joint undertaking, maple sugar produc-

tion, carving hundreds of wooden taps and sap buckets for the harvest, and acquiring an essential processing tool, a sap evaporator, through a fortuitous exchange of a freshly-killed mink, a story of Stanley luck and forbearance passed down for generations. The success of their maple sugaring enterprise not only raised enough money for the fabric for matching school suits (giving rise to the first of many "identical twin" tales – their mother measuring out two sets of sewing patterns only to discover that one set would have sufficed) but also allowed for the purchase of an advanced mathematics textbook, Greenleaf's *National Arithmetic*, through which the young scholars achieved some measure of local fame by "ciphering" all the way through it, well in advance of their years. (R.W. Stanley 1932: pp.13-23.)

The outbreak of the Civil War found the Twins too young for service, but their older brother Isaac (and a number of other young men from Kingfield) enlisted in the 28th Maine Regiment, serving eleven months from September 1862 to August 1863, primarily in Louisiana and Florida. (Chenowith 1985?) This is not to say that the fourteen-year-old Twins were unaffected by the distant war, as the passions of the conflict erupted in their own tiny Maine community in July 1863, in what has come to be known as the Kingfield Rebellion, an incident of such significance that it later inspired both Twins to write down their individual recollections. (F.E. Stanley 1916; F.O. Stanley 1934.)

A faction of Kingfield residents, unsupportive of the war and outraged by military conscription, took up arms and seized control of the town, burning draft edicts, shutting down and defacing shops that housed the post office and government agencies, and attempting a "lock-down" of all loyalist residents who disagreed with them, including Solomon Stanley and his family. Solomon, an abolitionist with a son fighting for the Union, refused to back down to the "copperheads" even though sick with pneumonia, challenging their edicts by traveling to the doctor in nearby New Portland with his son, Freel.

Later the elder Stanley, fearing the worst upon learning that the armed men had gotten "a lot of whisky," somberly told his sons: "you had better get out your bullet moulds and make a quantity of bullets, for we may need them," and the Twins began to erect defenses around the Stanley farmhouse. Fortunately the tense situation was defused by the timely arrival of 87 soldiers from the Lewiston Light Infantry of the State Militia, and the Kingfield Rebellion was put down without bloodshed. Their father's courage standing up to an armed mob of his fellow townsmen further reinforced the Twins' conviction to "stick to the right, regardless of its unpopularity." (F.O. Stanley 1934: pp.16-17, 34.) A month later the brothers got to experience the inglorious side of war when their brother Isaac returned home from the Port Hudson campaign, sick with camp fever and a wasted shell of his former self, forced to travel the last 40 miles to Kingfield on foot. (*Stanley Family Reunion* 1982: p.3.)

Given that their father was a school teacher and that the Twins possessed educational talents (their older brother Isaac was in line to inherit the family farm), it is no surprise that the Stanley Brothers first set out from home to find careers for themselves as teachers. In 1869 they enrolled in the two-year teaching program at the Western State Normal School in Farmington (now the University of Maine at Farmington), and F.O. graduated in 1871. F.E. withdrew from the school in his first year after

Augusta May Walker and Frank E. Stanley. *F.E. Stanley married his fellow teacher Augusta May Walker on January 1, 1870; this tintype dates to the time of their marriage. Augusta was known in the family as "Gustie" or "Gus." F.E. at this time used the name "Frank E. Stanley."*

Stanley Museum Archives.

a Geography instructor questioned his integrity over a class assignment – a map of the United States drawn from memory so accurately it aroused suspicion – an insinuation one of Solomon Stanley's sons could not tolerate. (The Normal School later issued F.E. an honorary diploma in 1906.) F.E. quickly found a position at the school in North New Portland where he had previously taught "penmanship," now assuming the role of schoolmaster. There he became engaged to the school's elementary teacher, Augusta May Walker (1848-1927), and they were married January 1, 1870.

F.O. Stanley taught in the Maine District Schools of Auburn, Farmington and Lisbon for a year following his graduation, then entered Hebron Academy to "fit" for college, enrolling at Bowdoin College in Brunswick in the fall of 1873. While at Bowdoin, F.O. became embroiled in a student "revolt" against the military edicts of Joshua Chamberlain, the former Bowdoin professor, turned-Civil War Hero, turned-College President, who reacted to a student petition against uniforms and drills by rusticating the entire student body, their reinstatement conditional on their renouncing their petition and obeying his directives. F.O. would later say that he could not afford the required uniform, although he could also look back at his brother Isaac's unrewarding military career and the capricious way some men in power wield authority, and decided not to return to the college. (Bowdoin later conferred an honorary degree on F.O. in 1919.) F.O. returned to teaching in the Maine towns of Industry and Mechanic Falls; at the latter he met and later married a fellow teacher, Flora Jane Record Tileston (1847-1939), on April 18, 1876. F.O. and Flora then moved out of state to Columbia,

F.O. Stanley, circa 1875. *A graduate of the teachers' program at the Western State Normal School, Farmington, Maine, in 1871, F.O. served as schoolmaster at several rural Maine localities, including the school at Mechanic Falls where he met his future wife, Flora Jane Record Tileston. Curtis Photographer, Lewiston, Maine.*
Stanley Museum Archives.

Flora Jane Record Tileston. *The daughter of descendents of Danish settlers in the Poland, Maine, area, Flora met F.O. Stanley while teaching at Mechanic Falls and they were married April 18, 1876. The couple was given board during the school year, but spent their summers alternating between their parents' homes in Poland and Kingfield according to the 1880 census. Photo by F.E. Stanley.*
Stanley Museum Archives.

Penn., for a few years, F.O. serving as the local school's headmaster and Flora as elementary school teacher. (Merrick 2002: pp.18-19.)

F.E. Stanley had assumed the Principal's position in the town of Strong, Maine, in 1873 when he was recommended for the Assistant Superintendent's position at the Maine State Reform School in Cape Elizabeth. The school's previous administrator had been dismissed in the wake of a scandal involving the death of a child following an ill-advised disciplinary action, and F.E. was brought in to restore public confidence in the program. Both of the Stanley Twins favored a modern approach to practical education which relied on class competition and incentives instead of strict discipline, and F.E. and Augusta Stanley were successful in turning the program around during their year in residence.

They returned to Strong, but with one

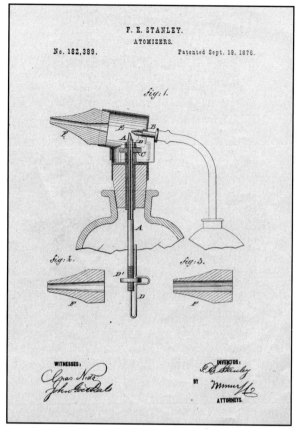

F. E. STANLEY.
ATOMIZERS.

No. 182,389.   Patented Sept. 19, 1876.

Fig: 1.

Fig: 2.   *Fig: 3.*

WITNESSES: INVENTOR:
                              BY
                              ATTORNEYS.

Airbrush patent drawings. *U.S. Patent #182,389, "Improvement in Atomizers," granted to Frank E. Stanley of Auburn, Maine, on September 19, 1876. F.E. designed this device to finish off the backgrounds and extraneous details of his "crayon portraits" more rapidly, sometimes duplicating intricate lace patterns by using a piece of the lace itself as a template, while leaving more time to concentrate on the facial features of his subjects. His portraitures won prizes at the 1876 Centennial exhibitions in Portland and Philadelphia.*
                    U.S. Patent and Trademark Office.

three-year-old child in the household (their daughter, Blanche) and another on the way, the Stanleys' meager teachers' salaries kept them barely at the subsistence level. F.E. decided to draw upon his artistic talents, turning to portraiture to supplement the family income, thinking perhaps that he might also set aside some money for law school. Working with liquefied charcoal as a medium, Stanley experimented with an atomizer, an early air brush, culminating in his first successful patent applica-

tion, granted by the U.S. Patent Office on September 19, 1876. F.E.'s initial attempts to solicit patrons door-to-door in the city of Auburn led to a referral to a prominent shop where samples of his work received window space, and he soon found himself with so many customers that he retired from active teaching, set up a profitable portrait studio in the city, and soon forgot about law school as he found his new career more rewarding. (A. M. Stanley 1919: p.xxi.)

Apphia Kezar French Stanley (1819-1874), the Twins' mother and the dominant influence in the Stanley household, died of tuberculosis in September 1874. Tuberculosis would become a scourge in the Stanley family – the three younger brothers, Solomon Liberty (1881), Calvin (1883), and Bayard (1915) all succumbing to the disease – and it would have a major impact on the Twins' lives.

F.O., in particular, had recurring bouts with the affliction, the earliest indication of which seems to have occurred when he was teaching in Pennsylvania. Blanche Stanley recalled that her father, F.E., had once traveled to Pennsylvania to stand in for his brother when F.O. was too ill to teach, taking over his classes for several weeks, apparently with none of F.O.'s students realizing that another Mr. Stanley was at their teacher's desk. (Hallett 1954: p.64.) In 1880, F.O. returned to Maine, taking an instructor's position on the faculty of his alma mater, the Western State Normal School in Farmington, but his illness reasserted itself and he retired from teaching in 1881 "to go into some less sedentary position." (Purington 1889: p.68.)

For F.O. Stanley, a "less sedentary position" meant rolling up his sleeves and returning to the spirit of manufacturing enterprise of his youth. As a teacher concerned with practical education he had been frustrated by the scarcity of cheap, accurate drawing sets for geometry students, so he designed a compact boxed set of drawing tools (including a simple compass, protractor, ruler, right triangle and square) to fill this need. In 1881 he set up shop in a former cheese factory in Mechanic Falls, Maine, outfitted his plant with steam-powered machinery supplied by the local firm of J.W. Penney and Sons, and began mass producing the Stanley Practical Drawing Set to satisfy a growing influx of orders. The success of this venture was abruptly ended a year later when a fire of unknown origin destroyed the factory and all of its contents. F.O. suddenly found himself in a state of financial ruin equal or worse to that which had plagued his father years before. As a temporary measure he took a cashier's job with the Damon Safe Company in Cambridge, Mass.,

Stanley's Practical Drawing Set. *F.O. designed an economical boxed set of accurate drawing tools for school children, inspired during his earlier years as a teacher. The set contained a metal compass, right triangle, and a right angle or square, accompanied by a paperboard protractor and six-inch ruler, all designed to fit in a compact wooden case, 6 1/4" x 2 1/2" x 5/8". Very similar sets are carried by school children today. The drawing sets were produced in Mechanic Falls until the factory was burned out in 1882, the F.O. Stanleys briefly relocating to Cambridgeport, Massachusetts. Photo by John S. Dillon.*

Courtesy John S. Dillon.

F.E. Stanley in his portrait studio, Lewiston, Maine, mid-1880s. *F.E. expanded his portrait business to include photography, initially to speed up the sitting time of his clients and later to provide photographic portraits as well. He became quite skilled with the camera, snapping this self-portrait in the "operating room" of his Lewiston studio. He began to experiment with his own formula for photographic dry plates and his success led to the formation, with his twin brother, of the Stanley Dry Plate Company. Photo by F.E. Stanley.*

Stanley Museum Archives.

and with a loan from his twin, struggled to restart his own business. (F.O. Stanley 1936: pp.4-6.)

F.E. Stanley had expanded his portrait studio into new quarters on Lisbon Street in Lewiston, and had taken up photography, first as a method of reducing his subjects' sitting time, later as a means of producing the portraits themselves, becoming so successful with the camera that he listed his occupation as "photographer" for the 1880 census. Stanley began by using the "wet plate" photographic methods common in the late 1870s, but soon began

F.E. Stanley, early 1880s. *When the Stanley Twins reunited in partnership in 1883/1884 they began to emulate each other's dress and appearance. Here F.E. has yet to adopt the full beard that would be characteristic of the Stanley Brothers.*
Stanley Museum Archives.

F.O. Stanley, late 1880s. *Once reunited in partnership with F.E., F.O. added a full beard to his earlier moustache to match that of his twin brother. To the outside world their identities merged to the extent that many business associates and reporters opted to refer to them both simply as "Mr. Stanley." Photo by J. Walden Smith.*
Stanley Museum Archives.

experimenting with the new gelatin "dry plates" just coming onto the market. His experiments led to a successful dry plate formula of his own in 1881, and finding a ready market for his plates among other area photographers, he decided to commence commercial production. F.E. acquired space in the basement of the Manufacturers National Bank of Lewiston for hand-coating and packing dry plates, but his efforts at production stalled due to a succession of intemperate shop foremen who were dismissed for drinking on the job. His wife suggested that he approach his twin brother, still unable to make good on his debts, and offer him a partnership in the dry plate shop. (F.O. Stanley 1936: pp.4, 6; *Stanley Family Reunion 1982*: p.24.)

F.O. considered his brother's offer for a time in 1883 before accepting, and in 1884 the Stanley Dry Plate Company was incorporated with F.E. Stanley as president, F.O. Stanley as treasurer, and Clarence Emerson of Lewiston, a close family friend and attorney, as clerk. The Twins' re-partnership after 15 years on their own was a striking success, so much so that they soon began to mimic each other in style and fashion, semiconsciously adopting a single persona of "Mr. Stanley" in their dealings with the outside world.

The brothers collaborated on an invention for a machine and a process for producing dry plates which would automate the industry. The U.S. Patent Office at first refused to grant the patent application until they had been assured that both of the Twins had signed it (their signatures were deemed indistinguishable), but the official Letters Patent was finally issued on July 13, 1886. Whereas 60 hand-coated dry plates could once be produced in an hour, the new Stanley apparatus could wash and machine-coat 60 dry plates in a minute. The

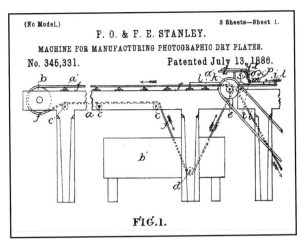

(No Model.)　　　　　　　　　3 Sheets—Sheet 1.

F. O. & F. E. STANLEY.

MACHINE FOR MANUFACTURING PHOTOGRAPHIC DRY PLATES.

No. 345,331.　　　　　Patented July 13, 1886.

FIG. 1.

Machine for Manufacturing Photographic Dry Plates. *F.O. and F.E. collaborated on this, their first joint patent, to revolutionize the production of photographic dry plates. A skilled worker, in an hour, could produce 60 plates coated by hand; the Stanleys' machine could coat 60 plates a minute. The process established the Stanleys as one of the top producers of photographic dry plates in the U.S., but the patent did not provide them with a monopoly as their competitors quickly found ways to duplicate the process. The Stanleys' invention nonetheless made them successful and wealthy manufacturers.*

U.S. Patent and Trademark Office.

breakthrough allowed the Twins to cut their prices in half and still double their profits. Although they were not able to block others from copying their process (their patent had been drafted too narrowly for clear protection), their invention brought them to the forefront of the business and also ensured that the Stanley Brothers would now be ranked as prosperous manufacturers and wealthy men.

With a comfortable income, the Twins turned to avocational pursuits, their preference leaning to those involving speed and transportation, and they began acquiring fast pace horses and trotters, building a large stable on Canal Street in Lewiston. They also took keen interest in the cutting-edge engineering challenges of their day, which included early concepts of aeronautics and of self-propelled "road

wagons." Some of their interests are reflected in a "class prophesy" delivered by Blanche Stanley before her high school graduating class in 1889, in which she foretells "the success of the flying machine, of a machine that would wash dishes [*a key dry plate machine component*], and a horse that would go a mile in two minutes" (Hallett 1954: p.36) – all dreams of her father and uncle.

For the road wagon, the Stanleys need only to have looked next door at Edwin Field's, whose machine shop sat adjacent to their stables on Canal Street. Field, an eccentric Lewiston inventor, had built a wood-fired steam road wagon in his shop in 1887 and had even run it in August of that year for a short distance, stopping frequently to rebuild steam pressure. (Foster 2004: pp.35-36.) The Stanleys were familiar with and amused by Field's experiments – Field recalled that both Twins, F.O. in particular, would come into his shop and engage in long arguments over the futility of his designs. (*The Motor World*, March 3, 1904, p.1005.)

In 1890 the Stanleys decided to move their dry plate business to a major port city to centralize the importing of glass plates (produced in England) and the shipping of their finished dry plates to customers all over the country. They settled on a site in Watertown, Mass., just outside of Boston on the Charles River, near major rail lines and convenient to nearby residential neighborhoods in Newton where the Twins built new homes.

The city water supply to the new factory was eventually found to be deficient in a necessary mineral, leading to a serious problem of defective dry plates on the market, a crisis that threatened to ruin the company in 1892/93. The Stanleys decided to have an artesian well drilled to the water table on their property, leading to an incident that illustrates their determination and scientific skepticism, and something of their humor as well.

They contracted the work to a local well-driller who, much to the Twins' dismay, arrived on the job with "a man past 60, very fat, and decidedly seedy," recalled F.O., "and with him he had a divining rod." The well-driller explained that he wanted his dowser to check to see if there was water where the Twins wanted the well drilled or if they would need to choose another site.

The dowser's rod indicated water right where the Stanleys wanted their well, but they

F.E. demonstrating the speed of Stanley Dry Plates, circa 1893. F.E. is captured in mid-air, leaping over a puddle outside the Watertown, Mass., factory in an exuberant demonstration of the speed of the Stanley Dry Plate. Once the Twins relocated their business to Watertown they continued to strive to introduce faster dry plates to meet photographers' needs.

Stanley Museum Archives.

couldn't resist asking the driller to have his dowser repeat the procedure blindfolded. His eyes bound, the dowser was led over the area again, indicating the presence of water everywhere but where he had determined it to be initially. The Stanleys were satisfied that their blindfolding-the-dowser test had shown that the divining rod was "entirely destitute of any virtue," but, as they expected, this failed to convince the well-driller, whose drill eventually struck water, 300 feet down through ledge. (F.O. Stanley 1936: pp.19-20.)

The Stanleys continued to raise horses and were frequent visitors to country fairgrounds and harness racing tracks where they turned a connoisseur's eye on fine equine stock. They were also avid cyclists, admiring the precise mechanics and simple engineering of the new "safety" bicycles (bicycles with similar-sized fore and aft wheels, replacing the old "high-wheelers") as well as the speed of the light-weight machines. It is said that F.E. Stanley, while out riding one day, conceived the idea of a racing sulky built of light-weight tubing riding on bicycle wheels with pneumatic tires. The Twins suggested the idea to their neighbor, bicycle manufacturer Sterling Elliott, who carried it to fruition at his Hickory Wheel plant next door to the Stanleys' dry plate factory.

The new "bike sulkies" were an instant success. Speed records were lowered and the elusive two-minute mile brought within reach, finally achieved by the pacer Star Pointer who led one of the new sulkies around the Readville track in Boston a mile in 1:59 1-4, on August 29, 1897. (Barrett 1998: pp.8-9.) F.E. was not so successful at bringing his wife up to speed with the new bicycle technology. Augusta Stanley, a matronly woman lame from a knee injury after a carriage accident in 1887 (the local doctors would have amputated her leg had her husband not insisted on a second opinion), suffered from inactivity and lack of exercise, which her husband hoped to remedy by getting her out in the fresh air on a bicycle. According to family history passed down by her daughter Emily, Mrs. Stanley did not take to the wheel very well, falling to the ground despite numerous attempts to remain upright. Resigned, her husband is said to have reassured her: "Never mind, my dear. I will build something so we can ride together, side by side." (Joy 1956: p.32.)

In the autumn of 1896 the Stanleys visited the Brockton Fair, south of Boston, the fairgrounds there a prominent stop on the professional harness racing circuit. A novel attraction at the track was a demonstration on October 1st of a new horseless carriage owned by George H. Morrill, Jr., of Norwood, Mass. (*Boston Globe*, October 2, 1896, p.9.) Believed to be an early gasoline-explosive French De Dion, the horseless carriage broke down, immobile, on its first lap around the track. On the train ride back to Boston the hapless vehicle and its performance were dissected by the Stanley party, and F.E. is said to have declared: "Well, boys, before another fall I will show you a self-propelled carriage that will go around the track not only once but several times without stopping." (C. Stanley 1945: p.23.)

Design work on the first Stanley carriage began soon after. "In the fall of 1896," recalled F.O., "my brother and I began to make drawings of a steam automobile." (F.O. Stanley 1930: p.2.) Whether the design of the first car was a joint effort or the principal work of F.E., it is hard to imagine that either of the Twins would have undertaken such a project without some input from his brother. It is clear that both brothers were studying contemporary motor carriages then being worked on by other local inventors.

George E. Whitney, a well-established steam engineer who built and patented several steam cars in the late 1890s, recalled that both Stanley brothers had visited his East Boston workshop on occasion in 1896. Whitney was also adamant that both brothers had taken excessive liberties in examining his steamer when it was on display in the basement of the Mechanics Hall in Boston during the annual bicycle show in February 1897. (Bacon 1980: pp.62-63, 72-73.) By the following summer work on the Stanleys' first car was underway, as F.E. wrote to his wife touring in Europe:

"I wrote you some time ago about motor carriages. Well I am building one. I am making the plans and it will only weigh 350 pounds and will be four inches wider and five inches longer than our buggy. It will cost me about $500 and will be finished the first of September or soon after you get home. It will not be afraid of a steam roller and will have no bad habits. It will stand without hitching (and perhaps that is all it will do)." (F.E. Stanley letter to Augusta Stanley, July 11, 1897, Stanley Museum Archives.)

The prototype steamer was rolled out on the back street adjacent to the Stanley factory sometime in September or October 1897, both Twins aboard. The Stanleys had commissioned a 14-inch fire-tube boiler from the Roberts Iron Works Company and a 2 1/2 x 4-inch, two-cylinder engine from the Mason Regulator Company (their selection of Roberts and Mason may have been influenced by the strong temperance stance of both men, as much as for their engineering work). The boiler weighed over 200 lbs, however, and the engine more than 400, which combined far exceeded the 350 lbs F.E. had projected as the total weight of the finished car in his letter to his wife.

The first test ride of the steamer was suc-

The Stanley Brothers in their first car, September 1897. *The Twins roll out their first steamer on what is now Hunt Street, Watertown, Mass., adjacent to their dry plate factory (off camera, left), in this famous photograph taken in the fall of 1897. F.E. Stanley, closest to camera, has his hand on the throttle; his brother, F.O., beside him. The car rides on a chassis of rigid bicycle tubing built by Piper and Tinker of the Comet Bicycle Works a few miles away in Waltham. George Tinker recalled that both Twins came to his shop to take delivery of the chassis and running gear, one sitting on a board placed on top and steering while the other pushed the chassis down the road toward Newton - even without an engine, Stanley-powered.*

Stanley Museum Archives.

cessful - except for a frightened workhorse - and the Stanleys got to work trimming the weight of the car's power plant. They turned to their friends in Mechanic Falls, A.R. Penney and J.W. Penney and Sons who had supplied F.O.'s drawing set factory and the Stanley Dry Plate factories with steam equipment. The Penneys provided them with a 2 1/2 x 3 1/2 inch-engine

weighing 35 lbs. The boiler was redesigned by the Twins themselves: made of thin copper tubes encased in a copper shell with steel heads, and wrapped with "three layers of high grade steel wire" (influenced, it is said, by a somewhat similar method used in munitions to reinforce large gun barrels). The Stanley boiler was the same size as the Roberts boiler, but was

J. W. Penney & Sons, Steam Engine Works, Mechanic Falls, Maine. *Penney had supplied F.O. Stanley with steam machinery for his drawing set factory, and likewise for both Stanley dry plate factories in Lewiston and Montreal. When the Twins needed a lightweight engine for their steam carriage the competent Maine firm quickly produced a 2 1/2 x 3 1/2-inch engine weighing 35 pounds which the Stanleys used to power their first cars. Penney briefly considered expanding into the automotive market, but apparently abandoned the idea when the much larger Mason Regulator Company of Boston began to mass produce steam engines for the new industry.*

*Stanley Museum Archives
courtesy Harland Penney.*

capable of producing 125-200 lbs of pressure and weighed only 90 lbs. (Dolnar 1898a: p.726; F.O. Stanley 1930: p.3.)

Using the new power plants, the Stanleys produced three cars in the latter part of 1897 and early 1898, assembled in carriage bodies supplied by Currier and Cameron of Amesbury, Mass., and supported on rigid bicycle tube frames produced in the Comet Bicycle Works in Waltham, Mass., by James W. Piper and George M. Tinker. Tinker recalled that both Twins visited the shop while the chassis were being made and took delivery of the first one together. (Richardson 1956: pp.16-19, 35.) One of the new carriages was a two-seated surrey that did not meet the Twins' approval and was dismantled; they split ownership of the other two runabouts.

A.R. Penney visited the Stanleys in June and found only one of the cars operational and still needing refinements, but F.O. was able to give him a three-mile test ride in six minutes. (*Mechanic Falls Ledger* June 23, 1898.) In July, F.E. attempted to drive his car from Newton to Poland Spring, Maine, but had to abandon his first attempt due to tire trouble. In his second attempt he reached Kennebunkport, but "his

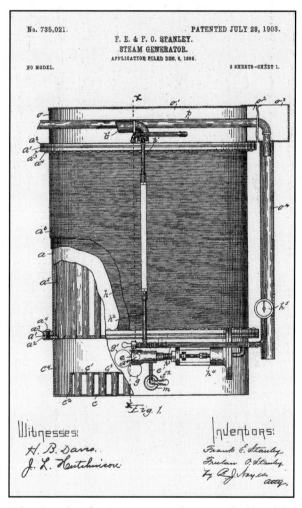

The Stanleys' wire-wrapped steam boiler. *The Stanleys considered all types of boilers before deciding that the fire-tube boiler's simplicity and power storage capability were key features they wanted in their steam car. They redesigned the boiler, reducing its weight without compromising its strength by applying wire wrapping. They applied for a patent on this design on December 6, 1898, which was finally granted as U.S. Patent #735,021 on July 28, 1903.*

U.S. Patent and Trademark Office.

F.E. and F.O. Stanley at Charles River Park, November 9, 1898. *F.E., at the tiller, left, with his brother F.O. holding a stopwatch, puts the Stanley steam carriage through its paces at this public demonstration at Charles River Park, Cambridge, Mass., November 9, 1898. Stanley drove a mile in 2:11, the fastest time of the day on the oval, concrete bicycle track , and scaled a 90-foot wooden ramp in the artificial hill-climbing contest with a single trial, out-performing all of the official contestants. After the exhibition public demand for the car convinced the brothers to enter the automotive business. Photo by N. L. Stebbins.*

Stanley Museum Archives.

Mass., on November 8, 1898, after a last-minute invitation to participate arranged by John C. Kerrison of the *Boston Herald.* The Stanley wowed the velodrome crowd with a fast mile run of 2:11, followed by an impressive climb up an artificial wooden ramp, 90 feet in length, catching the official handlers off-guard. Both victories were unofficial, but stirred up intense interest in the Stanleys' machine, and the brothers were surrounded with admirers, peppered with questions, and besieged with orders. The demand convinced the two that a new business focused on manufacturing the Stanley carriage would be a worthwhile venture.

steering bar broke when he was going at a high speed, and the carriage ran plum into a ledge breaking both front wheels and damaging the body badly." (F.O. Stanley letter to Flora Stanley, July 9, 1898, Stanley Museum Archives.) F.E. was unhurt, but had to continue on to Poland Spring by train, his car towed or shipped back to Newton. (*Boston Globe* July 17, 1898, p.29.) Several months later F.O. sold his carriage to a "Mr. Methot of Boston" (probably L.T. Ebens Methot, a Boston dentist of Canadian origin), confident that he and his brother could build a better one. (F.O. Stanley 1930: p.2; Merrick 2005: pp.6-7.)

F.E. Stanley took his remaining car to the Charles River Park Exhibition in Cambridge,

They began by ordering and stockpiling parts and bodies to assemble an initial lot of 100 cars, and purchased Sterling Elliott's now-vacant Hickory Wheel factory next door in Watertown to begin production. They also began hiring a group of talented machinists: Worthy Channing Bucknam, formerly of Mechanic Falls and the J.W. Penney plant where the first engines were produced; Howard O'Grady of Waltham, hired away from the Comet Bicycle Works where the first chassis were produced; and George Killam and Frank Hatch, hired away from rival steam car producer George E. Whitney's East Boston shop. Perhaps the Twins' most significant hire at this time, though, was a young mechanic from the

Fred Marriott, mid-1890s. *Fred Marriott of Needham in his early 20s, shortly before he began to work for the Stanley Brothers in 1898. Photo by Lynn Photo Company.*
Boston Post, Stanley Museum Archives.

Union Cycle Company in Hylandville by the name of Fred Marriott.

Fred Marriott (1872-1956) was born in the Hylandville section of Needham, Mass., on December 31, 1872, the eldest child of Mr. and Mrs. George Marriott. The young Marriott grew

Fred Marriott, with racing goggles, outside his home in Needham. *Marriott served as the foreman of the Stanley Motor Carriage Company's Repair Department. He made his auto racing debut for Stanley at the 1904 Commonwealth Avenue Hill Climb, and also competed at the Readville track in 1905.*
Fred Marriott Collection,
courtesy Joe and Rhoda Green
via Clarence Coons.

up in a small house on Central Avenue and attended the local public schools, serving an apprenticeship at the Pettee Machine Works, a producer of textile machinery in Newton, Mass. Marriott was a rising star on the local bicycle tracks, winning numerous cups, ribbons and trophies, and was acclaimed at the height of his cycle racing career as the champion of Needham.

Marriott was soon hired as a mechanic at the Union Cycle Company, where he developed exceptional skills at quickly diagnosing and repairing problems. It was this trait, and his keen interest in the exciting new mechanics in light-weight steam cars, that soon brought him

The Stanley Pacing Tandem, Buttonwood Track, New Bedford, Mass., 1899. *This special steam cycle was meant for motor pacing bicycle racers, and was built by the Stanleys for cycle champion Eddie McDuffee, right. McDuffee set the mile paced record of 1:32 behind motor pace for the first time with this machine on the Buttonwood Track in New Bedford, Mass., on June 30, 1899. The pacer was guided by the steersman, Billy Saunders, who sat astride the water tank emblazoned with the Stanley motto, "On! Stanley On!" The mechanic, Tech Hammond, operated all of the pacer's controls from the rear seat, behind the central boiler and vertically-mounted engine. The paired cylindrical tanks apparently carried the fuel supply. A commercial version of this pacer, with two 14-inch boilers for added power, was briefly marketed by Locomobile in early 1900.*
Yankee, Stanley Museum Archives.

to the Stanleys' attention. Marriott was hired to head the company's repair department, a position he would hold until he retired from the company in 1919. In the Stanley factory the repair department oversaw sophisticated redesign and experimental work, and frequently, the "experimental work" meant race cars.

Almost as soon as the November 1898 Charles River Park Exhibition had ended, the Stanleys were reported to be working on a special racer. "Stanley is now building a racing steam wagon for one passenger, which will weigh only about 275 pounds empty, and with which he expects to make the mile in 80 seconds, on a straightaway track." (Dolnar 1898b: p.973.) Nothing more is known of this early racer, and there is no record of it ever appearing on a track, if it was ever finished.

The Stanleys were approached at about this time by Eddie McDuffee, a champion middle-distance cyclist of the day, who was referred to the Stanleys in his quest for a pacing machine to enable him to break the mile-paced record. The following spring the Twins produced a tandem pacer – a two-seated, two-wheeled machine, operated by a mechanic in the rear and driven by a "steersman" in the front – which McDuffee used to set a new motor-paced mile record of 1:31 1-5 at the Buttonwood Track in New Bedford on June 30, 1899. (McDuffee 1955: pp.34-37.) The Stanley pacer had mixed success on the track, sometimes failing to function as required, but the Stanleys' were quite pleased with the speed attained by the machine – F.O. Stanley even issued an open challenge, to animal or

F.E. Stanley with his special racer at Readville, 1903. *F.E. stands with his special streamlined steam racer, sometimes called the "Torpedo" or "Turtle," with which he set a steam track record at Readville on May 30, 1903. Note the Stanley logo on the side of the car, which the race organizers required be covered up in competition (see photo on p.25). Standing behind, far left, is Stanley driver Frank Durbin.*
Stanley Museum Archives.

"Front view of the Stanley steam-driven racing car." The British journal The Autocar published this photo under that caption on October 8, 1904. It appears to be a transitional prototype racer between the Stanley "Torpedo" racer of 1903 and the Stanleys' Ormond Beach racer built in 1905. The car has outboard elliptical springs and a trailing funnel as in the earlier racer, but has a similar (though smaller) canoe-derived body like that of the later racer. The driver appears to be Frank Durbin. There is no record of this car appearing in any race, although Durbin is reported to have driven the earlier 1903 Stanley racer in a five-mile steam race against Louis Ross in his Wogglebug at Narragansett Park in September 1904, just a few weeks before this photo appeared. It may be that the 1903 racer was modified to test this canoe-derived body.

The Autocar, Stanley Museum Archives.

machine, to race the new Stanley pacer. (*Boston Globe* July 13, 1899, p.2; *The Horseless Age* June 26, 1899, p.19.)

The Stanleys seem to have taken a break from auto racing from about 1900 to 1902, during the period when their company was owned by Walker (Mobile) and Barber (Locomobile) and they were no longer actively involved as managers in the firm. Once they resumed the manufacture of cars under their own name, they took up racing again and designed a special streamlined racer that debuted at the Decoration Day races at Readville in 1903, driven by F.E. Stanley to a new world steam track record. His brother was represented at the track that day by his wife,

Flora; F.O. had come down with a serious case of tuberculosis, and had hastily relocated to Colorado that March under doctor's orders, his future uncertain. F.E. was reportedly working on a new racer later in 1903, perhaps intending to race it at Ormond in the 1904 races before he decided to sit out the 1904 tournament.

During 1904, Louis Ross designed and built his own freak steamer ("freak" denoting a specialized car, usually a racer, totally unsuited for touring or any normal street use), apparently with Stanley's blessing. There is some evidence that Stanley was also working on a new racer with a canoe-like body, a photograph of which appeared in *The Autocar* in October 1904, apparently piloted by Frank Durbin. Shortly before, on September 10, 1904, the Stanley's 1903 racer was reportedly driven by Frank Durbin to a second-place finish behind Louis Ross's Wogglebug in a five-mile race at Narragansett Park in Rhode Island. There are no details on this early canoe-bodied racer, and it may be that the earlier Stanley racer had been outfitted with a new canoe body as an experiment.

The success of Ross's Wogglebug at Ormond, winning the Dewar Trophy and setting steam records in the mile and kilometer, was the impetus for F.E. Stanley finally designing and building a special racer for the land speed record and bringing it to Ormond, according to Fred Marriott. (Marriott 1956.) The Stanley racer, built sometime toward the end of 1905, would borrow some of the winning elements used on the Wogglebug the year before, but it would have a Stanley chassis, with perch poles, and its body would not draw on automotive technology, but on that of state-of-the-art canoe design.

It is not known where or when Stanley got the idea to adapt an inverted canoe to a race

F.E. Stanley in the Stanley racer, Watertown, Mass., early 1906. *F.E. Stanley poses in the Stanley racer prior to its shipment to Ormond, outside the Stanley Motor Carriage Company's Repair Department where Fred Marriott served as foreman. With a streamlined body built by the J. R. Robertson Canoe Company of Auburndale, Mass., and a 30-inch boiler and a 30 hp engine, the racer was too fast to test at speed on local roads. A few short hill climbing trials and static tests in the factory had given some indication of what the racer was capable of, but no one knew for sure what it would do until it was tried out on Ormond Beach.*
Stanley Museum Archives.

car body, but the wooden canoe of 1905 was considered peerless for its combination of light weight, strength, rigidity, minimal frontal area and streamlining. Stanley is said to have designed an apparatus for determining the aerodynamic resistance of different canoes, towing them behind a car while attached to a spring scale. (Foster 2004: p.189.) Whether he already had a particular boiler dimension in mind which might have affected the design criteria of the canoe (e.g.: width of beam), or whether he aimed for the most aerodynamic shape he could find and then designed a boiler to fit, is not known, but Stanley selected a canoe produced by the J. R. Robertson Canoe Company of Auburndale, Mass. Vintage canoe experts believe the Stanley racer's body may have been formed on the same canoe moulds used for Robertson's popular "Riverside" model. (Sobel 2002: pp.8-10.) The total frontal area of the new racer, including its tires, was a mere nine square feet.

Inside, the racer had a special 30-inch diameter boiler, 18 inches high, with 1,475 tubes and a total heating surface of 285 square feet, producing a steam pressure of 800-900 psi. As in the Wogglebug the boiler and its "smoke-stack" were situated behind the driver, but Stanley chose to depart from Ross's use of twin engines and installed a single 4 1/2 x 6 1/2-inch engine, geared .5 to 1, the wheels making two turns for each engine revolution. (Foster 2004: p.189; *Scientific American* February 10, 1906, p.134.)

The racer had a listed rating of 30-50 hp, but its top speed was unknown, the only road tests that could be done in Massachusetts near the factory took place on the same hills that were used to test stock cars – there were no roads nearby that would allow testing the racer to anywhere near its hoped-for speed of two miles per minute. Static tests were done at the factory from which Stanley estimated that the car could achieve 120 mph – all that remained was to take it to Florida and try it out for certain on the beach and see what it could do. All that remained, that is, except for deciding who would drive the car.

CHAPTER FIVE

Let the Races Begin.

"Dear Blanche,

"Probably before you receive this letter, you will hear of the wonderful time your father's car made today in a trial. 30 2/5 seconds for a mile, according to your father's watch - and by several others under 31 - so it dont matter very much. <u>Against</u> <u>the</u> <u>wind.</u> It surprised your father, and to say it pleased him, would be putting it mildly.

"I didnt see it, as I have been kept indoors nursing a cold. I have a fearful cold - with white spots in my throat. I have Dr. Stubbs remedies and have taken them - and think I feel better tonight.

"It surprised everybody - that the car could do so well - Fred Marriot (sic) drove it - and is to in the races.

"This is the worst climate I ever saw - just like dog days in August. So much humidity. It makes the perspiration start every time you move. Of course after getting used to it one dont mind so much.

"It seems strange to go from white to summer so quickly. It seems strange to see the young ladies sitting around on the ground with nothing but shirtwaists etc on - and everyone carrying parasols - just like summer. Still the temperature at noon today was only 70 - but the dampness makes it seem so much worse. And there is considerable in getting worked up to hot weather.

"I dont like [it] here - Should not want to stay here - The hotel is almost empty - except for a few automobilists there are very few guests. There are several hotels about here - So not nearly everyone stops here.

"There are a great many cottages here where people spend the winter months - Oh dear! How can they do it! But they say it is unusually hot for this place today - So I am living in hopes of a cool day.

"And think of me with nothing but jersey underdraws - and flannelett nightgowns! I think I shall soon swet out my cold.

"The Hathaways are here and we are at the table with them.

"Our rooms are fine - one and bath. Our room has three windows being on the corner - so we get air both ways - There is also a window in the bathroom - There is a big closet.

"Your father dont think of running a car himself - I am happy to say. Frank [Durbin] ran the little car today a mile in 42 - He is going to run that one.

"Got a Boston Herald today with a picture of your father and the car in it.

"Well your father is going to write to Ed - so I wont write any more. Hope the baby is all right - and that Raymond is all right too - We wish we had taken him - your father especially.

"Write to us -

Lovingly,
A. M. Stanley"

(A. M. Stanley letter to her daughter Blanche Stanley Hallett,
Tuesday Evening, January 16, 1906. Stanley Museum Archives.)

"Dear Ed,

"Fred [Marriott] went a mile in the racer yesterday in 30 3/5 sec. under very unfavorable conditions. He went against a 10 mile wind striking on the quarter which was worse for that machine than a direct head wind. The last half of the mile the beach was rough still the machine seemed to run very smoothly. But on examining the tracks we saw that the front wheels only struck the top of the high places. We are confident now that with wind and beach favorable we can make the 2 miles in 1 m. He carried 700 [lbs] steam and finished with nearly 600, so that if he can start with 800 he can go the two miles and still have between 500 & 600 and go each mile under 30 s. The Fiats are not working well, none of them can show better than 45 s. and it looks now as though the watch is the only hard thing we shall have to beat. When an automobile has to go a mile while the second hand of a watch is making half a revolution it is giving the watch quite a handicap.*

"The stock car H is fully as satisfactory as the racer. Frank [Durbin] ran that a mile in 42 2/5 against the wind over the same course that Fred ran the racer. He made the last [half] in 20 sec. The time of the racer for halfs (sic) was 15 2/5 and 15 1/5 and the last half was the roughest.

"He – Frank – only carried 600 lbs steam so that if we put the steam up to 800 and go with the wind we can beat Ross' time of 38 sec. Burt [Holland] ran the touring car a mile in 1 m – 2 s with three passengers only carrying 450 lbs steam with one pump running and finished with 400 lbs. So a mile a minute is easy for that car. That is a fine running car.

Truly yours,
F.E. Stanley"

(F.E. Stanley letter to his son-in-law and plant manager,
Edward M. Hallett, January 17, 1906. Stanley Museum Archives.)

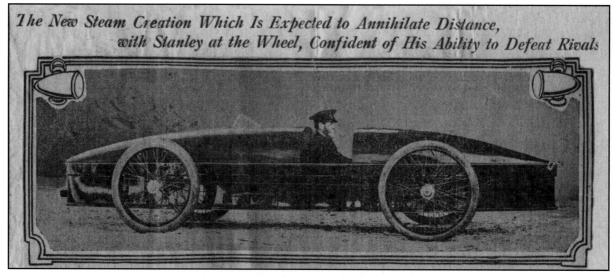

"Got a Boston Herald today with a picture of your father and the car in it." *Augusta Stanley's letter of January 16 to her daughter Blanche refers to this, the first published photo of the Stanley racer, which appeared in the Boston Sunday Herald on January 14, 1906, p.18 (the photo also appeared the same day in the Boston Sunday American, p.44). An example of an early publicity photo, the factory repair department in the background (as seen in the photo on p.54) has been airbrushed out. Stanley's proclaimed confidence in his ability to defeat his rivals may have irked his rivals almost as much as the presence of his car.*

Boston Herald, Stanley Museum Archives.

F.E. and the racer with beach and surf. *Yet another variation of the factory image, this time with a background of Ormond beach airbrushed in some years later by F.E.'s son, Raymond Stanley.*
Stanley Museum Archives.

~ EVENTS ~

THE SCHEDULING of races on Ormond/Daytona Beach was dependent on the tides, which ordinarily permitted racing to occur during four-hour periods within each tidal stage when there was a beach surface wide enough on which to drive several cars abreast. Poor weather and darkness could shorten the beach racing periods (three-hour time windows were not uncommon) and occasionally only one tidal stage a day was suitable for racing even though the tournaments were scheduled to maximize open beach during daylight hours.

Races at distances from one to fifteen miles could be run on the Ormond/Daytona Beach as straightaway events without turns, although races over five miles were often run out and back with at least one turn. Distances over thirty miles required multiple turns. In the early days of racing the direction in which the races were started would often be determined by prevailing winds, as officials were just as interested in seeing new speed records as were participants and spectators. The shorter races were often run with the wind for favorable results. The practice of requiring paired trials in opposite directions and averaging the times of both to nullify the effects of the wind was not instituted until much later.

The race officials tended to group similar events of like distances or attempted to balance long races with short ones to make best use of the available beach. The first day of the 1906 tournament, Tuesday, January 23, was devoted to the one-mile championship competitions. Wednesday, January 24, was set aside to run all the five-mile competitions with an additional 15-mile race at the end. On each day three of the four scheduled events were concluded with one postponement, some, like the 15-mile Price handicap race, put off till the next day.

Thursday, January 25, was intended for the running of the 100-mile race and one of the ten-mile amateur championships (in 1906, two races were set aside for amateur owner-drivers), but the officials decided to postpone the longer race in hopes of running some of the shorter races postponed earlier. In this they were only partially successful. Even under favorable conditions competitive races with standing or rolling starts (in which contestants had to cross the starting line in unison) were often delayed by false starts. Events with more than four cars entered required multiple, time-consuming elimination heats. Problems with the timing apparatus, spectators and private cars on the open beach, and temperamental drivers, owners, and officials alike, caused further delays.

On Friday, January 26, the individual mile and kilometer record trials were run in addition to two ten-mile competitions. The events went fairly smoothly and a number of World records were set, including historic runs by Fred Marriott in the Stanley racer in the mile and the kilometer. Only two short races were postponed.

Saturday, January 27, was set aside for two rescheduled races, the Two-Mile-a-Minute race and the 100-mile competition. The special two-mile race was postponed when both cars broke down in the first heat. The 100-mile race was sent off, but only after a lengthy delay. Sunday was an off-day with no races scheduled on the Sabbath.

On Monday, January 29, the final day of the 1906 meet, officials attempted to squeeze in all the remaining events on the schedule. Whether intentionally or not, the steam camp got caught in the squeeze: forced to scramble and make a late start in the 30-mile race; matched up in two combined ten-mile races where the steamer was only eligible to win one; denied a third trial in the Two-Mile-a-Minute race; and completely shut out of the five-mile steam championship which was apparently cancelled. The officials did manage to see that all the remaining gas car events were completed, and that the outcomes,

no matter how lopsided, were duly recorded.

The tables which follow list all the 1906 events in numerical order, the order in which they were scheduled and ran, and the cars and drivers scheduled to compete in each event. The latter charts include many last-minute changes – cars added or withdrawn, driver substitutions or disqualifications, etc. – and final race results are tabulated when known. In many cases the times for only the first place and runner-up finishers were recorded. Occasionally there are conflicting data on the cars and drivers who took part.

Events 1 through 6 were championship competitions open to all, differentiated by distance. Many of these were competitions for special trophies, including the Minneapolis Cup for the 100-mile event, the Sir Thomas R. Dewar Trophy for the one-mile competition, and the *Florida Times-Union* "Automobile Speed King" trophy for the Two-Mile-a-Minute race. There were special trophies and prizes for other races as well, and those that are known are listed in the table below.

Events 7 through 12 were championship competitions for gasoline-powered cars, broken down by distance and weight classes. The weight classes then recognized by the racing board of the Automobile Association of America were: 551 to 851 lbs for lightweight cars, 851 to 1,432 lbs for middleweight cars, and 1,432 to 2,204 lbs for heavyweight cars.

Events 13 and 14 were competitions for steam cars of any weight, at one and five mile distances. The Stanley Motor Carriage Company was the only steam car entrant in 1906. In the one-mile event the Stanley team entered three cars: their special racer, a stock roadster (the Model H) and a stock touring car (the Model F), to make it an official race. The five-mile event, postponed three times, was apparently not run.

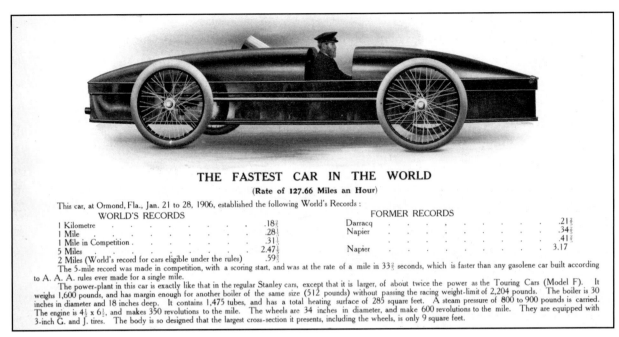

THE FASTEST CAR IN THE WORLD

(Rate of 127.66 Miles an Hour)

This car, at Ormond, Fla., Jan. 21 to 28, 1906, established the following World's Records :

WORLD'S RECORDS		FORMER RECORDS	
1 Kilometre	.18$\frac{2}{5}$	Darracq	.21$\frac{2}{5}$
1 Mile	.28$\frac{1}{5}$	Napier	.34$\frac{2}{5}$
1 Mile in Competition	.31$\frac{1}{5}$		.41$\frac{2}{5}$
5 Miles	2.47$\frac{1}{5}$	Napier	3.17
2 Miles (World's record for cars eligible under the rules)	.59$\frac{3}{5}$		

The 5-mile record was made in competition, with a scoring start, and was at the rate of a mile in 33$\frac{3}{5}$ seconds, which is faster than any gasolene car built according to A. A. A. rules ever made for a single mile.

The power-plant in this car is exactly like that in the regular Stanley cars, except that it is larger, of about twice the power as the Touring Cars (Model F). It weighs 1,600 pounds, and has margin enough for another boiler of the same size (512 pounds) without passing the racing weight-limit of 2,204 pounds. The boiler is 30 inches in diameter and 18 inches deep. It contains 1,475 tubes, and has a total heating surface of 285 square feet. A steam pressure of 800 to 900 pounds is carried. The engine is 4$\frac{1}{2}$ x 6$\frac{1}{2}$, and makes 350 revolutions to the mile. The wheels are 34 inches in diameter, and make 600 revolutions to the mile. They are equipped with 3-inch G. and J. tires. The body is so designed that the largest cross-section it presents, including the wheels, is only 9 square feet.

"The Fastest Car In The World." *Stanley Motor Carriage Company catalog illustration, again using the familiar image of F.E. in the car. The 1907 Stanley catalog lists the racing accomplishments and characteristics of the car. The most detailed contemporary description of the car, based on information furnished by F.E. Stanley himself, appeared in the Scientific American on February 10, 1906 (see below).*

1907 Stanley Motor Carriage Company Catalog, Stanley Museum Archives.

"...the following facts regarding the [Stanley steam racer] have been sent us by the inventor, Mr. F.E. Stanley.

"The wheelbase of the racer is 100 inches and the tread 54 inches. The rear or driving wheels are fitted with 34 x 3 1/2 and the front by 34 x 3-inch standard G. & J. [Gormully & Jeffery] clincher tires. The wheels are of the wire spoke type, the tires being bolted to the rims with eight tire bolts and being so perfectly balanced with counterweights that there was no vibration when the wheels were making upward of 1,200 revolutions per minute. The running gear is the same as that used on the Stanley touring car with the exception of the wheels, which have wire instead of wooden spokes. The body of the car is built entirely out of wood, and mounted on four full-elliptic springs. The springs are placed on the inside of the body, so as to reduce the air resistance to a minimum. Ball bearings of the two-point type, with 3/4-inch balls, are used in the running gear.

"The body is 16 feet long and 3 feet wide at the widest part. It is pointed in front, and terminates at the rear in a circle with 8-inch radius, tapering to 3-foot width and to the point in front with cycloidal curves, or curves with constantly diminishing radius. The bottom of the car is perfectly straight and smooth. It has a clearance of 10 1/2 inches. The sides are vertical to a height of 18 inches, and from that line the removable top is oval, curving both transversely and longitudinally. The largest cross section, including the wheels, amounts to 9 square feet.

"The power plant consists of a boiler 30 inches diameter and containing 1,476 tubes of 33-64 inch outside diameter and 18 inches long. The boiler contains 285 square feet of heating surface. The steam was superheated, by passing it through tubes surrounded by the contents of the boiler and through coils of pipe in the firebox, to a temperature of about 700 deg. F.

"The engine is of the two-cylinder double-acting type, with cylinders 4 1/2-inch bore by 6 1/2-inch stroke. It is fitted with Stephenson link valve gear and D slide valves. The engine makes 350 revolutions to the mile, while the 34-inch driving wheels make 600 revolutions to the mile. Linked up as the engine was in forward gear, the cut-off was about one-third stroke, and the mean effective pressure about one-half the steam chest pressure. The engine therefore develops 6 horse-power for each 100 revolutions per minute, and each 100 pounds steam chest pressure. The boiler will furnish steam for 50 horse-power continuously, and more than twice that amount for three minutes or more. About 275 pounds to the square inch steam pressure is carried. *(Continued on next page.)*

Events 15 and 16 were the two Corinthian competitions for amateur owner-drivers. "Corinthian" was a classical term for an amateur sportsman, a lover of sport for its own sake, a distinction of considerable significance in turn-of-the-century society. (Many contemporaries considered professional sports to be a corruption of the ideal, and the merits of both were subject to popular debate.) One of these was an open amateur event, the other a handicap race as were Events 17 and 18. Handicaps could be based on vehicle weight, engine characteristics (horsepower, number of cylinders, cubic inch displacement), or retail price. In Events 16 and 17 the handicap appears to have

been based on vehicle horsepower; in Event 18 the handicap was based on vehicle price.

Events 18 and 19 were restricted to American-built cars. European imports dominated early racing, and organizers of U.S. races often set aside a number of events to showcase domestic cars only.

The remainder of the races, Events 20 to 27, were individual record trials at the mile and the kilometer, broken down for gasoline-powered cars in the three weight categories, and for steam-powered cars. Either gas or steam cars could set World records for all classes, and slower performances could still set records within the established classes.

Fred Marriott in the cockpit of the Stanley racer. *Augusta Stanley notes in her January 16 letter that Marriott had driven the racer in its pre-race warm-ups to an unofficial world record of 31 2-5 earlier that day, and that he had been chosen to drive the car in the tournament. Whether Marriott had won the job on the basis of his success driving the car in the pre-race trials or whether he had already been chosen is unknown, but Mrs. Stanley's letter is the first mention of his selection. In an oral history interview Marriott (then 82) was asked why he thought he was chosen. His earthy response, partially garbled, seems to have been: "Oh I dunno, I probably I may'd [may of had] more balls than any o' the others." (Marriott 1956.)*

Larz Anderson Auto Museum.

(Caption continued from previous page) "The arrangement of parts of the power plant is as follows: The boiler is placed just back of the center of the body, the water tank between that and the rear axle. The engine is geared to the driving axle by spur gears, and is placed horizontally at the rear of the axle, so that the driving force of the engine tends to lift the front axle and transfer the load to the rear axle, thus giving the greatest possible traction to the driving wheels.

"In making the record of 28 1-5 for the mile, the power developed was probably about 120 horsepower. The engine made 750 1/2 R.P.M. and the 34-inch driving wheels 1,286 1/2 R.P.M.

"The total weight of the machine was 1,675 pounds. The boiler weighed 525 pounds; engine, 185; burner and fire-box, 75; pumps, tanks, etc., 50 pounds; making the total power plant 835 pounds, or less than half the total weight of the machine." (Scientific American February 10, 1906, p.134.)

Event 1 – 100 Miles International Championship for the Minneapolis Cup. Free-for all. Staggered or Standing Start. Must be won twice to obtain permanent possession. The race will be run with turns. [*15-mile straightaway with seven turns.*] In case the number of contestants exceeds six, the cars will be started one minute apart and the winner will be determined by time instead of position. [*Otherwise*] a standing start will be made.

Trophy: Silver. Donated by the Automobile Club of Minneapolis.

Event 2 – One Mile International Championship for the Sir Thomas R. Dewar Trophy. Rolling Start. Not more than four cars will be started in each heat; a second round of heats will be run if necessary. The winner of each (or second round of heats, as the case may be) and the fastest second car will compete in the final.

Trophy: Silver. Donated by Sir Thomas R. Dewar.

Event 3 – Two-Miles-a Minute Trophy Race. Flying Start. The winner must equal or exceed 120 miles an hour. To be run as time trials.

Trophy: Gold, silver and enamel, depicting a crown of gold over a winged wheel, enclosed by Roman laurel and palm wreaths, encased in a royal purple lined wooden case. Made by Dieges & Clust of NY. Value: $1,000. Commissioned and donated by the *Florida Times-Union* of Jacksonville.

Event 4 – Five Miles Open Championship. Standing Start.

Event 5 – Ten Miles Open Championship. Standing Start. (In 1906 this event was run concurrently with Event 9, the Ten Miles Heavyweight Championship for Gasoline Cars.)

Event 6 – Fifteen Miles Open Championship. Standing Start.

Trophy: Silver. Clyde Line Trophy. Donated by William P. Clyde & Co. (steamship line).

Event 7 – One Mile Heavyweight Championship, Gasoline Cars. Rolling Start.

Event 8 – Five Miles Heavyweight Championship, Gasoline Cars. Rolling Start.

Event 9 – Ten Miles Heavyweight Championship, Gasoline Cars. Rolling Start. (In 1906 this event was run concurrently with Event 5, the Ten Miles Open Championship.)

Event 10 – One Mile Middleweight Championship, Gasoline Cars. Rolling Start.

Event 11 – Five Miles Middleweight Championship, Gasoline Cars. Rolling Start.

Event 12 – Ten Miles Middleweight Championship, Gasoline Cars. Rolling Start.

Event 13 – One Mile Championship, Steam Cars. Rolling Start. (In 1906 this was an all-Stanley event which allowed for a collaborative flying start.)

Event 14 – Five Miles Championship, Steam Cars. Rolling Start. (This event was postponed three times, and was apparently the only event on the program that was not run.)

Event 15 – Ten Miles Corinthian Championship. Standing Start. For amateur owner/drivers. Amateur – an amateur driver is one who does not race for hire, or who is not actively engaged in the automobile trade, or who does not make his livelihood or any part of it as a result of his racing, or who has never been declared a professional by any sport governing body.

Trophy: Bronze, depicting a statue of Victory. Made by Tiffany Studios in NY. Commissioned and donated by George W. Young of NY.

Event 16 – Ten Miles Corinthian Handicap. Staggered Start. For amateur owner/drivers.

Event 17 – Ten Miles Handicap. Staggered Start.

Event 18 – Fifteen Miles Price Handicap for American Touring Cars Fully Equipped. Staggered Start. (Cars handicapped one second for every $100 difference in price from most expensive car entered: in 1906, the $3,500 Wayne. The Stanley Model H was adjudged to be worth $1,000 and was thus handicapped 25 seconds.)

Event 19 – Thirty Miles Championship for American-Built Cars. Standing Start.

Event 20 – One Mile Record Trials, Lightweight Gasoline Cars. Flying Start.

Event 21 – One Mile Record Trials, Middleweight Gasoline Cars. Flying Start.

Event 22 – One Mile Record Trials, Heavyweight Gasoline Cars. Flying Start.

Event 23 – One Mile Record Trials, Steam Cars. Flying Start.

Event 24 – One Kilometer Record Trials, Lightweight Gasoline Cars. Flying Start.

Event 25 – One Kilometer Record Trials, Middleweight Gasoline Cars. Flying Start.

Event 26 – One Kilometer Record Trials, Heavyweight Gasoline Cars. Flying Start.

Event 27 – One Kilometer Record Trials, Steam Cars. Flying Start.

~ January 23, 1906 ~

Event No. 2. One Mile International Championship for the Sir Thomas R. Dewar Trophy.

(Not more than four cars will be started in each heat; a second round of heats will be run if necessary. The winner of each (or second round of heats, as the case may be) and the fastest second car will compete in the final.)

Car #	Machine	Power	HP	#Cyl.	Weight	Driver	Owner	Status	Time	Results
1	Fiat	Gas	110	4	2204	Fletcher, Harry W.	Young, George W.	OK		eliminated
2	Stanley Racer	Steam	30-50	2		Ross, Louis S. or other*	Stanley Motor Car	OK	32 1-5/33	1st, World Record (1st heat)
4	Napier	Gas	80	6	2204	Clifford Earp, Walter	Edge, S.F.	OK	40/-	eliminated
7	Fiat	Gas	110	4	2180	Cedrino, Emanuel	Hollander & Tangeman	OK	38 1-5/38	2nd
8	Fiat	Gas	110	4	2180	Lancia, Vincenzo	Hollander & Tangeman	OK	37 3-5/-	3rd
10	Ford	Gas	105	6	1800	Ford, Henry or Kulick, Frank	Ford Motor Co.	DNS		
12	A.G. Vanderbilt	Gas	250	8	2204	Sartori, Paul	Vanderbilt, A.G.	DNS		
20	Darracq	Gas	200	8	2204	Hémery, Victor	A. Darracq & Cie.	Withdrawn		
21	Darracq	Gas	100	4		Guinness, A.L.	Guinness, A.L.	No Show		

Ford did not start due to team error; Vanderbilt due to mechanical problems. Darracq withdrawn by Hémery in protest after weigh-in. Guinness did not attend meet.

Event No. 7. One-Mile Heavyweight Championship (Gasoline).

Car #	Machine	Power	HP	# Cyl.	Weight	Driver	Owner	Status	Time	Results
1	Fiat	Gas	110	4	2204	Fletcher, Harry W.	Young, George W.	OK	39 4-5/ 37 3-5	2nd
4	Napier	Gas	80	6	2104	Clifford Earp, W.	Edge, S.F.	OK	40 3-5/-	eliminated
7	Fiat	Gas	110	4	2180	Cedrino, Emanuel	Hollander&Tangeman	OK	39 3-5/-	3rd
8	Fiat	Gas	110	4	2180	Lancia, Vincenzo	Hollander&tangeman	OK	42/37	1st
9	English Daimler	Gas	90	4	2190	Downey, Joseph	Harding, J.R.	OK		eliminated
12	A.G. Vanderbilt	Gas	250	8	2204	Sartori, Paul	Vanderbilt, A.G.	DNS		
20	Darracq	Gas	200	8	2204	Hémery, Victor	A. Darracq & Cie.	Withdrawn		
21	Darracq	Gas	100	4		Guinness, A.L.	Guinness, A.L.	No Show		

Vanderbilt did not start due to mechanical problems. Darracq withdrawn by Hémery in protest after weigh-in. Guinness did not attend meet.

Event No. 10. One-Mile Middleweight Championship (Gasoline).

Car #	Machine	Power	HP	# Cyl.	Weight	Driver	Owner	Status	Time	Results
6	Fiat Jr.	Gas	24-30	4	1420	Cedrino, Emanuel	Hollander&Tangeman	OK		
16	Wayne	Gas	40-50	4	1400	Holmes, Deacon D.	Wayne Auto Co.	OK		
18	Reo	Gas	32	4	1432	Wurgis, Dan	Reo Motor Car Co.	OK		
22	Darracq	Gas	80	4		Hémery, Victor	A. Darracq & Cie.	Withdrawn		

Darracq withdrawn by Hémery in protest after weigh-in. Event postponed to Thursday, January 25, 1906.

Event No. 13. One-Mile Championship (Steam).

Car #	Machine	Power	HP	# Cyl.	Weight	Driver	Owner	Status	Time	Results
2	Stanley racer	Steam	30-50	2		Ross, Louis S.*	Stanley Motor Car	OK	31 4-5	1st; world record
15	Stanley Model H Steam		15	2		Durbin, Francis P.	Stanley Motor Car	OK	45	2nd
	Stanley Model F Steam		20	2		Holland, Burton C.	Stanley Motor Car	OK	60 4-5	3rd

Louis Ross replaced as driver by Fred Marriott. Also entered: 15 hp Stanley Model H "Gentlemen's Speedy Roadster" driven by Frank Durbin, and Stanley Model F Touring car driven by Burt Holland.

~ January 24, 1906 ~

Event No. 4. Five-Mile Open Championship.

Car #	Machine	Power	HP	# Cyl.	Weight	Driver	Owner	Status	Time	Results
1	Fiat	Gas	110	4	2204	Fletcher, H.W.	Young, George. W.	OK	3:02/3:02	2nd
2	Stanley racer	Steam	30-50	2		Marriott, Fred	Stanley Motor Car	OK	2:47/3:03	3rd, World Record (1st heat)
4	Napier	Gas	80	6	2204	Clifford Earp, W.	Edge, S.F.	OK		eliminated
7	Fiat	Gas	110	4	2180	Cedrino, Emanuel	Hollander&Tangeman	DNS		
8	Fiat	Gas	110	4	2180	Lancia, Vincenzo	Hollander&Tangeman	OK	2:54 3-5/ 3:01 1-5	1st
12	A.G. Vanderbilt	Gas	250	8	2204	Sartori, Paul	Vanderbilt, A.G.	DNS		
20	Darracq	Gas	200	8	2204	Hémery, Victor	A. Darracq & Cie.	Disqualified		
21	Darracq	Gas	100	4		Guinness, A.L.	Guinness, A.L.	No Show		

Hémery disqualified from competition after refusing to re-run 1st heat after false start. Vanderbilt did not start due to mechanical problems. Guinness did not attend meet. Marriott cracked burner in 1st heat—finished 3rd in final.

Event No. 8. Five-Mile Heavyweight Championship (Gasoline).

Car #	Machine	Power	HP	# Cyl.	Weight	Driver	Owner	Status	Time	Results
1	Fiat	Gas	110	4	2204	Fletcher, H.W.	Young, George W.	OK		DNF
4	Napier	Gas	80	6	2204	Clifford Earp, W.	Edge, S.F.	OK	2:56	1st
7	Fiat	Gas	110	4	2180	Cedrino, Emanuel	Hollander&Tangeman	DNS		
8	Fiat	Gas	110	4	2180	Lancia, Vincenzo	Hollander&Tangeman	OK		DNF
9	English Daimler	Gas	90	4	2190	Downey, Joseph	Harding, J.R.	OK	3:29 1-5	2nd
12	A.G. Vanderbilt	Gas	250	8	2204	Sartori, Paul	Vanderbilt, A.G.	DNS		
14	Christie	Gas	110	4	2100	Christie, J.W.	Christie, J.W.	DNS		
20	Darracq	Gas	200	8	2204	Hémery, Victor	A. Darracq & Cie.	Disqualified		
21	Darracq	Gas	100	4		Guinness, A.L.	Guinness, A.L.	No Show		

Hémery disqualified from competition after refusing to re-run 1st heat in 5-mile open after false start. Vanderbilt and Fletcher did not start due to mechanical problems. Guinness did not attend meet.

Event No. 11. Five-Mile Middleweight Championship (Gasoline)

Car #	Machine	Power	HP	# Cyl.	Weight	Driver	Owner	Status	Time	Results
6	Fiat Jr.	Gas	24-30	4	1420	Cedrino, Emanuel	Hollander&Tangeman	OK	3:53 3-5	1st
16	Wayne	Gas	40-50	4	1400	Holmes, D.D.	Wayne Auto Co.	OK	5:46	2nd
18	Reo	Gas	32	4	1432	Wurgis, Dan	Reo Motor Car Co.	DNS		
22	Darracq	Gas	80	4		Hémery, Victor	A. Darracq & Cie.	Disqualified		

Hémery disqualified from competition after refusing to re-run 1st heat in 5-mile open after false start.

Event No. 14. Five-Mile Championship, Steam Cars.

Car #	Machine	Power	HP	# Cyl.	Weight	Driver	Owner	Status	Time	Results
2	Stanley racer	Steam	30-50	2		Marriott, Fred	Stanley Motor Car	OK		

Event postponed to Thursday, January 25, 1906.

Event No. 18. Fifteen Miles Price Handicap for American Touring Cars Fully Equipped.

Car #	Machine	Power	HP	# Cyl.	Weight	Driver	Owner	Status	Time	Results
2	Stanley racer	Steam	30-50	2		Marriott, Fred	Stanley Motor Car	DNS		
11	Stoddard-Dayton	Gas	30	4	2100	Bristol, J.E.	Bristol, J.E.	OK		
15	Stanley Model H	Steam	15-20	2		Stanley, F.E.	Stanley Motor Car	OK		
16	Wayne	Gas	40-50	4	1400	Holmes, D.D.	Wayne Auto Co.	OK		

Stanley Racer not entered in this event; Stanley Model H driven by Frank Durbin (not F.E. Stanley). Event postponed to Thursday, January 25, 1906.

~ JANUARY 25, 1906 ~

Event No. 18. Fifteen Miles Price Handicap for American Touring Cars Fully Equipped.

Car #	Machine	Power	HP	# Cyl.	Weight	Driver	Owner	Status	Time	Results
2	Stanley racer	Steam	30-50	2		Marriott, Fred	Stanley Motor Car	DNS		
11	Stoddard-Dayton	Gas	30	4	2100	Bristol, J.E.	Bristol, J.E.	OK	17:11 2-5	2nd (12 1/2 sec handicap)
15	Stanley Model H	Steam	15-20	2		Stanley, F.E.*	Stanley Motor Car	OK	13:42 2-5	1st (25 sec handicap)
16	Wayne	Gas	40-50	4	1400	Holmes, D.D.	Wayne Auto Co.	OK	?	3rd (no handicap)

Stanley Racer not entered in this event; Stanley Model H driven by Frank Durbin (not F.E. Stanley). Event rescheduled from Wednesday, January 24, 1906.

Event No. 1. Free-for-All Championship. 100 Miles International Championship for the Minneapolis Cup (which must be won twice to obtain permanent possession). The race will be run with turns. In case the number of contestants exceeds six, the cars will be started one minute apart and the winner will be determined by time instead of position. Otherwise a standing start will be made.

Car #	Machine	Power	HP	# Cyl.	Weight	Driver	Owner	Status	Time	Results
1	Fiat	Gas	110	4	2204	Fletcher, H.W.	Young, George W.	DNS		
3	Thomas	Gas	90	6	2190	Coey, C.A.	Coey, C.A.	DNS		
4	Napier	Gas	80	6	2204	Clifford Earp, W.	Edge, S.F.	OK		
7	Fiat	Gas	110	4	2180	Cedrino, Emanuel	Hollander&Tangeman	OK		
8	Fiat	Gas	110	4	2180	Lancia, Vincenzo	Hollander&Tangeman	OK		
9	Mercedes	Gas	90	4	2190	Downey, Joseph	Harding, J.N.	DNS		
12	A.G. Vanderbilt	Gas	250	8	2204	Sartori, Paul	Vanderbilt, A.G.	DNS		
14	Christie	Gas	110	4	2100	Christie, J.W.	Christie, J.W.	OK		
17	Napier	Gas	90	4	2200	Hilliard, W.L.	Napier Motor Co. USA	OK		
19	English Daimler	Gas	46	4	2200	Harding, H.N.	Sutphen, E.W.	OK		
20	Darracq	Gas	200	8	2204	Vaughan, Guy	A. Darracq & Cie.	DNS		
21	Darracq	Gas	100	4		Guinness, A.L.	Guinness, A.L.	No Show		
22	Darracq	Gas	80	4	2204	Vaughan, Guy	Stevens, S.B.	Withdrawn		

Event postponed to Saturday, January 27, 1906.

Event No. 10. One-Mile Middleweight Championship (Gasoline).

Car #	Machine	Power	HP	# Cyl.	Weight	Driver	Owner	Status	Time	Results
6	Fiat Jr.	Gas	24-30	4	1420	Cedrino, Emanuel	Hollander&Tangeman	OK		
16	Wayne	Gas	40-50	4	1400	Holmes, Deacon D.	Wayne Auto Co.	OK		
18	Reo	Gas	32	4	1432	Wurgis, Dan	Reo Motor Car Co.	OK		
22	Darracq	Gas	80	4		Hémery, Victor	A. Darracq & Cie.	OK		

Darracq driven by Guy Vaughan in replacement of Hémery. Event rescheduled from Tuesday, January 23, 1906. Postponed to Friday, January 26, 1906.

Event No. 14. Five-Mile Championship, Steam Cars.

Car #	Machine	Power	HP	# Cyl.	Weight	Driver	Owner	Status	Time	Results
2	Stanley racer	Steam	30-50	2		Marriott, Fred	Stanley Motor Car	OK		

Event rescheduled from Wednesday, January 24, 1906. Postponed. There is no record of this event being run.

~continued~

F.E. and Marriott with the racer at weigh-in, January 22, 1906. *The official weigh-in for competing cars was held on Monday, January 22, the day before the races began. The car would receive its official entry number, No. 2, once it passed inspection. Weighing in at 1,675 pounds, the Stanley racer easily came in under the 2,204 lb limit, so much so that the factory team could have added the weight of a second boiler and still kept the car within the weight limit. Tight space restraints may have precluded adding a second boiler to the car, and the added steam pressure from a second boiler might have caused more engine problems.*

Stanley Museum Archives.

Event No. 15. Ten Miles Corinthian Championship. Amateur Championships: - Amateur.

An amateur driver is one who does not race for hire, or who is not actively engaged in the automotive trade, or who does not make his livelyhood or any part of it as a result of his racing, or who has never been declared a professional by any sport governing body.

Car #	Machine	Power	HP	# Cyl.	Weight	Driver	Owner	Status	Time	Results
9	Mercedes	Gas	90	4	2190	Downey, Joseph	Harding, J.R.	OK	7:32 2-5/-	eliminated
22	Darracq	Gas	80	4	2204	Stevens, S.B.	Stevens, S.B.	Late Entry	6:36 2-5/ 9:28	1st
24	Mercedes	Gas	60			Breese, James L.	Breese, James L.	OK	10:37/ 9:47 3-5	2nd
25	Fiat	Gas	90			Barron, C. W.	Barron, C.W.	OK		DNF
	Maxwell Runabout	Gas	10			Reeves, Alfred	Reeves, Alfred	Late Entry	12:51 1-5/-	eliminated

J.R. Harding protested S.B. Steven's late entry of Darracq challenging his ownership of the car; protest not allowed.

~ JANUARY 26, 1906 ~

Event No. 12. 10-Mile Middleweight Championship. (All Powers.)

Car #	Machine	Power	HP	# Cyl.	Weight	Driver	Owner	Status	Time	Results
6	Fiat Jr.	Gas	24-30	4	1420	Cedrino, Emanuel	Hollander&Tangeman	OK	7:50	2nd
	Darracq	Gas	20-30			Vaughan, Guy	A. Darracq & Cie.	OK	7:00	1st (record for class)

Event No. 16. 10-Mile Corinthian Handicap. (Amateurs.)

Car #	Machine	Power	HP	# Cyl.	Weight	Driver	Owner	Status	Time	Results
9	Mercedes	Gas	90	4	2190	Harding, J.W.	Harding, J.W.	OK		DNF
19	English Daimler	Gas	45	4	2200	Harding, H.N.	Sutphen, E.W.	OK	8:48 4-5	1st (3:30 allowance)
22	Darracq	Gas	80	4	2204	Stevens, S.B.	Stevens, S.B.	OK	9:42 2-5	2nd (no allowance)
24	Mercedes	Gas	60			Breese, J.L.	Breese, J.L.	OK	10:50 2-5	3rd (3:00 allowance)
25	Fiat	Gas	90			Barron, C.W.	Barron, C.W.	OK		DNF
	Maxwell Runabout	Gas	10			Reeves, Alfred	Reeves, Alfred	OK	?	4th (6:00 allowance)

Event No. 24. One Kilometer Record Trials for Lightweight Gas Cars.

Car #	Machine	Power	HP	# Cyl.	Weight	Driver	Owner	Status	Time	Results
	Maxwell Runabout	Gas	10			Fleming, Charles	Fleming, Charles	OK	59	1st

Event No. 25. One Kilometer Record Trials for Middleweight Gas Cars.

Car #	Machine	Power	HP	# Cyl.	Weight	Driver	Owner	Status	Time	Results
16	Wayne	Gas	40-50	4	1400	Holmes, D.D.	Wayne Auto Co.	OK	41 1-5	3rd
18	Reo	Gas	32	4	1432	Wurgis, Dan	Reo Motor Car Co.	OK	34 2-5	2nd
	Darracq	Gas	80			Vaughan, Guy	A. Darracq & Cie.	OK	25	1st

Event No. 26. One Kilometer Record Trials, Heavyweight Gas Cars.

Car #	Machine	Power	HP	# Cyl.	Weight	Driver	Owner	Status	Time	Results
7	Fiat	Gas	110	4	2180	Cedrino, Emanuel	Hollander&Tangeman	OK	22 4-5	3rd
10	Ford	Gas	105	6	1800	Kulick, Frank	Ford Motor Co.	OK	24 4-5	4th
20	Darracq	Gas	200	8	2204	Chevrolet, Louis	A. Darracq & Cie.	OK	19 2-5	1st (record for class)
4	Napier	Gas	80	6	2204	Clifford Earp, W.	Edge, S.F.	OK	21 3-5	2nd

Event No. 23. One Mile Record Trials, Steam Cars.

Car #	Machine	Power	HP	# Cyl.	Weight	Driver	Owner	Status	Time	Results
2	Stanley racer	Steam	30-50	2			Marriott, Fred	Stanley Motor Car Co.	OK	18 2-5	1st, World Record

~continued~

Event No. 3. Two-Miles-a-Minute Trophy Race. The winner must equal or exceed 120 miles an hour. To be run as time trials.

Car #	Machine	Power	HP	# Cyl.	Weight	Driver	Owner	Status	Time	Results
1	Fiat	Gas	110	4	2204	Fletcher, H.W.	Young, George W.	DNS		
2	Stanley racer	Steam	20-30	2		Marriott, Fred	Stanley Motor Car Co.	OK		
3	Thomas	Gas	90	6	2190	Coey, C.A.	Coey, C.A.	DNS		
7	Fiat	Gas	110	4	2180	Cedrino, Emanuel	Hollander&Tangeman	DNS		
8	Fiat	Gas	110	4	2180	Lancia, Vincenzo	Hollander&Tangeman	DNS		
10	Ford	Gas	105	6	1800	Ford, Henry of Kulick, Frank	Ford Motor Co.	DNS		
12	A.G. Vanderbilt	Gas	250	8	2204	Sartori, Paul	Vanderbilt, A.G.	DNS		
14	Christie	Gas	110	4	2100	Christie, J.W. or Chevrolet, L.	Christie, J. Walter	DNS		
20	Darracq	Gas	200	8	2204	Vaughan, Guy	A. Darracq & Cie.	OK		
21	Darracq	Gas	100	4	2204	Guinness, A.L.	Guinness, A.L.	No Show		

Event postponed to Saturday, January 27, 1906.

Event No. 20. One Mile Record Trials, Lightweight Gas Cars.

Car #	Machine	Power	HP	# Cyl.	Weight	Driver	Owner	Status	Time	Results
	Maxwell Runabout	Gas	10			Fleming, Charles	Fleming, Charles	OK	1:29 2-5	1st

Event No. 21. One Mile Record Trials, Middleweight Gas Cars.

Car #	Machine	Power	HP	# Cyl.	Weight	Driver	Owner	Status	Time	Results
16	Wayne	Gas	40-50	4	1400	Holmes, D.D.	Wayne Auto Co.	OK	1:06	3rd
18	Reo	Gas	32	4	1432	Wurgis, Dan	Reo Motor Car Co.	OK	52 3-5	2nd
22	Darracq	Gas	80	4		Vaughan, Guy	A. Darracq & Cie.	OK	40 3-5	1st (record for class)

Event No. 22. One Mile Record Trials, Heavyweight Gas Cars.

Car #	Machine	Power	HP	# Cyl.	Weight	Driver	Owner	Status	Time	Results
	Fiat	Gas	110	4	2180	Cedrino, Emanuel	Hollander&Tangeman	OK	36 3-5	2nd
10	Ford	Gas	105	6	1800	Kulick, Frank	Ford Motor Co.	OK	40	4th
20	Darracq	Gas	200	8	2204	Chevrolet, Louis	A. Darracq & Cie.	OK	30 3-5	1st (record for class)
4	Napier	Gas	80	6	2204	Clifford Earp, W.	Edge, S.F.	OK	37 2-5	3rd

Event No. 27. One Kilometer Record Trials, Steam Cars.

Car #	Machine	Power	HP	# Cyl.	Weight	Driver	Owner	Status	Time	Results
2	Stanley racer	Steam	30-50	2		Marriott, Fred	Stanley Motor Car Co.	OK	28 1-5	1st, World Record

Event No. 10. One-Mile Middleweight Championship (Gasoline).

Car #	Machine	Power	HP	# Cyl.	Weight	Driver	Owner	Status	Time	Results
6	Fiat Jr.	Gas	24-30	4	1420	Cedrino, Emanuel	Hollander&Tangeman	OK		
16	Wayne	Gas	40-50	4	1400	Holmes, Deacon D.	Wayne Auto Co.	OK		
18	Reo	Gas	32	4	1432	Wurgis, Dan	Reo Motor Car Co.	OK		
22	Darracq	Gas	80	4		Hémery, Victor	A. Darracq & Cie.	OK		

Darracq driven by Guy Vaughan in replacement of Hémery. Event postponed to Monday, January 29, 1906 (originally scheduled for 1/23/1906).

~ JANUARY 27, 1906 ~

Event No. 3. Two-Miles-a-Minute Trophy Race. The winner must equal or exceed 120 miles an hour. To be run as time trials.

Car #	Machine	Power	HP	# Cyl.	Weight	Driver	Owner	Status	Time	Results
1	Fiat	Gas	110	4	2204	Fletcher, H.W.	Young, George W.	DNS		
2	Stanley racer	Steam	30-50	2		Marriott, Fred	Stanley Motor Car Co.	OK		
3	Thomas	Gas	90	6	2190	Coey, C.A.	Coey, C.A.	DNS		
7	Fiat	Gas	110	4	2180	Cedrino, Emanuel	Hollander&Tangeman	DNS		
8	Fiat	Gas	110	4	2180	Lancia, Vincenzo	Hollander&Tangeman	DNS		
10	Ford	Gas	105	6	1800	Ford, Henry of Kulick, Frank	Ford Motor Co.	DNS		
12	A.G. Vanderbilt	Gas	250	8	2204	Sartori, Paul	Vanderbilt, A.G.	DNS		
14	Christie	Gas	110	4	2100	Christie, J.W. or Chevrolet, L.	Christie, J. Walter	DNS		
20	Darracq	Gas	200	8	2204	Demogeot, Victor	A. Darracq & Cie.	OK		
21	Darracq	Gas	100	4	2204	Guinness, A.L.	Guinness, A.L.	No Show		

Event rescheduled from Friday, January 26, 1906. Darracq and Stanley both brokedown and failed to make any official run. Event postponed to Monday, January 29, 1906.

Event No. 1. Free-for-All Championship. 100 Miles International Championship for the Minneapolis Cup (which must be won twice to obtain permanent possession). The race will be run with turns. In case the number of contestants exceeds six, the cars will be started one minute apart and the winner will be determined by time instead of position. Otherwise a standing start will be made.

Car #	Machine	Power	HP	# Cyl.	Weight	Driver	Owner	Status	Time	Results
1	Fiat	Gas	110	4	2204	Fletcher, H.W.	Young, George W.	DNS		
3	Thomas	Gas	90	6	2190	Coey, C.A.	Coey, C.A.	DNS		
4	Napier	Gas	80	6	2204	Clifford Earp, W.	Edge, S.F.	OK	1:15:40 2-5	1st, World Record
7	Fiat	Gas	110	4	2180	Cedrino, Emanuel	Hollander&Tangeman	OK	1:16:39 4-5	2nd
8	Fiat	Gas	110	4	2180	Lancia, Vincenzo	Hollander&Tangeman	OK		DNF
9	Mercedes	Gas	90	4	2190	Downey, Joseph	Harding, J.N.	DNS		
12	A.G. Vanderbilt	Gas	250	8	2204	Sartori, Paul	Vanderbilt, A.G.	DNS		
14	Christie	Gas	110	4	2100	Christie, J.W.	Christie, J.W.	OK		DNF
17	Napier	Gas	60	4	2200	Hilliard, W.L.	Napier Motor Co. USA	OK	1:21:05 4-5	3rd
19	English Daimler	Gas	46	4	2200	Harding, H.N.	Sutphen, E.W.	OK		DNF
20	Darracq	Gas	200	8	2204	Vaughan, Guy	A. Darracq & Cie.	DNS		
21	Darracq	Gas	100	4		Guinness, A.L.	Guinness, A.L.	No Show		
22	Darracq	Gas	80	4	2204	Vaughan, Guy	Stevens, S.B.	Withdrawn		

Event rescheduled from Thursday, January 25, 1906. Stevens' Darracq withdrawn under protest. Fletcher and Sartori unable to start due to mechanical problems. Guinness did not attend meet.

~ JANUARY 29, 1906 ~

Event No. 19. 30 Mile Championship for American-Built Cars.

Car #	Machine	Power	HP	# Cyl.	Weight	Driver	Owner	Status	Time	Results
2	Stanley racer	Steam	30-50	2		Marriott, Fred	Stanley Motor Car Co.	OK	34:18 2-5	1st (5:40 delayed start)
10	Ford	Gas	105	6	1800	Kulick, Frank	Ford Motor Co.	OK		DNF
14	Christie	Gas	110	4	2100	Christie, J.W.	Christie, J.W.	OK	7:35 3-5	2nd

Marriott started 5 min. 40 sec. after the others (uninformed of race start time).

Event No. 6. 15 Mile Open Championship.

Car #	Machine	Power	HP	# Cyl.	Weight	Driver	Owner	Status	Time	Results
7	Fiat	Gas	110	4	2180	Cedrino, Emanuel	Hollader&Tangeman	OK		DNF
8	Fiat	Gas	110	4	2180	Lancia, Vincenzo	Hollander&Tangeman	OK	10:00	1st, World Record
17	Napier	Gas	60	4	2200	Hilliard, W.L.	Napier Motor Co. USA	OK	11:36 3-5	2nd

Cedrino broke connecting rod and was out of the remainder of the competition.

Event 5 and Event 9 (Combined 10 Mile Open Championship and 10 Mile Heavyweight Championship, Gasoline Cars).

Event No. 5. 10 Mile Open Championship.

Car #	Machine	Power	HP	# Cyl.	Weight	Driver	Owner	Status	Time	Results
2	Stanley racer	Steam	30-50	2		Marriott, Fred	Stanley Motor Car Co.	OK	7:35 3-5	2nd
8	Fiat	Gas	110	4	2180	Lancia, Vincenzo	Hollander&Tangeman	OK	6:19 3-5	1st
17	Napier	Gas	60	4	2200	Hilliard, W.L.	Napier Motor Co. USA	OK		DNF

Event run concurrently with the 10 Mile Heavyweight Championship.

Event No. 9. 10 Mile Heavyweight Championship.

Car #	Machine	Power	HP	# Cyl.	Weight	Driver	Owner	Status	Time	Results
2	Stanley racer	Steam	30-50	2		Marriott, Fred	Stanley Motor Car Co.	OK	7:35 3-5	2nd*
8	Fiat	Gas	110	4	2180	Lancia, Vincenzo	Hollander&Tangeman	OK	6:19 3-5	1st
17	Napier	Gas	60	4	2200	Hilliard, W.L.	Napier Motor Co. USA	OK		DNF

Event run concurrently with the 10 Mile Open Championship.

Event No. 17. 10 Mile Handicap.

Car #	Machine	Power	HP	# Cyl.	Weight	Driver	Owner	Status	Time	Results
8	Fiat	Gas	110	4	2180	Lancia, Vincenzo	Hollander&Tangeman	OK	6:18 2-5	1st (no allowance)
9	Mercedes	Gas	90	4	2190	Downey, Joseph	Harding, J.R.	OK	?	3rd (2:48 allowance)
17	Napier	Gas	60	4	2200	Hilliard, W.L.	Napier Motor Co. USA	OK	8:03 4-5	2nd (1:00 allowance)

~continued~

Event No. 10. One-Mile Middleweight Championship (Gasoline).

Car #	Machine	Power	HP	# Cyl.	Weight	Driver	Owner	Status	Time	Results
6	Fiat Jr.	Gas	24-30	4	1420	Cedrino, Emanuel	Hollander&Tangeman	DNS		
16	Wayne	Gas	40-50	4	1400	Holmes, Deacon D.	Wayne Auto Co.	DNS		
18	Reo	Gas	32	4	1432	Wurgis, Dan	Reo Motor Car Co.	DNS		
	Darracq	Gas	30			Vaughan, Guy	A. Darracq & Cie.	OK	not recorded	1st

Darracq driven by Guy Vaughan in walkover. Event rescheduled from Friday, January 26, 1906 (originally scheduled for 1/23/1906 and rescheduled for 1/25/1906).

Event No. 3. Two-Miles-a-Minute Trophy Race. The winner must equal or exceed 120 miles an hour. To be run as time trials.

Car #	Machine	Power	HP	# Cyl.	Weight	Driver	Owner	Status	Time	Results
1	Fiat	Gas	110	4	2204	Fletcher, H.W.	Young, George W.	DNS		
2	Stanley racer	Steam	20-30	2		Marriott, Fred	Stanley Motor Car Co.	OK	1:03/ 59 3-5	2nd
3	Thomas	Gas	90	6	2190	Coey, C.A.	Coey, C.A.	DNS		
7	Fiat	Gas	110	4	2180	Cedrino, Emanuel	Hollander&Tangeman	DNS		
8	Fiat	Gas	110	4	2180	Lancia, Vincenzo	Hollander&Tangeman	DNS		
10	Ford	Gas	105	6	1800	Ford, Henry of Kulick, Frank	Ford Motor Co.	DNS		
12	A.G. Vanderbilt	Gas	250	8	2204	Sartori, Paul	Vanderbilt, A.G.	DNS		
14	Christie	Gas	110	4	2100	Christie, J.W. or Chevrolet, L.	Christie, J. Walter	DNS		
20	Darracq	Gas	200	8	2204	Demogeot, Victor	A. Darracq & Cie.	OK	1:01 3-5/ 58 4-5	1st
21	Darracq	Gas	100	4	2204	Guinness, A.L.	Guinness, A.L.	No Show		

Event rescheduled from Saturday, January 27, 1906 (previously scheduled for 1/26/1906). Event closed after second heat despite Stanley request for third trial as permitted. Demogeot crowned King of Speed. Stanley protest disallowed.

F.E. and Frank Durbin at the Model H weigh-in, January 22, 1906. *Durbin (hatless, behind car) looks on as F.E. Stanley (to his left, behind scale enclosure) watches the scale reading. The stock Stanley has had its seats removed for the weigh-in. The 15 hp Model H, the "Gentlemen's Speedy Roadster," was clocked in the mile steam championship at 80 mph. Durbin also drove it to victory in the 15-mile Price handicap championship for American touring cars. In Fred Marriott's view the Model H (later upgraded to 20 hp) was the best all-round Stanley for stock car racing on hill, beach or track.*

Stanley Museum Archives.

~ COMPETITORS 1906 ~

Barron, Charles W. Owner/driver, 90 hp Fiat.

Basle, Charles. Professional driver, 120 hp Mercedes "Flying Dutchman." (Did not compete.) Basle was mentioned in some press accounts as a possible replacement for the disqualified Victor Hémery before that assignment was split between Louis Chevrolet and Victor Demogeot.

Bowden, Herbert L. Owner, 120 hp Mercedes "Flying Dutchman." (Did not compete.) Bowden's special (and overweight) Mercedes set an unofficial mile record at Ormond in 1905. At Readville in 1906, Bowden allegedly challenged F.O. Stanley to a match race, his Mercedes against one of the Stanley Vanderbilts, for a side bet of $1,000. Stanley agreed, but proposed a hill race with the Stanley climbing and the Mercedes descending, the first car to reach the other's starting location to be judged the winner. Bowden refused to race on those terms. (Elliott 1945: pp. 33, 35.)

Fred Marriott in the Stanley racer prior to the races, Ormond 1906. *Marriott poses in the racer on the beach for a pre-race photograph, possibly the same day as the weigh-in (Monday, January 22). The racer has yet to have its number, No. 2, painted on the side.*

Stanley Museum Archives.

    In letters and diaries of the day, the Stanleys themselves referred to the car simply as the "Racer" or the "Big Racer," and sometimes as the "Florida Racer." The car acquired a number of nicknames in press accounts, including "Flying Teapot" or "Teakettle," which, like "Steamer," were fairly generic terms for steam-powered race cars. Louis S. Ross's 1904/05 special Stanley-powered racer had been nicknamed the "Wogglebug," and since some outside observers considered the Stanley racer to be the descendent or successor to Ross's car, it, too, was sometimes called the "Wogglebug" or simply the "Bug." In keeping with this theme, some of the car's detractors called it an "Insect" or a "Cockroach." Still others called it a "Monster" or "Sea Monster" or "Sea Creature." It was often referred to as a "Freak" as that was a common term for special-built racing machines unequipped for touring or general road use. Some called it a "Flying Canoe" based on its construction. In action it was often described as a "Red Streak" or even a "Red Pencil Line." One of the most curious references to the racer comes from a 1918 Stanley Motor Carriage Co. pamphlet, "The Magic of Steam," in which some over-imaginative writer refers to the car as the "Armadillo," the only time it was ever called such.

    Fred Marriott, in an interview in the Boston Traveler on March 20, 1956, conveyed that the racer in 1906 was referred to as the "Bug" and that the upgraded car in 1907 was called the "Rocket." Very few period sources refer to the car as the "Rocket" but in later years that became a commonly used name. Because the scope of this history is the 1906 and 1907 races, the car has been referred to herein as the Stanley racer.

Walter Clifford Earp, at the wheel of his Napier, Ormond 1906. An accomplished Napier team driver respected for his professionalism and sportsmanship, Clifford Earp drove a 80-100 hp Napier owned by S. F. Edge. Photo by Penfield.

New York Times,
Stanley Museum Archives.

Breese, James L. Owner/driver, 35 hp Mercedes, 60 hp Mercedes.

Bristol, J. E. Owner/driver, 30 hp Stoddard-Dayton.

Cedrino, Emanuel. Professional driver, 24 hp Fiat Jr., 110 hp Fiat.

Chevrolet, Louis. Professional driver, 110 hp Christie, 200 hp Darracq. Chevrolet came to Ormond in the employ of J. Walter Christie, assigned to drive Christie's 110 hp front-wheel-drive racer. When the ownership and management of the Darracq company's cars were transferred to S.B. Stevens, Christie consented to a temporary "loan" of Chevrolet's services to the Darracq team. Chevrolet replaced Victor Hémery as driver and drove the 200 hp Darracq to new gasoline car records in the mile and kilometer speed trials. He later returned to Christie's service for the 100-mile race.

Christie, J. Walter. Owner/driver, 110 hp Christie "Blue Streak." Christie built distinctive front-wheel drive racers with transverse engines. Most of the driving of Christie's car was done by Louis Chevrolet. In the 30-mile race for American-built cars, Christie is credited in some accounts as driving the car to a second place finish himself, while in others Chevrolet is named as the driver. Still others state that Christie drove while Chevrolet accompanied him as his mechanician.

Clifford Earp, Walter. Professional driver, 100 hp Napier.

Coey, C. A. Owner/driver, 90 hp Thomas.

Demogeot, Victor. Professional driver, 200 hp Darracq. Demogeot was Victor Hémery's mechanician, although he may have been marked for driving one of the smaller Darracqs in the team's fleet.

Downey, Joseph. Professional driver, 90 hp Mercedes, 110 hp Mercedes.

Durbin, Francis P. (Frank). Professional driver, 15 hp Stanley Model H, 20 hp Stanley Model F. Durbin, a foreman in the Testing Department in the Stanley factory, was one of the company's earliest drivers, seeing professional duty at the Readville track and the Commonwealth Avenue hill climb as early as 1903. In addition to racing the company's stock cars, Durbin also raced the 1903 Stanley special racer in a five-mile race against Louis Ross at Narragansett Park, September 10, 1904. He was one of the prime candidates to drive the Stanley racer at Ormond, but published accounts claim that his wife, Ella, implored him not to accept the dangerous assignment, and the opportunity went to Fred Marriott. (*Boston Post* February 1906)

Frank Durbin in the Stanley Model H, Ormond 1906. Durbin was reported to be first in line to replace Louis Ross as the driver of the Stanley racer, but acquiesced to his wife's objections and piloted the "Gentlemen's Speedy Roadster" instead.
The Illustrated Outdoor News,
Stanley Museum Archives.

Edge, Selwyn Francis. (S. F.) Owner, 100 hp Napier driven by W. Clifford Earp. Edge was the distributor and tireless promoter of Napier cars. A former racing cyclist, he campaigned Napiers in Europe, winning the Gordon Bennett race in 1902.

Fleming, Charles. Owner/driver, 10 hp Maxwell Runabout.

Fletcher, Harry W. Professional driver, 110 hp Fiat. Fletcher, like Marriott and Hémery, was involved in the most famous "false start" in Ormond history, occurring in the second heat of the 5-mile Open. Fletcher and Hémery took off even though Marriott's car was not in position, and were recalled to the line. Fletcher, like Hémery, also protested the late recall, but unlike Hémery, Fletcher did as requested and returned to the starting line.

Ford, Henry. Owner/driver, 105 hp Ford. (Did not compete.) Ford was listed in the scheduled as a possible driver. He appears to have been preoccupied with fixing the last-minute problems with his racer, leaving the driving to Frank Kulick.

Gould Brokaw, W. Owner/driver, 60 hp Renault. (Did not compete.) It was reported that Gould Brokaw had commissioned a special Stanley steam racer capable of a 25-second mile to be delivered six months after the 1906 Ormond races, but the proposed racer was not built. Gould Brokaw eventually bought two front-wheel drive racers built by J. Walter Christie and entered them in the 1908 races.

Guinness, Algernon L. (A. L.) Owner/driver, 100 hp Darracq. (Did not attend.) Guinness (sometimes called "Arthur") was a wealthy amateur racing enthusiast from London, considered in some pre-race accounts as a major contender, but did not attend the meet.

Harding, H. N. Professional driver, 45 hp English Daimler.

Harry W. Fletcher in his 110 hp Fiat, Ormond 1906. A professional driver with experience in previous tournaments at Ormond, Fletcher drove a Fiat owned by New York banker George W. Young. Mechanical problems with the car put it out of action after the first few days of racing.
Photo Era, Stanley Museum Archives.

Harding, Josiah R. Owner/driver, 90 hp Mercedes. Harding protested S. B. Stevens's entry of the 80 hp Darracq (the 1905 Vanderbilt Cup winner) in the 10-mile Corinthian Championship for amateur owner/drivers, claiming that Stevens was not legally registered as the owner of the car. His challenge was disallowed.

Hémery, Victor. Professional driver, 200 hp Darracq. (Disqualified from competition.) Hémery's abbreviated performance in the 1906 races amounted to an unofficial record in the second heat of the five-mile Open, negated due to a false start. Hémery, as was his nature, twice ran afoul of the officials at Ormond – first protesting a disputed weigh-in, and then refusing to accept the false start, leading to his disqualification. Hémery's earlier racing experience in the U.S. included a victory in the 1905 Vanderbilt Cup race. During that event Hémery and a number of the other foreign gas car drivers were contemptuous of the driving of Walter White in one of the White steam racers, and were vocal in their complaints regarding the steamer's participation in the contest. The English-speaking press often referred to the temperamental Frenchman as "Auguste Hémery" and his name is so inscribed on the Vanderbilt Cup.

Burt Holland in the Stanley Model F Touring car, Ormond 1906. Holland, a Stanley factory mechanic, raced Stanleys at Readville and other local tracks, and represented the company in hill climbs, most notably the 1905 Climb to the Clouds on Mt. Washington where he established the steam course record.
The Bulb Horn,
Stanley Museum Archives.

Hilliard, William H. Professional driver, 80 hp Napier. Hilliard won the 1905 Climb to the Clouds driving the Gordon Bennett Napier, edging out Burt Holland driving a Stanley Model H.

5L. Vincenzo Lancia in his 110 hp Fiat, Ormond 1906. Lancia drove for the Fiat factory team in Europe, venturing overseas for the 1905 Vanderbilt Cup race and losing to Victory Hémery after a collision with J. Walter Christie. Competing at Ormond for the first (and last) time, Lancia was popular with many of his fellow drivers and other attendees, including the Stanleys.
Larz Anderson Auto Museum.

Holland, Burton C. (Burt or Bert). Professional driver, 20 hp Stanley Model F. Holland worked for Stanley in the Testing Department, and drove stock Stanleys on tracks and hill climbs. On July 18, 1905, Holland set the steam course record on Mount Washington during the second Climb to the Clouds, driving a prototype Model H to the summit in 27:17 2-5. Known as Burt (or Bert – some sources have his name as "Bertram" or "Albert") he was a good friend of Fred Marriott.

Holmes, Deacon D. Professional driver, 40 hp Wayne "Kite."

Jay, Webb. Professional driver, White steam cars. (Did not compete.) Webb Jay

Fred H. Marriott on Ormond Beach, 1906. *Marriott had begun his racing career as an amateur cyclist, winning numerous races on road and track, and was recognized as the bicycling champion of Needham. When he began work as a mechanic at the Union Cycle works in Hylandville (part of Needham), he most likely turned pro to race for the factory team. His early racing experience provided him with skills and competitive savvy for excellence in motor racing when he began driving for Stanley at local venues, such as the 1904 Commonwealth Avenue Hill Climb and the 1905 Readville races. Acclaimed for his fearlessness and daring, Marriott was also considered a cautious racer with an appreciation for race tactics. At Ormond he competed "under the direct supervision of F.E. Stanley, who gives Marriott specific directions at the beginning of each race, and holds him responsible, in so far as the race is concerned. Marriott, of course, is expected to use his head if conditions change during the race." (Motor Age February 1, 1906, p.5.) Larz Anderson Auto Museum.*

had raced his White steamer at Ormond in 1905, but later that summer was severely injured in a bad crash in Buffalo, NY, and was a spectator at the 1906 races.

Keene, Foxhall P. Owner/driver, 120 hp Mercedes. (Did not attend.)

Kulick, Frank. Professional driver, 105 hp Ford.

Kull, A. L. (Frank). Professional driver, 30-40 hp Wayne.

Lancia, Vincenzo. Professional driver, 110 hp Fiat. Fiat test driver-turned-racer Lancia and his teammate Cedrino came to Ormond with powerful Fiats. Set up for road racing, they were too slow in competition with the beach racers at the meet. Despite this, the crafty Lancia managed to win his share of races, including several match-ups with Fred Marriott in the Stanley racer. Lancia later manufactured an automobile under his own name.

Marriott, Fred H. Professional driver, 30-50 hp Stanley racer. Marriott, a former bicycle racer, was the foreman of the Stanley Repair Department, and had begun to race stock cars for the firm in 1904 at Readville and the Commonwealth Avenue hill climb. Family lore says that he added the middle initial "H" to his name at that time in mock dignity as his name began appearing in the auto racing columns. Given his inexperience in high-speed racing, he was regarded by some as an unlikely, last-minute choice to drive the Stanley racer. Stanley, however, praised his foreman for "courage and a good head," indicating that Fred was chosen for his fearlessness and decisiveness to pilot the racer.

Reeves, Alfred. Owner/driver, 10 hp Maxwell Runabout.

Ross, Louis S. Amateur driver, 20 hp Stanley-powered "Wogglebug." (Did not attend.) Ross had achieved an unprecedented series of victories in his home-built steamer at Ormond in 1905, and many believed he would be chosen to drive the new Stanley racer, given his experience and proven track record. In fact, up until a month before the

Paul Sartori and his boss, Alfred Gwynn Vanderbilt, Ormond 1906. Sartori, left, explains the problems with the 250 hp racer to its owner, A. G. Vanderbilt, right, as a Mr. Spencer, center, listens in. Vanderbilt had spent a small fortune on a special 250 hp racer on which he had high hopes of setting the Land Speed Record, but Sartori and his crew were unable to get the untried car running and it appeared in none of the races.

Photo Era, Stanley Museum Archives.

1906 races Ross was the designated driver for the Stanley racer. On December 20, 1905, Ross and Stanley broke off their partnership in this endeavor, reportedly over a disagreement involving the custody of prizes and awards that might be won by the Stanley racer at Ormond. Ross apparently believed that as an amateur, driving for Stanley without pay, he had a legitimate claim to any prizes and honors won through his efforts, but Stanley presumably thought otherwise. (*Boston Globe* December 22, 1905, p.9.) For a time between 1906 and 1910, Ross was a rival steam car manufacturer to Stanley, but according to a number of sources they remained on friendly terms.

Sartori, Paul. Professional driver, 250 hp Vanderbilt racer "Spooner." (Did not compete.) Sartori was also mentioned as a potential replacement for Victor Hémery, but continued to work on A.G. Vanderbilt's troublesome race car, which finally made its first test run on the beach on the last day of the races, making no mark in competition.

Stanley, Francis E. (F.E.). Owner/driver, Stanley cars. (Did not compete.) F.E. drove his first special racer at the Decoration Day races at Readville in 1903, setting a World track record for steam cars. There are some undocumented assertions that F.E. Stanley may have entertained the notion of driving the Stanley racer in competition at Ormond himself, before being dissuaded by his wife's objections. If so, it may be that Stanley made a practical judgment that his car's chances of victory in the high-speed races might be improved under the hand of a younger man, rather than any concern of personal risk, but what factors might have influenced him are a matter of conjecture.

Stevens, Samuel B. (S. B.). Owner/driver, 80 hp Darracq. Stevens, the wealthy heir to local iron concerns in Rome, NY, had raced Mercedes at Ormond in 1904 and 1905. After purchasing the 80 hp Darracq (the winner of the 1905 Vanderbilt Cup) on the third day of the 1906 Ormond tournament, he gained the dubious distinction of having the car challenged twice during the next 48 hours. First J. R. Harding (who had purchased the Mercedes Stevens had previously campaigned at Ormond) protested Stevens's entry of the car in the ten-mile Corinthian Cup race (for amateur owner/drivers), charging that he was not actually the legal owner at race time – this challenge was disallowed. On Saturday a group of the foreign gas car drivers challenged the Darracq's entry in the

F.E. Stanley and his driver, Fred Marriott, at the weigh-in of the Stanley Racer. Stanley was the only steam car manufacturer taking part in the 1906 Ormond Beach tournament. At 56, Stanley was a self-made man and an individualist, but was also adept at fitting in wherever circumstance found him, be it involved with school children, concert violinists, auto manufacturers, mechanics, economists, politicians, farmers, or high society. At Ormond Beach, the scene of his greatest racing triumph, he appears to have been regarded as a true maverick.

Stanley Museum Archives.

100-mile race for not being equipped with a differential gear. This time Stevens withdrew his car before it could be officially disqualified. The second challenge lead to a threatened challenge to the 200 hp Darracq (likewise improperly equipped) by F.E. Stanley.

Sutphin, T. W. Owner, 45 hp English Daimler driven by H. N. Harding.

Vanderbilt, Alfred Gwynn. Owner, 250 hp Vanderbilt racer "Spooner," driven by Paul Sartori. Vanderbilt was the cousin of William Kissam ("Willie K.") Vanderbilt, Jr., instigator of the Vanderbilt Cup races and an Ormond competitor in 1904 and 1905.

Vaughan, Guy. Professional driver, 30 hp Darracq, 80 hp Darracq.

Wurgis, Dan. Professional driver, 32 hp Reo "Bird."

Young, George W. Owner, 110 hp Fiat driven by H. W. Fletcher.

Ormond Beach Trophies, 1906. *A group of race trophies to be won are assembled for viewing by the grandstand area at Ormond Beach. Left to right: the Automobile Speed King Trophy, commissioned by the Times-Union newspaper of Jacksonville, Fla., to be awarded to the winner of the Two-Mile-a-Minute race; the Clyde Line Trophy, commissioned by William P. Clyde & Co. [steamship line] to be awarded to the winner of the 15-Mile Open Championship; the Minneapolis Cup, commissioned by the Automobile Club of Minneapolis, to be awarded to the winner of the 100-Mile International Championship. The other tall trophy, third from right, bottom row, is the Hotel Ormond Trophy, presented by the Hotel Ormond most likely to the winner of the One-Mile Heavyweight Championship. The other trophies are unidentified.*

Stanley Museum Archives.

~ COMPETITORS 1907 ~

Adriance, William A. Owner/driver, 20 hp Stevens-Duryea.

Baker, Walter C. Owner/driver, 30 hp Peerless. Baker manufactured electric cars under his own name; his "Torpedo Kid," driven by W. J. Hastings, set a world's record for electric cars at Ormond in 1904.

Baldwin, Leon F. N. Professional driver, 25 hp Stanley Model K, 30 hp Stanley Vanderbilt racer. Baldwin was an early steam car pioneer in Providence, RI, and later the Stanley agent in several southeastern New England markets. He drove Stanleys in many local hill climbs, tracks and beach races. Nicknamed "Lucky," his fortunes were few at Ormond, but he went on to drive the Stanley Vanderbilt racer to many triumphs and record-setting performances.

Blackinton, Byron F. Professional driver, Stanley team. (Did not compete.) Blackinton was Baldwin's partner in the Providence dealership and a veteran of many local races. He may have served as a mechanician at the Ormond races.

Blakeley, Edward B. (Ned). Owner/driver, 70 hp American Mercedes. Blakeley was a Harvard tutor, fairly new to motor racing. With few other gas car owners competing, Blakeley drove his American Mercedes to a number of victories, dominating the meet without setting any records.

Bond, R. M. Owner/driver, 30 hp Cleveland.

The Sir Thomas R. Dewar Trophy. *Sir Thomas Dewar, the Scottish distillery heir and sportsman, donated this trophy for the One-Mile International Championship to be held annually at Ormond Beach. It was won by Louis S. Ross in 1905 and by Fred Marriott in 1906 and 1907, before it was retired from competition. Although open to all cars of all weights and all powers, it was never won in competition by a gasoline car, only by Stanley-powered steamers.*
Clarence Coons Collection,
courtesy Joe Green and Fred Marriott.

Curtiss, Glenn. Owner/driver, 14 hp Curtiss motorcycle, 40 hp Curtiss motorcycle. Motorcycle and aviation pioneer Curtiss previously raced at Ormond in 1904, setting a world record at 10 miles. For 1907, he brought a special motorcycle powered by a V-8 airship engine and was clocked in an unofficial trial run at 26 2-5, eclipsing the existing mile record. His machine broke down before he was able to make an official trial, and he apparently never rebuilt the machine nor constructed another to make another attempt at the record. Curtiss did drive his other motorcycle to a world's record in the lightweight class at the 1907 races.

Durbin, Francis P. (Frank). Professional driver, 20 hp Stanley Model F. Durbin returned with the Stanley team to drive the Model F Touring car. Apparently his wife was still uneasy over his competing, as it was reported that Burt Holland might take his place.

Fales, Warren R. Owner/driver, 30 hp Stanley Vanderbilt racer driven by L. F. N. Baldwin. (Did not compete.) Fales is listed in some press reports as the driver of his Vanderbilt racer. It was common to list the owner of a winning car instead of the driver, which leads to some confusion over who actually drove. Fales appears to have left the driving of the Vanderbilt to Baldwin, F.E. Stanley, or H. Ernest Rogers.

Harper, Daniel Walter. Professional driver, Stanley team. (Did not compete.) Harper was the Stanley Philadelphia dealer, and drove Stanleys at many mid-East venues. His wife, Mary, also drove Stanleys in local races, sometimes under her husband's name when women were barred from competition. The Harpers apparently attended the Ormond meet but did not compete.

Harroun, Ray. Owner/driver, 40 hp Harroun racer. (Did not compete.) Harroun's 1907 car was a special racer of his own manufacture. He later drove for Marmon, winning the inaugural Indianapolis 500 race in 1911.

Holland, Burton C. (Burt or Bert.) Professional driver, Stanley team. (Did not compete.) Holland was mentioned as a possible replacement for Frank Durbin. During the 1907 events he probably served as a mechanician on one of the Vanderbilt cars.

Hutton, C. E. Owner/driver, 20 hp Rolls-Royce also driven by R.A. McCready. Marriott easily defeated Hutton's out-matched Rolls-Royce touring car in the 5-mile Open. It was Hutton's car which later came to his rescue, however, transporting Marriott from the crash site on the beach to medical help at the Florida East Coast A.A. clubhouse.

Kull, A. L. (Frank). Professional driver, 35 hp Wayne.

Laughlin, J. Owner/driver, 30 hp Cleveland.

McCarthy, John H. Owner/driver, Wayne.

McCready, R. A. Professional driver, 20 hp Rolls-Royce owned by C. E. Hutton.

Marriott, Fred H. Professional driver, 30-50 hp Stanley racer. When Marriott returned to Ormond for the 1907 races he was now considered as one of the top drivers, having earned his credentials at the 1906 tournament. He was also one of the race favorites, popular with spectators, officials and other drivers alike.

Owen, Ralph. Owner/driver, 35 hp Oldsmobile "Mud-Lark."

Paine, Asa. Owner/driver, 20 hp Autocar, 30 hp Winton. Paine, from Minneapolis, was also the president of the Florida East Coast Automobile Association. With such a depleted field of contestants at Ormond, Paine pressed his own private touring cars into action to try to fill out the entry slots in several events.

Perlman, L. H. Owner/driver, 50 hp Welch.

Rogers, Henry Ernest. Owner/driver, 25 hp Stanley Model K, 30 hp Stanley Vanderbilt racer. Rogers, an amateur sporting enthusiast, drove a Peerless in the first Climb to the Clouds in 1904. Converting to steam cars soon after, he had achieved a number of steam successes at Readville, Atlantic City, and other venues. His wife, Margaret, was also an accomplished driver, driving Maxwells to victory in her class at Dead Horse Hill, and competing in match races against Joan Cuneo and other prominent woman racers of the day.

Rose, G. D. W. Owner/driver, 30 hp Stoddard-Dayton.

Seabring, George E. Owner/driver, Winton.

Stanley, Francis E. (F.E.). Owner/driver, 20 hp Stanley Model F, 30 hp Stanley Vanderbilt racer. Despite having a fairly large number of team drivers in attendance, Stanley decided to take part in the action during the 1907 meet. He apparently decided to drive one of the Vanderbilt racers in the 10-mile Open as a last-minute substitution for H. Ernest Rogers, who was occupied with repairs to his Model K. Later F.E. took the wheel of the Model F Touring car, setting a world record for steam touring cars in the mile trial.

Stinson, W. N., Dr. Owner/driver, 30 hp Franklin.

Wagner, Louis. Professional driver, 110 hp Darracq. (Did not attend.)

Wray, William H. Owner/driver, 14 hp Simplex-Peugeot motorcycle. Wray set a world's record for motorcycles in the middleweight class. Even though he had beaten Glenn Curtiss in this event, his triumph was overshadowed by Curtiss's unofficial time in the mile.

CHAPTER SIX

"Bravo, Stanley!"

"Dear Ed,

"The first day of the contest is over and the Stanley is on top. Fred [Marriott] beat the Napier in the trial heat nearly seven sec. 32 1/5 & 40 being the times. When you realize that Fred was going five rods while the Napier was going four you see it should hardly be called a race. The track was unusually slow on account of the heavy rains and they had a direct cross wind which is worse for our car than a head wind. So you see our machine is faster even than we estimated. I am satisfied now that we can do the two miles in one minute if we can have good or I will say the best conditions.

"When the mile steam competition was run Fred, Frank [Durbin] with the H and Bert [Holland] with the touring car made the race and Frank and Fred had to score with Bert so was going only about a 60 second clip when they crossed the tape and then Fred went in 31 4/5 and Frank in 45 and Bert in 60 1/5.

"Yesterday Bert ran the touring car over the same course in 54 4/5 the difference being due wholly to the condition of the beach and the wind.

"From that you can see what the possibilities are with our racer.

"The cylinders came to night but the engine we are using is all right and we shall use it through the meet if it does not give out. The trouble with the others has been the pistons have been too tight and either brake (sic) the connecting rod or the piston in the last case when they stick.

"Tomorrow we run in the five mile open and we expect to win.

"All well and having a fine time.

Yours,
F.E. Stanley"

(F.E. Stanley letter to Edward Hallett, January 23, 1906, Stanley Museum Archives.)

Attempting to start Vanderbilt's 250 hp car. *A curious F.E. Stanley, center, stands alongside A. G. Vanderbilt's 250 hp car and watches as the crew struggles to crank start it. Vanderbilt's car was first thought to be a serious contender but was unable to start in any of its scheduled races. In the Stanley Model F touring car in the background, F.E. Stanley's son, Raymond, waits for his father.*

Stanley Museum Archives.

Victory Hémery and Victor Demogeot in the 200 hp Darracq. Hémery, left, and his mechanician, Demogeot, prepare to take the 200 hp Darracq out for a warm-up run. The Darracq was considered the chief competition for the Stanley racer.

Harper's Weekly.

"RAIN AND DARK," wrote Mrs. Stanley in her diary on Tuesday morning, January 23, 1906, as contestants, race officials and spectators prepared for the start of the races. The beach itself was in fairly good shape, and as the morning fog began to lift and the rain tapered to a drizzle the officials delayed the scheduled 10:00

am start of the tournament for an hour or so, hoping to run some of the early races while the tides were still favorable. Unlike the 1905 meet when many insignificant and uninteresting races were clustered on the first day, Senator Morgan and his team elected to start the 1906 races off with a bang, leading off with a marquee event, the one-mile International Challenge for the Sir Thomas Dewar Trophy.

The bang threatened to turn into a whimper as several of the heavyweight players failed to make it to the starting line. A. G. Vanderbilt's 250 hp behemoth racer "Spooner," thought to be a major threat prior to the start of the races, was plagued with insurmountable troubles – the only threat it posed was as an obstacle on the beach. Henry Ford's Model K racer was also a no-show due to some pre-race miscommunications among the members of the Ford team.

The absence of the Darracq race cars was not due to miscommunication but to a fit of pique on the part of the French team's leader, Victor Hémery. The mercurial Hémery, upset over a disqualification of one of his cars deemed too heavy for its class at the weigh-in,

Ormond Beach Judges' stand, January 23, 1906. The judges and timers for the races were positioned on the smaller stand in front of the larger wooden platform; above and behind was the spectators' gallery. The clubhouse of the Florida East Coast Automobile Association (the event sponsor) stands to the left. The sign on the upper balcony reads "32 1-5," the current mile record just set a short time earlier by Fred Marriott in the first heat for the Dewar Trophy race. Marriott would lower the record still further in the one-mile steam championship later in the day. Photo by Edward G. Harris.

Stanley Museum Archives.

pulled all of the Darracqs from the first day of competition. His abrupt withdrawal angered the American Darracq Company's representative, and disappointed many race fans as the 200 hp Darracq was thought by many to have the only chance of defeating the Stanley steamer.

Lining up for the first heat for the Dewar Cup were the Englishman, W. Clifford Earp, in a 100 hp Napier, H. W. Fletcher, driving George A. Young's 110 hp Fiat, and Fred Marriott in the Stanley racer. After two false starts the trio was away, Marriott quickly running off with a seemingly easy victory in 32 1-5 seconds, a new world's record. Clifford Earp's British Napier had made an unofficial run of 31 seconds in pre-race trials, but here trailed at the finish by an eighth of a mile, almost eight seconds off the pace, Fletcher third. The second heat matched two 110 hp Fiats driven by Lancia and Cedrino, who went head-to-head over their mile run, Lancia pulling just ahead to win the heat in 37 3-5.

The final heat for the Dewar Cup pitted Marriott against the two other contestants with the best times, so Lancia and Cedrino lined up their Fiats once again. This heat also saw a pair of false starts, and the third start saw Marriott come across the starting line slowly, the two Italian cars getting away with an early lead. Marriott quickly recovered and drew even, pouring on steam and racing away with the first victory of the meet, his 32-second time easily leading Cedrino over the line by five seconds. Not only had the Stanley with the replacement engine performed brilliantly, it had also successfully "defended" the Dewar Trophy won by Louis Ross in 1905.

The outcome of the one-mile steam championship race held later that day could well have been considered a foregone conclusion as

The Starting line-up for the one-mile steam championship. *Fred Marriott, in the Stanley racer, lines up with Burt Holland in a Stanley Model F touring car. Frank Durbin, in the Stanley Model H, is just out of the picture to the left. Working in unison, all three Stanley cars were able to cross the starting line in a flying start, resulting in another world record for Fred Marriott.*

The Bulb Horn, Stanley Museum Archives.

it was an all-Stanley affair. For the race times to be ruled official there had to be at least three cars entered, so Marriott was joined at the starting line by his teammates Frank Durbin, in a 15 hp stock Model H "Gentlemen's Speedy Roadster," and Burt Holland, driving a stock touring car, a 20 hp Stanley Model F. All three cars had to cross the line together, requiring some coordination as the two faster cars worked to match the top speed of the touring car, pushed by Holland to its limit to give Marriott the fastest running start possible in an open race. Once over the line Marriott and Durbin took off, Marriott finishing in 31 4-5, another new world's record, Durbin following in 45 seconds. Burt Holland crossed the line in 60 4-5, making the race official and recording a very respectable 59.2 mph in the process. (Foster 2004: p.193.)

Wednesday, January 24th, the second day of the meet, saw the return of Hémery and the Darracqs, as the controversy over the weight of one of the team cars was resolved and all were cleared (at least for the moment) for competition. The key race of the day was the five-mile

Fireworks with Hémery and the Darracq. *Hémery, left, adopts an intimidating stance while lining up with Marriott in the Stanley racer. Illustration by Peter Helck.*

The Bulb Horn, Stanley Museum Archives.

open contest, a race which the Stanley team approached with expectations of victory, given their success the day before in the Dewar competition. Instead of making short work of it, however, the Stanleys found the race to be full of surprises and high drama, indicative of how quickly fortunes could turn on the beach.

The first heat saw Lancia drive his Fiat to a new record of 2:54 3-5, quickly eclipsing the five-mile record set by Arthur MacDonald the year before. Lancia's opponent, Clifford Earp, was left far behind when he had to turn out to avoid J. Walter Christie's new car that had broken down on the course. The gentlemanly Lancia, in an act of old-school sportsmanship, offered to re-run the heat despite his new record, but the officials ruled his time and the heat official.

The real fireworks began in the second heat, in which Hémery at first balked at participating, finding that he was pitted against Marriott in the steamer. It took the combined efforts of Clifford Earp and Lancia to persuade Hémery to come to the starting line. (*New York Times* January 25, 1906, p.7) When he finally did so, Hémery allegedly drew his 200 hp

Darracq up alongside Marriott's wooden-bodied car, revving his engine so as to spit fire from his exhaust pipes, probably more as intimidation than an actual attempt to set his rival on fire, though some witnesses weren't too sure. (Helck 1958: p.15.)

The second heat began, typically, with a false start, and Hémery, Marriott and Fletcher, with his Fiat, returned for another attempt. The second go-round was also ruled a false start but

Start of the final heat of the five-mile open championship. *Despite a cracked burner, Marriott sprints away from the line ahead of Fletcher, center, and Lancia, left, in their 110 hp Fiats. Forced to shut down his burner and finish on stored steam, Marriott was passed by Lancia and Fletcher in the final 200 yards. Marriott finished third, but his world record in that distance set during the first heat held up as official.*

Larz Anderson Auto Museum.

Hémery and Fletcher both sped down the beach, apparently neither man noticing the recall flag. Directed to return for another start, Hémery went into a rage and flatly refused. Senator Morgan and the other officials spent the next 30 minutes alternately persuading, cajoling, reasoning, imploring, then threatening, and finally ordering the Frenchman to comply, all to no avail. After a lengthy delay Hémery was disqualified from the rest of the meet, armed constables placed on his car so that he could disrupt the races no further.

When the second heat was finally run off, Marriott bested Lancia's fresh mark with another world's record in 2:47 1-5. The steamer had suffered a cracked burner which cast in doubt its participation in the final heat. Despite the Stanley's record time the officials were in no mood to grant further delays and ordered Stanley to run his car in the final or face having his record thrown out. Marriott ran the race with a leaking burner, as far as possible, to about the three-mile mark, then shut it down to run the remaining distance on stored steam. In the last half mile he began to slow down and lose ground, the race tightening until Lancia and Fletcher caught and passed him in the final 200 yards, Lancia winning in 3:01 1-5, Fletcher following in 3:02, Marriott coasting in just behind in 3:03. The Stanleys were disappointed in the result, "but," as Augusta Stanley admitted, "it was a great race." (A. Stanley *Diary*, January 24, 1906.) The Stanleys' disappointment was mitigated by the fact that Marriott's world record in the five-mile distance held up and went into the record books as official.

By 6:00 pm that evening the Stanley racer had been fitted with a replacement burner and was all ready to continue its record-breaking performance. Some of the competing gas cars, showing signs of the stresses of intense racing,

were not so fortunate. Fletcher's Fiat was out for the rest of the meet, needing a new engine and crankcase. Lancia's Fiat faced a day or two of repairs, during which time he would drive one of the spare Fiats at the factory team's disposal. Hopes for A. G. Vanderbilt's 250 hp car were rapidly dimming, Ford was still having trouble getting his racer to run right, and Chevrolet had broken down in Christie's new car just driving down the beach.

Adding to the peculiarities of the day's events was a report that surfaced in the *Philadelphia Inquirer*, dateline January 24, that offers some insight into the casual interactions of owners, race car drivers and spectators who were free to intermingle on the sidelines of the beach. A young New York socialite, Mrs. Ella Burt Claussen, was watching the trial heats from her touring car on the beach when the Stanley racer "went by like a streak of lightning." Mrs. Claussen, the daughter of the head of the Panamanian Railway and the wife of the Resort Editor of the *New York Herald*, was said to remark, "How I wish I could ride in that car." According to the *Inquirer* "an elderly gentleman in the next touring car spoke up, 'Pardon me, madame, I am afraid you would not care to go that fast.' 'Oh, yes I would, and if I knew Mr. Stanley I would ask him.' 'Well, I declare!' exclaimed Mr. Stanley, for it was he. 'You shall have your wish.'"

Stanley signaled Fred Marriott, who brought the car around and took on Mrs. Claussen. The racer was designed to hold one person, the driver, in a seated position, but photos exist which show that it was possible to carry a kneeling passenger alongside, although the cockpit would then be a tight fit. Marriott was instructed to try another timed mile but to slow down if his passenger so wished. Mrs. Claussen, however, showed "plenty of pluck" and urged him to go "Faster!" as Marriott throttled up to full speed, tearing through the mile unofficially in 31 2-5. "The fastest mile ever traveled by a woman," the paper declared, and a steam car mark that may still stand today. (*Philadelphia Inquirer* January 25, 1906.)

Thursday, January 25, was "rainy all day," wrote Mrs. Stanley. "Crowds here greatly disappointed in regard to races." (A. Stanley *Diary*, January 25, 1906.) Highlighting the news at Ormond was the dismissal of Victor Hémery by order of the French Darracq Company, and their approval of the sale of the 80 hp Darracq to S. B. Stevens, to whom their American representative, Charles D. Cooke, was directed to turn over the management of the team cars for the duration of the races. Samuel B. Stevens of Rome, NY, was a wealthy amateur owner-driver who had raced Mercedes at Ormond the previous two meets, finishing second three times in 1905 to Louis Ross's steamer.

Stevens's action was applauded by many racing enthusiasts because it permitted the re-entry of the Darracqs, particularly the 200 hp car, in the remaining races. The applause was muted among the contestants of the ten-mile Corinthian Cup race for owner-drivers, however, as Stevens quickly entered his new 80 hp Darracq with himself as driver, defeating James L. Breese in a 40 hp Mercedes with a time of 9:28. There was some grumbling that the last minute purchase and entry by an amateur of what was essentially a factory team car exceeded the spirit if not the letter of the rules, but an official protest was overruled. (*Boston Herald* January 25, 1906.)

The solitary steam action of the day took place in the 15-mile Price Handicap race for stock touring cars fully equipped, in which the Stanleys entered their stock Model H, the "Gentlemen's Speedy Roadster," driven by

Frank Durbin in the Model H, Ormond 1906. *Durbin won the 15-mile Price Handicap race for stock touring cars fully equipped in Stanley's "Gentlemen's Speedy Roadster."*

Brown Brothers.

Frank Durbin. A prototype of the Model H had set the steam course record in the 1905 Climb to the Clouds on Mount Washington in New Hampshire the previous July. Durbin's Model H, built for the Decoration Day races at Readville, was handicapped 25 seconds (one second for each $100 difference in value, factored against the most expensive car in the race, a $3,500 Wayne), and easily won its event in 13:42 2-5, defeating J. E. Bristol in a 30 hp Stoddard-

The timers look over their apparatus. *The timing of the races was performed by both electronic apparatus and by hand-held watches under the supervision of experienced timers, including John C. Kerrison, right, the president of the Chronograph Club of Boston. Photo by Nathan Lazarnick.*

Courtesy George Eastman House.

Marriott sets the world's kilometer record.
Marriott returns to the pit area after setting the kilometer record at 121.6 mph in his first record trial on January 26, 1906. Beside him, wheeling in the car, is Stanley team member Burt Holland.
Larz Anderson Auto Museum.

Dayton by some three and a half minutes. (*New York Times* January 26, 1906, p.6.)

Friday, January 26, was cold and damp, the beach only in fair condition, but the lack of wind made racing conditions favorable for the mile and kilometer speed trials scheduled. Problems with the electrical timing apparatus delayed the races until 1:00 pm, and then the one-kilometer trials began from the Daytona end of the course. The first to go was Fred Marriott, who drove back and took a two-mile

Louis Chevrolet in the 200 hp Darracq.
Chevrolet was "loaned" by his employer, J. Walter Christie, to the Darracq team to drive the 200 hp Darracq in the record trials in the absence of the disqualified Victor Hémery. Although Chevrolet had never driven the car before, he set new records for gasoline-powered cars in the mile and the kilometer, falling short of Marriott's records.
Photo Era, Stanley Museum Archives.

flying start to the line, flashing over the course and tripping the timers and watches at the finish in 18 2-5 seconds, 121.6 mph, the first world record performance of the day and the first time the two-mile-per-minute barrier had been crossed (if only at the kilometer distance). The Stanley record was received with a great cheer from the crowd. Chevrolet drove the 200 hp Darracq to a new gas car record at the kilometer distance, 19 2-5. Following Chevrolet were Clifford Earp's Napier in 21 3-5; Cedrino's Fiat in 22 4-5; and Ford's Model K in 24 4-5.

About two hours later the mile heavyweight trials began. Earlier in the week many spectators watched the Stanley in the rolling starts for the Dewar Trophy and wondered what it might do with a full flying start. They were about to find out. Clifford Earp led off the mile trials with a run of 37 2-5, then it was Marriott's turn, Fred again taking the racer back to about two miles before the starting line to begin his run. James T. Sullivan, the automotive correspondent of the *Boston Globe*, described the scene:

"The day was good for fast time as there was no wind. It was a foregone conclusion that the mile record would be broken, judging from the time in the kilometer. Finally, about 3, the word was passed, 'car coming,' and every one began to crane his neck. Two miles away, under the bridge, was a little object that looked like a bit of driftwood thrown on the beach. It was but a speck, but each second it grew larger as it raced toward the start. No bullet from a rifle ever sped a straighter course. Each second it increased its speed and when it shot over the line the spectators saw only an object shaped like a cigar, a blur of red and white and they held their breath until it was lost in a cloud of steam an eighth of a mile away. There was no

"Getting ready for the Mile record." *Marriott, center, looks on as the Stanley crew prepares the racer for the mile record, its rear carapace removed. The man in the coat with his back to the camera, leaning into the rear engine compartment, may be Burt Holland. Leaning on the stern of the car is Prescott Warren, F.E. Stanley's son-in-law, who had delivered a spare engine from the Stanley factory just prior to the races.*
Larz Anderson Auto Musuem.

"All ready for the mile." *Marriott prepares to climb into the Stanley racer as the mile record trials are about to begin.*
Stanley Museum Archives.

sound of rapid explosions such as accompanies a gasoline car. Just a whistling sound like that from the 'hot peanuts' can, only 100 times louder.

"One mile down the beach there was a crowd gathered at the finish and toward this the steamer was headed, growing less distinct momentarily until at last it was but a black speck. It crossed the line and two red flags dropped.

"'Just 28 1-5 seconds,' said one of the timers. The word was quickly passed and even before the announcer had time to raise his megaphone all those within a few hundred feet of the stand

"Start of the Mile record." *Marriott crosses the line in a flying start at the beginning of his mile record attempt.*

Larz Anderson Auto Museum.

knew that the old record was shattered badly. When the announcement was made there was a wild shout of delight, and for the first time since the meet began there was much enthusiasm evinced by the spectators." (*Boston Globe* January 26, 1906, p.7.)

Marriott's time of 28 1-5 indicated a speed of 127.66 mph, the first time the speed of two miles per minute had been exceeded in pursuit of the mile record – the new Land Speed Record. It was the hoped-for breakthrough event of the tournament, and everyone instantly recognized it, "the crowd of spectators… jumped to their feet with an exclamation of astonishment and recognition of the phenomenal speed at which it traveled. F.E. Stanley, its builder, was standing on the beach and bowed to the plaudits of the crowd." (*New York Times* January 27, 1906, p.1.)

"It was a great Stanley day," wrote Mrs. Stanley, "as Fred drove the racer a kilo in 18 2-5

sec. and a mile in the wonderful time of 28 1-5 sec. – the mark no one here thought could be reached. Frank's genius has been recognized – and his judgement proved to be good in letting Fred run the car." (A. Stanley *Diary* January 26, 1906.) Accolades in the press and from friends and associates continued to pour in. A delighted F.O. Stanley telegrammed from Colorado: "Wonderful, Wonderful, Wonderful is all I can say." From France, steam pioneer Léon Serpollet's telegram was even more succinct: "Bravo Stanley!" it read. (Stanley Museum Archives.)

For F.E. Stanley's part, he said: "I wish to give every possible credit to my driver, Fred H. Marriott of Boston, who piloted the steamer. Without him the feat would have been impossible. He is extremely modest, and laid it all to the machine, but I know it took courage and a good head to guide the steamer as it flew over the beach at the highest speed anything had

Fred Marriott surrounded by a crowd of admirers. *Marriott stands beside his victorious machine, surrounded by a congratulatory crowd. Augusta Stanley (in large hat) standing just beyond Fred Marriott, center, beams at the Stanleys' driver with pride.*
Stanley Museum Archives, courtesy Fred Heim via Don Davidson.

ever traveled on wheels up to that time." (*Portland (Me.) Advertiser* February 1, 1906.)

"I am proud of my car," said Marriott, "and proud to think that I traveled faster than two miles a minute, the mark we have all been aiming at. When the beach is in good condition for speeding I am certain I will do better." (*The World (NY.)* January 27, 1906, p.3.) There were others among the contestants who were determined to do better as well.

F.E. Stanley congratulates Fred Marriott. *The photo of this handshake graced the pages of the Sunday New York Times on February 4, 1906, following the close of the races. Photo by Penfield.*
New York Times,
Stanley Museum Archives.

CHAPTER SEVEN

"For $1,000 or an Orange."

"The most glaring weakness in the present system of racing is shown in the eligibility of such palpably freak machines as the Stanley steamer to compete in the same classes with and win honors from cars of rational construction, like the Fiats and Napiers, which are serviceable for touring as well as for racing. Even F.E. Stanley admits that his freak creation is of absolutely no use except for sprint racing on a perfectly level, straightaway course."

(*New York Herald* January 28, 1906. p.10.)

"The gasoline contingent would like to get back at Stanley, but no course seems apparent."

(*St. Louis (Mo.) Globe Democrat* January 29, 1906.)

BY THE END of the first week of the races the promotion of Florida as a land of sunshine was for many visitors the focus of much jest and scorn. Finally, however, the damp, forbidding weather lifted and Saturday, January 27, dawned as the first bright sunny day of the meet. After all the foul weather and heavy traffic the beach was not in the best of shape, and strong winds began to kick up later in the day, but this did not deter thousands of spectators from crowding special trains to make their way to Ormond Beach. For today was the day for the much-

Working on the Stanley racer. F.E. Stanley, right, strides away from the busy crew area while Marriott, behind, listens to J. F. Hathaway. Young Raymond Stanley sits on the front of the racer, left, while behind him Burt Holland leans over the car.
Stanley Museum Archives.

vaunted Two-Mile-a-Minute race, promoted near and far as a must-see event.

As viewed from today, a two-mile sprint might seem an oddity, a distance event not worthy of special promotion, nor a record that would seem to stir a great deal of interest. In 1906, a mere decade into the horseless age, the barely imaginable two-mile-a-minute barrier ("the mark no one here thought could be reached" – Augusta Stanley) was now almost within reach by the most powerful of specialized race cars. To lay down the challenge of a

Marriott in "freak" racer. *A "freak" car was one deemed unsuitable for touring. Although many of the gasoline contingent did not care for the Stanley racer there was still a sense of comaraderie among many of the drivers. Here Guy Vaughan, an Ormond veteran and one of the Darracq drivers, stops by to exchange pleasantries with Fred Marriott.*
Stanley Museum Archives.

Clifford Earp in his Napier by the Ormond Garage. *Clifford Earp and his crew prepare their Napier for an upcoming race. An interested Fred Marriott stands behind the car to the right.*

Harper's Weekly.

special race to highlight this speed barrier ("the mark we have all been aiming at" – Fred Marriott) covering the two miles' distance in one minute or less, seemed logical and fitting, and stirred up keen anticipation. The influential *Florida Times-Union* of Jacksonville had put up an unusual "Automobile Speed King" trophy for the occasion and had spent weeks not only promoting the race, but also sponsoring a concurrent contest for the "Prettiest Girl in Florida," whose primary task would be to crown the new Speed King. On hand at the beach was the contest winner, Miss Mary Simrall of Ormond. (That Miss Simrall was also the niece of Joseph D. Price, one of the managers of the Hotel Ormond, one of the sponsors of the speed tournament, does not appear to have raised as many eyebrows as it might today.)

Also on the day's program was the 100 Mile International Open Championship for the Minneapolis Cup, which had the unforeseen effect of reducing the field for the Two-Mile-a-Minute race to just two entrants: the 200 hp Darracq, now driven by Victor Demogeot, and

the Stanley racer driven by Fred Marriott. Organizing two major events, one long and one short, on the same day was seen as a scheduling blunder that effectively split the field, with many of the heavyweight gasoline racers opting to prepare for the 100-mile event. (Many of the drivers realized, too, that they stood little chance against the big Darracq and the Stanley at two miles.)

The hydrocarbon branch was prone to assert that their cars, of "rational construction," were capable of competing in events both short and long – their versatility being part of what distinguished them from cars of "freak construction." In reality their versatility was enabled by laborious mechanical makeovers, so that competing in short versus long distance events required changing gearing, fuel tanks, wheels and tires, sometimes even seating configurations. The rational, versatile race cars of the period could not effectively compete at widely different distance events on the same day. W. Clifford Earp, in fact, had mistakenly set up his Napier for the 100-mile race a day too early, but had still felt obligated to participate in the one-mile trials on Friday, finishing well out of the running. His sportsmanship was widely noted and praised in the press, and his endeavors would win him more than praise at the end of the day.

The Two-Mile-a-Minute race was to be waged by individual time trials, which were scheduled to commence at the Florida East Coast Automobile Association's clubhouse in Daytona at 1:30 pm. For the second day in a row there were last-minute problems with the electrical timing apparatus, normally a smooth-running facet of the beach events when the tides didn't intervene, and there was an hour's delay in getting the problems resolved. The timing apparatus was designed and operated by Alden L McMurtry, who headed up an experienced international team of eight official timers, including John C. Kerrison, a correspondent with the *Boston Herald*, who was president and one of the original founders of the Chronograph Club of Boston. The Chronograph Club, founded in 1896, was one of the earliest organizations of sports timekeepers in America. (*Boston Globe* March 8, 1896, p.23.)

The timers' stand, Ormond 1906. *The timers and other officials take their stations around the timing devices on the judges' stand at the 1906 Ormond races.*

Harper's Weekly.

For a complex and lengthy tournament such as Ormond a large group of timers was required by established convention, for in addition to the automatic electrical timing devices, at least three hand-held stopwatches were to be used on every race trial. The integrity of the timekeepers was usually considered beyond reproach, but a story in the Stanley camp, passed down by Raymond Stanley, holds that J. F. Hathaway was standing near the timers' stand and 'caught' the timers trying to reset a clock after an official Stanley run, whereupon the timers were put on notice that they would be closely monitored for the rest of the tournament. (R. Stanley 1984.)

After the timing problems were resolved there was another half hour delay for the contestants to get ready, but around 3 pm the first trial was called and Victor Demogeot brought the 200 hp Darracq around to start his first run. Demogeot, who had served as Hémery's mechanic, was virtually unknown in American racing circles, but was judged a competent race car handler. The young Frenchman was installed as the new driver of the Darracq by Charles Cooke, the American representative, who felt it fitting that one of the original Darracq team drivers should have the chance. (Louis Chevrolet, who had driven the car in the mile trials, now went back to Walter Christie as he was scheduled to drive the Christie racer in the 100-mile contest.) Demogeot brought the Darracq thundering down the beach over the two-mile course, only to find that the timing device had failed again and his first run was not recorded. Minutes afterward, the timers again signaled their readiness.

Marriott then took his position down the beach and began his first run. Just after he crossed the starting line there was a loud report as an engine cylinder head blew out,

Webb Jay wishes Fred Marriott good luck.
Webb Jay drove steamers competitively for the White Company and had competed at Ormond in 1905 and at the Climb to the Clouds in 1904 and 1905. An accident in Buffalo, NY, the previous summer kept both Jay and the White Company from participating in the 1906 tournament.
                    Larz Anderson Auto Museum.

tearing a hole in the body of the Stanley and bringing the racer coasting to a halt, out of commission for several hours. (The racer was promptly towed back to the Ormond Garage and had a new engine installed by 6 pm.) No one was injured in the incident, though a frag-

F.E. Stanley working on the racer. *F.E. works on the rear of the racer outside the Ormond Garage. The rear carapace has been removed, revealing the large, 30-inch boiler partially obscured by the main water tank. The building in the background is the "Chauffeur's Barracks" where the race crews would have been housed.*
                    Stanley Museum Archives.

ment, from either the car or the engine, was said to have come close to a photographer on the sidelines. According to sources published after the fact, Mr. Cooke then approached the officials seeking a postponement of the race, "as he did not care for a walkover with the car"

Stanley working on the racer. *This newspaper photo shows another view of F.E. Stanley, left, working beside the rear end of the racer. The rectangular water tank can be seen just behind the drum-shaped boiler, and the insulated steam line feeding the engine. The crewman working with Stanley may be Burt Holland.*
                    Unidentified news-clipping,
                    Stanley Museum Archives.

with the Stanley disabled. (*Motor Age* February 1, 1906, pp.6-7.)

When the referees, mindful of the packed stands of spectators who had come especially for this race, directed that the Darracq make an attempt for the record anyway, it was determined that the car was unable to continue after its earlier run, as "two nuts were found to have shaken loose and lost. There were no others on hand to replace them, and in consequence the car was retired for the day." (*New York Times* January 26, 1906, p.9.) The *Motor Age* reporter implied that this was but an excuse by the

Darracq team to ensure a later desired match-up with the Stanley, a view likewise taken up by most of the gasoline contingent. For a major foreign auto manufacturer (whose purpose in attending Ormond was largely to showcase and sell their cars) to pass up an opportunity for a free demonstration in front of a large crowd was highly unusual. Most of the immediate accounts of the day only report that the Darracq was apparently first to be disabled, which suggests that the Darracq people may have seized upon the Stanley's accident to for-tuitously seek a postponement, a face-saving far preferable to admitting losing a pair of nuts.

Whatever the reason, the announcement of the postponement of the race brought howls of protest from the large crowd. Spectators were reported to be fed up with interminable delays, nonexistent communications, poor viewing areas, and perceived price-gouging by conces-sionaires. Even more embarrassing was the predicament that ensnared the large contin-gent of members from the Automobile Club of

Minneapolis. They had put up the handsome trophy for the 100 Mile International Championship for the Minneapolis Cup and had traveled from Minnesota by chartered train to view the race and see their cup presented. While they waited on the beach, delay after delay put off the start of the race until, forced to make their scheduled return charter, the entire Minneapolis delegation had to leave for home without even seeing the start of their sponsored race. (*Boston Post* February 4, 1906, p.13.)

One of the last minute delays of the 100-mile race involved a protest by a group of the European drivers, led by Lancia, Cedrino and Clifford Earp, challenging the eligibility of S. B. Stevens's 80 hp Darracq which had been entered in the race with Guy Vaughan as the driver. The Darracq, they pointed out, was not equipped with a differential gear as required by AAA rules, and thus was ineligible to partici-pate. Upon examination, the head referee, Robert L. Morrill, determined that the car was

Guy Vaughan in the 80 hp Darracq. Vaughan was entered in the 100-mile race but his car, the 1905 Vanderbilt Cup winner, was challenged by some of the European gas car drivers, including Cedrino, Lancia, and Clifford Earp, because it was not equipped with a differential gear as required. S. B. Stevens, the owner, withdrew the car when the European drivers refused to start with the Darracq competing.
Harper's Weekly.

indeed without a differential, but as the challenge had not been properly filed in writing, the Darracq could participate under protest. This was not good enough for Lancia and the others, and they refused to start the race if the Darracq was allowed to enter. This impasse was eventually overcome when Stevens, who professed not to know if his new car had a differential or not, withdrew his Darracq from the competition. (*New York Times* January 29, 1906, p.7.) Almost immediately suspicions arose concerning the other Darracqs, also thought to be without differentials, and rumors of additional challenges began to circulate.

After all the delays the 100-mile race began just before 3:30 pm. The diehard spectators

Clifford Earp and his Napier on the beach.
Clifford Earp and his mechanician, H. B. Baker, set out for a run on the beach. Their Napier was set up specially for beach racing based on recommendations from Arthur MacDonald and the Napier team from 1905. Their car won the 100-mile championship, setting a new record at the distance despite running most of the race on three tires.

Harper's Weekly.

who stayed to watch were treated to one of the most celebrated races in Ormond history. The starting field included Chevrolet in a 120 hp Christie, Clifford Earp in his 100 hp Napier, Lancia and Cedrino in their 110 hp Fiats, H. N. Harding in a 45 hp English Daimler, and W. H. Hilliard, the winner of the 1905 Climb to the Clouds, driving a 60 hp Napier. Starting 20 seconds apart, they followed a 15-mile straight-away course with seven turns.

Clifford Earp took the lead a quarter of the way through the race, but blew out a tire at mile 37. Stopping only to strip the remnants from the wheel, he continued on with a bare rim. The Englishman gambled that his wire-spoked wheel on the firm beach would allow him to overtake his opponents if they faltered, and his strategy paid off. Lancia was forced to withdraw halfway through with radiator trouble, Chevrolet and Harding dropping out ten miles later. One lap further, Cedrino was forced to slow down with tire trouble. Clifford Earp finally retook the lead at 75 miles, passing Cedrino who had stopped to exchange tires with his teammate Lancia's stranded Fiat. Pressing on, Clifford Earp rattled across the finish line in 1:15:40 2-5, less than a minute ahead of Cedrino, a new world's record for the 100 miles. (*Motor Age* February 1, 1906, pp.5-6.) That evening at a reception in honor of the winner, the Stanleys, whose racer had soundly whipped the Napier earlier in the Dewar Cup race, "wore the Napier colors, which was considered a very graceful thing on our part." (A. Stanley *Diary* January 27, 1906.)

Sunday was an off day for racing, but hardly an off day for backroom maneuvering and self-righteous posturing in and out of press-room and clubhouse. The previous day's insurrection by a coterie of European gas car drivers, challenging one of their own – the 80 hp

F.E. Stanley with Fred Marriott in the racer. *The rear of the racer has a piece of sheet metal attached as a temporary patch over the hole where it lost a cylinder head during the first runs of the postponed Two-Mile-a-Minute race on Saturday, January 27, 1906. This photo was probably taken on Sunday, January 28, an off-day for racing but not for controversy.*

Stanley Museum Archives.

Darracq's lack of a required differential – was resolved without rancor, undue deliberation, or even much attention. In contrast, word that steam man F.E. Stanley was going to enter a similar protest against the 200 hp Darracq touched off a veritable tempest in a teapot.

Stanley's action was widely condemned as unsportsmanlike, in effect eliminating the only car with a chance of defeating his steamer in the Two-Mile-a-Minute race, made all the more egregious, in the gas car crowd's view, by Stanley's irritating penchant for publicly declaring that his steamer was faster and superior to any other machine on the beach, and frequently proving it. They also contended, disingenuously, that the Darracq team had nobly offered to postpone the race to give Stanley a chance to repair his car, and now after benefiting from

the delay, Stanley was attempting to have the Darracq barred.

The press, too, was highly critical of his protest, even those who conceded that Stanley was well within his rights, focusing instead on the arguments for letting the Darracq compete as equipped: that it was entered in good faith by foreign guests who had brought it a great distance at considerable expense; that the differential gear was an obsolete requirement already abandoned in European racing; that it was the only serious competition to the Stanley, and without it the race would be meaningless. Left unsaid was the likelihood that a successful protest would also wreak havoc with the considerable betting on the race taking place on the sidelines. Few observers seemed to think it odd that the 80 hp Darracq should be challenged and removed without question, while the 200 hp Darracq equally at fault, should be allowed to compete.

For his part, Stanley was following his principles of honor and fair play. He had equipped his machine as required by the rules, and he expected the competing owners to do the same. He explained to the reporter from the *Brooklyn (NY) Eagle*:

"I followed [*the requirements for*] my machine in good faith under the rules of the A.A.A. specification stated in the entry blanks. My car absolutely fulfills all conditions. I have never examined the Darracq machine, but I have been told by men who have done so that it has no differential gear. Rule 19 of the A.A.A. regulations reads: 'Automobile, motor car, car – an automobile, motor car or car within the meaning of these rules, is a four wheel track or road vehicle, propelled by self-contained mechanical means, and provided with suitable brakes, a differential gear or its equivalent and a reverse gear.'

"In my opinion there is absolutely no grounds for misunderstanding this rule. If the Darracq car has a differential it is eligible. If it has not, it is ineligible. That is all there is to it, and the matter is in the hands of the committee to do as the rules direct."

The reporter then sought Stanley's opinion on a possible counter-challenge:

"It was suggested to Mr. Stanley that his car might be protested on the ground that it was unsafe as a speed vehicle. Rule 44 of the A.A.A. regulations reads: 'Prohibit – The referee shall have the power to prohibit a car which he considers unsafe, unsuitable or of improper construction to start in any event.'

"In answer to such a possibility Mr. Stanley said he would consider it a most preposterous action; that the Stanley steamer was safer than any of the gasoline cars competing, and that if it was protested on the ground of being unsafe, he would certainly make an appeal to the A.A.A." (*Brooklyn (NY) Eagle* January 29, 1906.)

Samuel B. Stevens, who had lost three races in the 1905 meet to a freak steamer, Louis S. Ross's 'Wogglebug', was determined to have his chance to avenge his losses against Ross's successor. Braced for a second protest against the Darracqs under his management, this time he had a counter-strategy already in place:

"When the protest is lodged, Mr. Stevens says, he will immediately withdraw the entry of the big 200-horse-power car, giving Stanley the trophy without any contest. He will, however, protest against the steamer on the ground that it is a freak and unsafe for racing purposes, calling the attention of the board of officials to the fact that it has at least twice blown out its cylinder and on one occasion a flying fragment struck one of the army of photographers located along the beach.

"He will seek a decision on this point and whatever the result he will challenge Stanley to send his steamer against his big Darracq for the two miles for $1000 or an orange, and oranges are most plentiful in this country." (*Boston Herald* January 29, 1906, p.4.)

In the end it appears that F.E. Stanley never filed a formal protest against the Darracq. There are indications that Stanley believed that all he needed to do was bring the matter to the attention of the referees, and that they would take the matter in hand and enforce the rules. Without a formal, written protest, the racing board could turn a blind eye to the alleged infraction, and allow the races to continue. When they showed no inclination to take up the enforcement of their rules after he had publicly pointed out that the Darracq was competing in violation of their rules, Stanley may have considered his efforts to be a lost cause, and concentrated on proving the superiority of his steamer on the beach instead.

Monday, January 29, the final day of the races, dawned bright and sunny with winds and tides favorable, but with a disconcerting start for the steam camp. F.E. Stanley arose early as was his custom, expecting to join his team later to prepare the Stanley racer for its first event, the 30-Mile Championship for American-Built Cars, scheduled to begin shortly before 9 am. Upon venturing out at 6:35 am, he noticed some unusual activity among cars and race officials down on the beach, and quickly checking a posted race schedule, he discovered that the start of the 30-mile race had been moved up to 7 am. Stanley rushed to the garage and the chauffeurs' barracks where the cars and their crews were housed, rousted Marriott and the rest of the team out of bed, and began getting steam up in the racer. (R. Stanley 1945: p.20)

Down on the beach the referees sent away Frank Kulick in the 105 hp Ford and Walter Christie driving his 120 hp Christie promptly at 7 am, the course being 15 miles down to the Inlet and back. Their cars were already out of sight when Fred Marriott, still barely awake, drove up to the starting line and asked when the race would start. Told that it was already underway, Marriott pulled the racer around and set off in pursuit, five minutes and 40 seconds behind. He first overtook Kulick at the turn around – the Ford had gotten bogged down in loose sand and would not finish. Further down the course Christie had developed a coolant leak and was forced to stop at the Clarendon Hotel to plug

his radiator and refill it with water. Marriott, seeing Christie stopped and thinking the race was over, pulled over himself. Startled, Christie explained the situation and Marriott jumped back in his car and pressed on to the finish, winning in 34:18 2-5 (his actual time 28:38 2-5), Christie second in 37:24 3-5. (*The Automobile* February 1, 1906, p.278; *St. Augustine Evening Record* January 29, 1906, p.1.) The officials later explained that they had moved up the start of the race due to a miscalculation of the tides, and in fact had to postpone the scheduled 15-mile race till the afternoon (*Motor Age* February 1, 1906, p.8), but the steam camp felt they had been purposely left in the dark in a most underhanded manner.

When the races resumed in the afternoon the officials made every attempt to step up the pace and speed things along so as to complete the remaining program of events by the end of the day and bring the 1906 tournament to a close. To this end they decided to combine the 10 Mile Open Championship and the 10 Mile

Lancia in his 110 hp Fiat. Lancia, left, listens to some advice from H. L. Bowden, right, before setting off on another event.
Harper's Weekly.

Demogeot in the 200 hp Darracq. *Demogeot was elevated to chief driver for the Two-Mile-a-Minute race. The car was allowed to compete even though it was not equipped with a differential gear required under American racing rules. F.E. Stanley had brought the infraction to the attention of the officials but did not file a formal protest, and the referees did not take any action.*

Larz Anderson Auto Museum.

Heavyweight Championship for Gasoline Cars, running the two events concurrently. Marriott lined up the Stanley racer alongside Lancia in his Fiat and W. H. Hilliard in his 60-80 hp Napier.

The trio set off, Marriott taking the lead followed by Lancia, then Hilliard. The Napier soon fell behind and was never in the race, dropping out with a broken spark plug at the six-mile mark. The Stanley developed a fuel line leak about halfway through the race, and Marriott found he wasn't able to hold the lead. It was Lancia first over the line in 6:19 3-5, exceeding his pessimistic pre-race predictions ("Stanley will win") by taking two head-to-head contests from the crippled Stanley (one five-mile and one of the two-combined ten-mile races), Marriott finishing second in 7:35 3-5. (*The Automobile* February 1, 1906, p.278; *Florida Times-Union* January 30, 1906, pp.1-2.)

All that remained was the Two-Mile-a-Minute Championship that had been postponed from Saturday; the Darracq, differential or no differential, was officially unchallenged and thus permitted to compete. The spectators' gallery was now less than filled and the beach was in worse condition, although the winds were calm and not a factor. Robert L. Morrill, the head referee, announced that "no limit would be placed on the number of trials" (*Motor Age* February 1, 1906, p.7) and that the Stanley would make the first trial. Marriott took his position for a flying start two miles down the beach, and at the starter's signal, began his first run. As he flew down the course "the frail looking car seemed to leap across the sands, and at times it looked as though he touched only the 'high spots,' if there are any on the beach." (*Boston Herald* January 30, 1906, p.2.) The unevenness of the beach took its toll on the lightweight car – Marriott was clocked at 1:03.

Demogeot was waiting with the Darracq four miles away and in due course began his first trial. "The great heavy car made a striking appearance in contrast to the low steamer. Its great weight, within eight pounds of the limit, aided it materially in going over the course. It gave more traction, and the eight exhausts belched forth fire and smoke, whereas [*before*] only the white exhaust of the steamer could be seen..." (*Boston Herald* January 30, 1906, p.2.) The Darracq was clocked at 1:01 3-5.

Marriott's second attempt was even rockier than his first. "Again and again," reported the *Boston Herald*, the racer "seemed to fairly leap from the ground, the wheels, owing to the lightness of the car, not getting the best traction possible. At the mile mark she struck a hump and went into the air several feet and it looked as though she was going over. Marriott's feeling at that moment must have been peculiar. He did not seem to mind it for a second, but steered the machine true and steady..." The timers caught the Stanley at 59 3-5.

The crowd reacted with "wild enthusiasm" – Marriott now had the singular distinction of having twice broken the two-mile-a-minute barrier, once at one mile and again at two miles. Backtracking to the finish line, he learned of his record time and was asked if he wished to go again. "Not unless my time is improved upon," replied Fred. "I know that I don't want to drive any faster. The car will not hold the course if

you give her any more speed, and I had one thump on that ride." (*Boston Herald* January 30, 1906, p.2.)

All eyes turned to the Darracq as the signal was given to begin its second trial. "Demogeot sat firmly in his seat and drove the car in a fearless and daring manner, taking no notice whatever of the few slight windrows left by the receding tide." (*Boston Herald* January 30, 1906, p.2.) The Darracq thundered down the beach, "all eight cylinders working in beautiful rhythm and hurling the thing of steel along like a thunderbolt." (*Motor Age* February 1, 1906, p.7.) His time: 58 4-5.

Once again, the crowd responded with a long, spirited ovation. Marriott at once approached the referees and requested another trial, as permitted under the rules. His request was granted, although the officials were apparently anxious to conclude the competition and proceed to the final award ceremonies, and had

Marriott breaks the two-mile-a-minute barrier. *Marriott crosses the finish line in the Two-Mile-a-Minute contest in 59 3-5 seconds, or 120.8 mph, becoming the first to exceed two-miles-a-minute at both the mile and two-mile distances. Although each contestant in this special event was allowed as many trials as needed, Marriott was denied a third trial to lower the record further.*
Larz Anderson Auto Museum.

their eyes on the clock. According to A. G. Batchelder writing in *The Automobile*, "there was a wait of a quarter of an hour to give Marriott a third trial, but before he got ready the recess was over and Referee Morrill called the meet to an end. Mr. Stanley then reappeared saying Marriott was ready, but the wires were disconnected and the sport finished." (*The Automobile* February 1, 1906, p.278.) The Stanley team could only watch in dismay and exasperation as Demogeot was crowned the "King of Speed."

This time, F.E. Stanley did file a formal protest – that Marriott had been unfairly denied another trial in spite of the rules permitting as many as requested. Once more, Stanley came under criticism for poor sportsmanship, and his protest was abruptly dismissed. The Stanleys and their team were convinced that they could have made better time with another trial, no matter what the outcome, and that they had been given short shrift simply because they were running a steam car. Leaving Florida, F.E. Stanley had the Land Speed Record and an automotive propulsion system he believed was superior to all others. He was beginning to see that it was one thing to have the former – he would have to come back to prove the latter.

CHAPTER EIGHT

Can Steam Go the Distance?

"Having just returned from a visit to Stanley's works in U.S.A., where I had the pleasure of seeing the racer which has done such phenomenal performances at Florida, I can most emphatically say that there was absolutely nothing of the freak about its construction. Every part of the car, without exception, was made in the same pattern, and put together in the same style as the ordinary stock cars, the only difference being that it was on a larger and stronger scale...

"[I]t was an absolutely untried car sent straight from the works to the races, there being neither time nor opportunity of testing it properly beforehand. That steam cars are not merely short distance sprinters...is surely disproved by the fact that the Stanley covered ten miles at the rate of eighty miles per hour, and thirty miles was run at the rate of sixty-two miles per hour... The results, I think, should prove to any fair-minded person that its designer had no reason to be ashamed of it..."

W. E. Galloway *[Stanley agent for Great Britain]*.
(Letter to the Editor, *The Autocar* February 17, 1906, p.214.)

THE 1906 ORMOND TOURNAMENT was considered a success by its organizers. The Stanley steamer had set phenomenal new records in the mile and the kilometer, and the 100-mile race had drama, excitement and a close finish. To many, though, it was the Two-Mile-a-Minute race with its close-fought, one-on-one match-up between the huge 200 hp French-built Darracq (cheered on by most of the visiting motorists, including many in the automotive press) and the small, sleek, 30 hp American-built Stanley (cheered on by most of the local public), which really saved the meet. The organizers did have problems with the weather and tides, as they had before, and there were many disgruntled spectators upset that the costly races were poorly set up for viewing, as before. For the officials, ironically, it was the Two-Mile-a-Minute race and its resulting controversy that would not go away.

In the weeks following the meet, a number of reporters who had been so harsh on F.E. Stanley and his protest over the Darracq began to reconsider and temper their earlier remarks.

Howard G. Reynolds wrote in the *Boston Post* that "While the designer of the Marriott steamer *[the Post, akin to the Boston Globe, appears to have adopted a 'no-name' policy in regard to the Stanleys, perhaps due to the brothers' aversion to supporting their local papers with paid advertising]* showed a rather unsportsmanlike spirit in talking about protesting this car, in a way he had a perfect right to call the matter before the referee. His argument was that he had built his car to come under the rules, and why should not others? Why should he contest against cars that were not?" Reynolds noted that the Stanley still had the Land Speed Record – "a record of a mile in 28 1-5 seconds should be satisfying to anyone" – but he wondered "Again, why was Marriott not given another trial in the two-mile-a-minute race? The referee announced after the first trials that they would each be given one or more. Yet when the builder of the steamer came up to the referee to ask for his third trial he was told that it was all off and that the meet for 1906 was over." (*Boston Post* February 4, 1906, p.13.)

Walter C. White in White steamer, Ormond 1905. *Walter C. White sits at the wheel of a 15 hp White touring car, stripped down to a special "wind shield" bonnet, at Ormond Beach, 1905. Web Jay drove this car to a second place finish behind Louis Ross's Wogglebug in the one mile steam championship for the R. C. Clowry Trophy. The White Company was the Stanley Motor Carriage Company's chief steam rival.*

*Old Motor Magazine,
Stanley Museum Archives.*

Others turned their attention to the curious rulings of the officials and their reluctance to enforce certain rules unless formally asked to do so. One prominent manufacturer to express his displeasure regarding the AAA's handling of the Stanley/Darracq controversy was Walter C. White of the White Company. White, the other major steam car manufacturer next to Stanley, had entered a White steam racer in the 1905 Ormond tournament, driven by Webb Jay to a second place finish behind Louis Ross's Wogglebug in the one-mile steam championship. (An accident to the White racer and the injuries to Jay in a crash at Buffalo, NY, late in the 1905 season had kept the company out of the 1906 races.) In his relationship to Stanley White was a cordial but formidable business rival, but an ally regarding antagonisms between gas and steam interests. Asked his opinion of the Darracq affair, Mr. White responded:

"I dislike to criticise such a good friend of mine as Robert Lee Morrill, chairman of the racing board of the A.A.A., yet I think he is wrong in the attitude he took at Ormond regarding the enforcement of the racing rules, particularly in the matter of protests, or grounds of protest. Because the Darracqs did not have differential gears Mr. Morrill, if correctly quoted, said it was the duty of the racing board to disqualify a car which did not comply with the rules only in the event of a car being protested by a competitor.

"The inconsistency of such an attitude lies here: The racing rules provide that a car shall be within a certain weight, that it shall have satisfactory brakes, that it be fitted with a reversing gear and that it have a differential or its equivalent. We all know how much stress is laid on the weight feature. Cars are towed miles from the course to a suitable scale, and if found overweight, a machine is disqualified and is not allowed to compete until by heroic efforts, enough metal is pared off to bring it within the prescribed limit.

"Brakes are also tested with no little ceremony and sometimes a car is run backwards. For some reason hard to explain cars are not examined to see if they have differentials, although the framers of the rules deemed such a requirement necessary. To enforce three of these requirements and let the fourth go by default is illogical.

"Imagine the awkward position in which a driver is placed who comes to the line with a car which has been built with proper regard for the rules and who finds that his competitor's car does not meet requirements.

"If a protest is filed, the protestant is scored

for not being a sportsman. If he does not protest, it is against his sense of justice that he should be compelled to race on equal terms with a car not complying with the rules...

"The officials should of their own initiative disqualify a car not conforming to the rules. They should not await a protest from the drivers of the cars... [F]or the officials to test a racing car for a part of the requirements and to leave the rest to the good nature of the competitors is indefensible." (*New York American* February 15, 1906, p.8.)

Duncan Curry of the *New York American* concurred and pressed the issue further:

"[W]hat the public would like to know is how the Darracq car was ever allowed to win the Vanderbilt Cup race without a differential and if road rules do not require a differential were the American manufacturers informed of the fact when they built their cars for the Vanderbilt trials? Many of them seriously weakened their cars trying to get within the weight limit and if they had known in time that differentials were not necessary it might have made a big difference in the result of the trial races.

"Another point the public can't understand is, if the 80-horsepower Darracq was ineligible for the 100-mile race at Ormond, by what right did the 200-horsepower car compete and win the two-mile-a-minute race?

"Was it because the Stanley steamer was a steam machine and had no friends at court, or what was the reason?

"Calling the Stanley car a freak machine does not make wrong right. The car complied with the rules and the Darracq did not. There should not be one rule for Darracq cars and another for Stanley steamers. Automobile racing, if it is ever to become popular, will have to be run on different lines than this, and the rules, good or bad, should be enforced on all

alike, or the end of the game is in sight." (*New York American* February 15, 1906, p.8.)

Notably absent from the debate was F.E. Stanley, who had apparently decided to concentrate his efforts on improving his car's performance, and on correcting some of the problems encountered during competition. Stanley had referred to tight engine pistons in a January 23, 1906, letter to his son-in-law, Edward Hallett (see p.83). In an interview in 1954, Fred Marriott further recalled:

"That car wasn't right in 1906. Stanley knew it wasn't right, and I knew it wasn't right. Seemed all right around Newton, but when we first tested her on the beach, we could see she wasn't right. You get her up over a certain speed and a tinglin' would come over her. Couldn't figure it out at first, it was like static electricity. I couldn't hold onto the wheel, my legs would get such a tinglin' they'd go completely to sleep. I wore heavy paddin' in the seat of my pants, up my back, and rubber pads on my soles helped some. We taped the wheel, then we completely taped my hands where they touched the wheel and up to above my wrists. Stanley said, 'Gee, cracky, what's the matter, Fred?' We made some trial runs and got our heads together. Stanley figured out what he thought it was, and I figured out what I thought it was and we came out with the same answer. We knew the trouble was in the engine; she was just crowdin' herself enough to be rough, not really like a rough engine, but it was such a slight vibration that it gave you this tinglin' sensation – and it would drive you crazy. We figured out we could fix her, but not 'till we got back to the factory, so we raced her anyway." (Marshall 1982: pp.20-21.) *[Note: Marriott's reference to a "wheel" here may be allegorical – the racer had tiller steering. While it is not conclusive, there is also no evidence, in docu-*

ments or photographs, of Marriott driving the racer with taped hands.]

Less urgent than the engine problems but no less troublesome was the tendency for the racer's nose and front wheels to lift off the beach when running at speed against the wind or over ripples and bumps in the sand. There are references to attempts to remedy this at Ormond by lowering the nose and by adding weights (either sand bags or rocks) to the front of the racer. (Tucker 1906: p.6.) Given the racer's flat bottom and the preponderance of weight toward the rear, the seriousness of this

Manufacturers, car owners and suppliers mingle on the sidelines at Ormond. F.E. Stanley, left, listens to a comment from E.V. Hartford of the Hartford Suspension Company, right. In the middle stands W. Gould Brokaw, a wealthy owner and amateur driver who had entered race cars and speed boats in Ormond competitions in previous years. During the 1906 tournament Gould Brokaw reportedly commissioned F.E. to build him a special steam racer capable of a mile in 25 seconds, but the deal apparently went uncompleted. Gould Brokaw had no car entered in the 1906 events but was still a photographer's favorite due to his penchant for extravagant attire, such as the full-length leopard skin coat he wears here.

Stanley Museum Archives.

problem of the front wheels only touching the "high spots" on the course may have been only partially understood. The Stanley team also experimented with the flue positioned aft of the racer's cockpit. Photographs show various configurations of "stove pipe" extending or exposing the top of the flue, perhaps to achieve beneficial draft.

"I have learned a great deal from these tournaments," Stanley understated, "and I think that a car of a little different design with a little heavier steam engine will be able to go a mile in 24 seconds, which I believe is the limit of speed under the weight limit of 2,204 pounds. Our mile in 28 1-5 seconds...is at the rate of 127.6 miles an hour, something that we would not have dreamed of a few years ago." (*The Motor Way* February 1, 1906, p.7.) Following the races it was reported that W. Gould Brokaw, one of the wealthy owner/drivers at Ormond, had commissioned Stanley to build a race car that would go a mile in 25 seconds, to be delivered by June 1, 1906, and that Marriott would probably be hired to drive the car. (*Boston Evening Record* February 5, 1906.) This rumored transaction appears to have been little more than that. Far more significant was an announcement by Stanley at the end of the tournament that appears to have received little notice in the press at the time but would have far-reaching repercussions:

"F.E. Stanley announced tonight [*January 29, 1906*] that if the Vanderbilt Cup race is held in this country this year, as now seems possible, he will build a steam racing machine for it capable of sustaining power for three hundred miles. He says it will be possible to build a car that will average ninety miles an hour for the entire distance of the race." (*New York Herald* January 30, 1906, p.12.)

It was one thing for the hydrocarbon

Marriott and F.E. Stanley in a Vanderbilt racer in front of the Stanley factory. *The Stanleys designed a long-distance 30 hp steam racer, building two specifically for the 1906 Vanderbilt Cup race on Long Island. The cars were unveiled at the Decoration Day races at Readville on May 30, 1906. Here Fred Marriott and F.E. Stanley pose in one of the Vanderbilt racers in front of the assembled Stanley workforce at the Stanley factory in Watertown. Problems with the new cars delayed their completion, and they did not compete in the Vanderbilt Cup race.*
The Bulb Horn, Stanley Museum Archives.

branch to undertake the fruitless pursuit of sprint records such as the land speed record for the mile in competition with freak steamers. The prospect of competing in the distance events against long-distance steamers was potentially daunting. Stanley had established his reputation as a competent designer and builder of steam-powered race cars in the international competition at Ormond. His competitors knew only too well that Stanley was also a man of his word, and if he said it was possible to build a steamer to compete in distance events like the Vanderbilt Cup race, they could almost expect to see him on the starting line.

Back at the Stanley factory in Watertown, Mass., work began on the design for a long-distance steamer equipped with the Stanleys' 30 hp power plant to compete in the Vanderbilt Cup race, and it was not long before the Stanleys received inquiries from prospective buyers. By early May the Stanleys had received orders for two Vanderbilt cars from a pair of Philadelphia sportsmen, Charles J. Swain and John N. Wilkins, Jr., both members of the Cape May Automobile Club. Negotiating the transaction on behalf of the Stanley Motor Carriage Company was F.O. Stanley, who had returned to Newton from his convalescence home in Estes Park, Colorado, on March 31st. It was apparently agreed that the two cars would be finished in time for the annual Decoration Day races at Readville on May 30, where they would debut for their first public tune-up.

The target date appears to have been overly ambitious. Perhaps the new racers presented unforeseen technical problems, or perhaps the time required for their completion was simply underestimated. Augusta Stanley first notes in her diary going down to the factory to see the completed "Vanderbilt racer" on May 23, just one week before their scheduled race debut. As they rushed to get the cars ready, F.E. Stanley

F.E. Stanley and Fred Marriott with a Vanderbilt racer. *F.E. Stanley confers with Fred Marriott outside the Stanley Repair Department as Marriott appears ready to set out on a trial run in one of the Vanderbilt racers.*

Fred Marriott Collection, Speed Age, Stanley Museum Archives.

was suddenly bedridden with a severe cold or the "grippe," and felt "very badly that he can't be helping get the racing cars ready for Readville Wednesday." (A. Stanley *Diary*, May 23 and 28, 1906.)

Swain and Wilkins, apparently unaware of any problems with their cars, were on hand at Readville for their debut. Swain recounted their side of the events in a letter transmitted to *The Automobile* by J. Hiscock, the secretary of the Cape May Automobile Club:

"Preliminary negotiation for the purchase of two Stanley steamers, guaranteed to do a mile in thirty seconds, and capable of standing up for the Vanderbilt Cup car journey, were made by Mr. Wilkins and myself in early May. The cars were to be tuned up for the meet at the Readville, Mass., track, and, following the directions from Mr. Stanley himself, we were on

hand at Readville on Decoration Day to witness their performances, fully expecting, as we had been assured, that the cars would come up to guarantee…

"The automobile world knows what happened that day. Mr. Wilkins witnessed his so-called world-beater lead Bowden's 'Flying Dutchman' for two miles, only to be ignominiously lapped on the ninth circuit. Marriott drove my car against the Fiat Junior, which broke down and so he took the heat. Then Marriott refused to go against the Mercedes in the final, as it was apparent that the car would not hold steam."

The *Boston Globe* described the race, a 10-mile free-for-all, as "the waterloo of the two steam cars that were expected to do wonders. They were built for the Vanderbilt elimination, and it was expected that they would show marvelous bursts of speed." That they failed to do so "surprised everyone." Frank Durbin drove one of the Stanley Vanderbilts in the first heat against Charles Basle in the Mercedes, barely leading what was considered to be the slower car for halfway before Basle pulled away to finish "more than a mile ahead in 9m 27 1-5s." Marriott drove the second Vanderbilt racer against Cedrino in the 24 hp Fiat Junior in the second heat, but faired little better even though expected to run away with the race. Cedrino lost a tire seven miles into the race, continuing to run on the flat and then a bare rim to the end; incredibly, Marriott was unable to catch the crippled Fiat until the last half-mile, winning in the slow time of 10:24 3-5. "To the great surprise of the spectators, Marriott decided not to compete" in the final "and the race, of course, went to Basle by default." Marriott did make a mile exhibition in 37 2-5, but his steamer was not identified. (*Boston Globe* May 31, 1906, p.5.) Augusta Stanley summed it up succinctly: "Frank was right. They didn't do anything. The big cars are a fizzle." (A. Stanley *Diary* May 30, 1906.)

F.O. Stanley, however, moved to reassure the new owners, according to Swain:

"Mr. Stanley had insisted from the outset that we should enter the cars, as he admits in his own letter we had purchased, in the Vanderbilt Cup contest, and we had signified our set purpose of so doing from the outset of negotiations, and, notwithstanding their disappointing showing on that day, he said to Mr. Wilkins, 'Go right ahead as though the cars are a success. What we need is forced draught, and that we will have. You make good with the entries and I will make good with the cars.'"

Swain and Wilkins proceeded with their plans for participating in the Vanderbilt competition, but at the deadline for the $1,000

entry fees, an anxious Swain decided to check in with Stanley one more time:

"I telegraphed Mr. Stanley, asking when we might expect the cars, and if everything was all right. Remember, we had had no word from him after his sweeping assurance at Readville, and you can imagine my surprise when I received a telegram from the Stanley Motor Carriage Co., saying 'Do not enter cars. See letter.' Then came a letter from Mr. Stanley himself, dated Estes Park, Col., in which he stated that owing to indisposition he had been obliged to leave hurriedly for the West and expected to remain there till fall. But here is the vital feature of the communication, so far as we and our cars were concerned:

'In reference to the machines, I fear, owing to my absence and the fact that my brother will be away more or less this summer, we shall be unable to complete them in season for the Vanderbilt races. Hence, of course, you are under no obligation to buy them. I fear this will greatly disappoint you and Mr. Wilkins, as, of course, it does me. There is no doubt but the machines can do all that we expected of them when we have time to put them in shape.'" (*The Automobile* September 6, 1906, p.297.)

Unbeknownst to Swain and Wilkins, F.O. Stanley was suddenly stricken with a recurrence of his chronic health problems a week after the Readville races, and was forced to rush back to Colorado on June 7th. His brother, meanwhile, had plans for a lengthy family vacation that summer in Maine and on the Massachusetts North Shore – a much-needed break before the effort to get ready for Ormond in 1907. In truth, neither of the Twins was available to prepare the Vanderbilt cars for their intended race in September. Their failure to communicate this to Swain and Wilkins is a bit more difficult to fathom.

Marriott in Vanderbilt racer. *Fred Marriott sits in one of the Vanderbilt racers in this undated photo. Not ready for the 1906 Vanderbilt Cup race, the Stanley specials were worked up for the 1907 Ormond Beach races.*

Antique Automobile, Stanley Museum Archives.

The Stanley Brothers could be quite reticent in expressing their intentions in certain ventures, especially those which combined social, business, and sporting interests. For example, Louis Ross, who had originally agreed to drive the Stanley racer at Ormond in 1906, broke off the agreement just a month shy of the event when he discovered that he and the Stanleys were of different minds as to who would retain the prizes and honors to be won at the races. (*Boston Globe* December 22, 1905, p.9.) The Stanleys may have also considered their special racing machines to be something more than typical car sales, perhaps more on par with their thoroughbred horses, which they would likely decline to sell to individuals they considered incompetent or intemperate. Their actions in this case suggest that they may have decided that they did not wish to have Messrs. Swain and Wilkins as customers.

F.E. and Mrs. Stanley did attend the Vanderbilt Cup elimination trials on September 22 and the finals on October 6. They had apparently arranged for reserved box seats which

would have provided excellent viewing if any of their cars had been entered, but no Stanleys took part in the races. A long-standing story exists which alleges that the steam cars were barred from the Vanderbilt competition because their visible steam exhaust was deemed a hazard to other (gas-powered) racers. (R. Stanley 1942: p.10.) The Vanderbilt Cup authorities were indeed concerned with ensuring good visibility for their drivers under race conditions, and the money raised from the sale of spectators' boxes was used to pay for oiling the roads on the course to reduce dust. No evidence has come to light, however, documenting that steam cars were prohibited from the race due to showing visible steam, and there is no mention of the specially-built Stanley racers being barred from the 1906 event in family diaries and correspondence of the day.

The day after the Vanderbilt Cup race, F.O. Stanley returned to Newton from Colorado for a month's stay, during which time he and his brother could collaborate and work out some of the problems which plagued the Vanderbilt cars earlier in the year. Two new customers with solid steam credentials emerged to take ownership of the cars: Warren R. Fales of Providence, RI, and H. Ernest Rogers of Brookline, Mass.

Fales, a member of the Rhode Island Automobile Club who had driven Stanleys at Narragansett Park in Rhode Island, engaged the Providence Stanley dealer, L. F. N. Baldwin to drive his car in the 1907 Ormond tournament. Leon "Lucky" Baldwin had been racing Stanleys at local tracks and hill climbs in Massachusetts and Rhode Island, and was part of a fraternity of drivers that made up what could be described as an unofficial factory team. (Foster 2004: pp.212-213.) Rogers was an amateur sportsman and auto racing enthusiast. He had driven a Peerless in the 1904 Climb to the Clouds, but had recently switched to Stanleys, with a record steam trial at Ventnor Beach at Atlantic City in April, a victory in the five-mile stock car

event at Readville in May and a first place in his class at the Crawford Notch Hill Climb in New Hampshire in July.

Rogers also planned to bring to Ormond his stock Stanley Model K "Semi-Racer" – a new, more powerful version of the popular Model H, the "Gentlemen's Speedy Roadster," geared for speed with a larger, 26-inch boiler. The Model K would eventually be equipped with a 30 hp engine, but even rated at 25 hp it was the fastest stock car Stanley would produce.

The entrance of the Stanley Vanderbilt cars in the upcoming 1907 Ormond races would create quite a stir. The *New York Times* reported:

"For the first time in the history of the Ormond Beach automobile races two fast steam cars will be entered in the 100-mile contest and speculation is already rife as to their chances of winning. These are the two Stanley steam cars originally built in expectation of

Stanley Vanderbilt racer in action. *A Stanley Vanderbilt car, driven by L.F.N. Baldwin, steams through a course ahead of its competition. Baldwin successfully campaigned one of the Vanderbilt cars at a number of venues over several years. This image may record his victory at the St. Louis, Missouri, fairgrounds in 1908.*

Stanley Museum Archives.

Baldwin in Vanderbilt racer, Old Orchard Beach, Maine. *Baldwin raced his Vanderbilt from Maine to Florida, as a number of other seaside communities organized beach races in the wake of the success of the Ormond/Daytona Beach tournaments. Here Baldwin prepares for a time trial during the inaugural races at Old Orchard Beach, Maine, held September 4-7, 1911.*

Joseph Freeman Collection.

running them in the Vanderbilt Cup race. They have undergone several improvements since last Fall, and their designer claims that they will go fifty miles at high speed without stopping for water. This claim will be put to a severe test during the week of January 21, when the Florida race meet opens…

"These Stanley cars will be one of the features of this year's meet… It is also claimed that these machines will average in the 100-mile race forty seconds per mile. This is fast going – at the rate of 1 1/2 miles each minute – but something pretty close to that figure will be necessary to break the 100-mile beach record of 1:15:40 2-5, made last year by Clifford Earp in the 80 (sic) horse power Napier. If the steam cars prove equal to their claims, it would mean a trifle over 1 hour and 6 minutes for the distance, about nine minutes under the existing record.

"A third Stanley steam car especially constructed for sprint work will be entered in the one, two, and five mile events. It will be driven by Marriott, who established new records for all distances at five miles and under, except the two-mile event, last year. A supreme effort will be made by Marriott to lower the figures of 0:58 4-5 made by Demogeot in the 200 horse power Darracq." (*New York Times* January 11, 1907, p.7.)

In all, the Stanley Motor Carriage Company would have five steam racers at Ormond: Marriott's 30-50 hp racer, the two 30 hp Vanderbilt cars, the 25 hp Model K "Semi-Racer," and a 20 hp stock Model F touring car. The Stanley team seemed prepared to cover all of the races, short, long, and in-between. What remained to be seen was how well the steamers would perform, and who else would show up to contest the races.

Marriott tests out the damaged Stanley racer on the beach, 1907. *During rail shipment of the Stanley cars to Ormond in 1907, the cars were "pretty well battered," the racer receiving visible damage to the top of its front cover, near the nose, and less-visible damage to the top of the rear cover, behind the vent. One or more of the cars may have broken loose and rolled back and forth into the other cars in the rail container. The Stanley crew made what make-shift repairs they could, but the damage may have contributed to the racer's woes during the races which followed.*

Stanley Museum Archives.

CHAPTER NINE

"Old Man Stanley."

*"Going to church in the morning. There was quite a good sermon by a Methodist Minister, dean of Boston University. It was a sermon to remember. He spoke of people living each one in a world of their own. Some in a world of music – some force – some mathematics and so on. I thought of Frank and concluded he lived in a world of **speed**."*

Augusta Stanley. (*Diary* July 13, 1913.)

THE STANLEYS, accompanied by Mr. and Mrs. J. F. Hathaway, arrived in Ormond by train on January 15, a week prior to the 1907 races, finding Florida in the midst of a lengthy drought. "It is dreadfully dusty as there has been no rain in Florida for three months," wrote Mrs. Stanley. (A. Stanley *Diary* January 15, 1907.)

Their cars did not arrive as scheduled, and after some anxious checking, the rail car carrying the Stanley race cars was found to be delayed in Jacksonville. Marriott and Baldwin went to investigate, and reported that the cars had been damaged in shipment – just how badly they wouldn't know until they unpacked them at Ormond.

In Ormond the outlook for good racing was pessimistic, even depressing. "They tell us here

that the beach is totally unfit for racing on account of the long spell of dry weather," wrote Mrs. Stanley. "Our only hope is rain. There are very few here, and hardly no interest shown in the races," she observed. "So unlike last year." (A. Stanley *Diary* January 16, 1907.)

The freight car containing the Stanley cars finally arrived at Ormond on Thursday, January 17, and the crew immediately began working on them at the Ormond Garage to get them ready. Judging from the visible damage to the top of the shell of the Stanley racer (as seen in period photographs), one or more of the cars may have come loose in shipment, rolling back and forth against the other cars. The damage was deemed not serious enough to prevent the cars from racing, although "They are pretty well battered," wrote Mrs. Stanley. "It seems too bad for it does not seem as though there would be much racing – as there are so few cars here." (A. Stanley *Diary* January 17, 1907.)

The foreign car manufacturers who had sent cars to Florida for previous tournaments had elected not to enter their cars in the 1907 meet. There were no Napiers, Fiats, Darracqs, or imported Mercedes on hand to contest the races, either with professional or owner-drivers. A. L. Guinness of London, who had purchased the 200 hp Darracq used in the 1906 races, had planned to attend but withdrew his entry due, it was said, to pressing business concerns. S. B. Stevens of Rome, NY, who had been central to the Darracq controversy the year before, had again entered his 80 hp Darracq but was also a late withdrawal. Louis Wagner was scheduled to bring his 110 hp Darracq with which he had won the Vanderbilt Cup, but failed to show up. The only foreign car to be found on the beach was a Rolls-Royce touring car. The absence of the powerful European race cars was thought to be a direct result of the unprecedented success of the streamlined

steam racers built and entered by Louis S. Ross and F.E. Stanley during the previous two years. The Stanley-powered steam racers had dominated the high-profile speed events, and seemed on the verge of doing so again. (Punnett 2004: p.61)

Missing also were many American manufacturers, some of whom, with Midwestern offices, were more concerned with attending to business at the Chicago Auto Show, scheduled too close on the heels of the Ormond Tournament for them to attend both. Others, among them reportedly Thomas, Locomobile and Haynes, were apparently discouraged from attending due to the announcement that Stanley had entered his two long-distance Vanderbilt cars in the races – there was genuine concern that the Stanley Vanderbilts might dominate the distance events in much the same way as the special racer had outclassed its competition in the sprint categories. (*New York Times* January 31, 1907, p.7.)

The Stanley team finally got their cars out on the beach for their first shakedown on Friday afternoon, January 18, finding the beach

Stanley and Marriott with their racer, Ormond 1907. *F.E. and Marriott look optimistic standing next to the racer prior to the start of the 1907 races, while an unidentified man tries out the cockpit. The racer's 30 hp engine had been reworked and the boiler's steaming capacity enhanced, and it was found to be very smooth in operation. The beach, however, was quite rough and threatened to retard any speed record attempts.*

Stanley Museum Archives.

very "rough – and hard to go over in an automobile," assayed Mrs. Stanley. The shakedown was rough, too: "Frank smashed the engine in his Vanderbilt racer, so that they had to put in a new one." (A. Stanley *Diary* January 18, 1907.) The beach proved troublesome even when not racing the cars. On Saturday, Frank Durbin took Mrs. Stanley, Mrs. Hathaway, and a guest in the Model F touring car on a trip down to the Inlet, and on the return the car "broke the connecting rod and blew out a cylinder head" stranding them 18 miles down the beach. Durbin set off on foot to find help; Burt Holland and H. E. Rogers came along in one of the racing cars and sped off to do likewise; finally F.E. came to the rescue with another car and a tow line, "and after considerable trouble we got home." (A. Stanley *Diary* January 19, 1907.)

By Sunday evening the Stanley team had gotten all the cars into "fine shape" and returned to the hotel just as the long-hoped-for rain arrived – finally, the prospects for the scheduled start of the races the next day looked favorable. The optimism was short-lived, however, as the morning found the beach swept by strong winds that had shifted during the night, and unusually high tides that left a minimal course for racing. The remaining beach surface, if anything, was worse than before: "It is very rough too, with runs in it – making it very dangerous to run a car fast on the beach." (A. Stanley *Diary* January 21, 1907.)

The officials postponed the scheduled time trials till Friday, but having become more sensitive to the needs of spectators following years of complaints, they persuaded some of the contestants to make exhibition runs. Running into a fierce wind and over a rough beach, Marriott managed to make a mile in 38 3-5 seconds. (*Motor Age* January 24, 1907, p.2.) Not so fortunate was "Lucky" Baldwin, who broke an

Marriott waits to be called for a speed trial, Ormond 1907. *The top of the front cover of the racer shows evidence of make-shift repairs to the damage received during rail shipment from Newton. The car also shows the large outboard brake drums added to the car for the 1907 trials. Now an experienced high-speed race car driver, Marriott sports a leather helmet and jacket, neither of which he used in 1906.*
Courtesy Buz McKim,
International Speedway Corporation.

engine on one of the Vanderbilt cars. More luckless still was Ray Harroun, whose special 468-lb skeletal racer powered by a V-8 engine, despite showing great promise earlier with an unofficial, pre-race timed run of 29 seconds, sustained a broken crankshaft and was out of the races before they began. (Punnett 2004: p.71.) Harroun's withdrawal would leave the Dewar Trophy uncontested in the 1907 meet. (Harroun would have to wait for the inaugural Indianapolis 500 in 1911 to achieve automotive fame.)

Tuesday, January 22, was "a glorious day for lazy loitering on the beach" according to the correspondent from *Motor Age*. Sadly, the beach was good for little more than that, as the previous day's storm "went too soon and before it had completed its task of smoothing the beach it left the surface rolling and with a lot of unfilled gullies that tossed the fast flyers off the sand and killed all chance of anything approaching record time." (*Motor Age* January 24, 1907, p.2.)

Despite conditions the first event, a five-mile, standing-start race for amateur

H. Ernest Rogers in his Stanley Model K Semi-Racer, Ormond 1907. *Rogers, a wealthy amateur sportsman from Brookline, Mass., had found success driving Stanleys the previous year with victories at Readville, Atlantic City, and Crawford Notch, NH. He purchased one of the Stanley Vanderbilt cars and this stock Model K and brought them to Ormond to compete for the Stanley team. In the background, right, Augusta Stanley sits in an earlier model Stanley Runabout, possibly belonging to J. F. Hathaway, with Fred Marriott standing beside.*

Stanley Museum Archives.

owner/drivers was sent off at 8:30 am. The entrants were E. B. Blakeley in a 70 hp American Mercedes, R. A. McCready in a 20 hp Rolls-Royce, and H. Ernest Rogers in his 25 hp Model K Stanley. Rogers quickly overtook the Mercedes and outpaced both cars until the three-mile mark when his car began to fail, "refused to steam" as Mrs. Stanley put it, and the others swept by, Blakeley winning in 4:25 almost a mile ahead of the second-place Rolls.

Next on the program was the five-mile open championship, flying-start, at which Marriott "slipped away without any fuss" to a relative walkover despite his "slow time" of 3:44 4-5, McCready's Rolls-Royce finishing second more than a minute later in 4:52 2-5. "Marriott didn't try to get all the speed possible out of his machine," noted the *Boston Globe*. "When he went over the rough spots the car bobbed like the clapper of a bell." (*Boston Globe* January 23, 1907, p.6.)

John C. Kerrison reported that Marriott also lost time during the race when he was "forced into the water to avoid striking a woman who

had walked out on the course." (Kerrison 1907: p.231.) For the racers and organizers, hazardous beach conditions made for slow times, which made for bored spectators, which made for additional course hazards – an exasperating cycle.

Frank Durbin was entered in the next event, the one-mile, flying-start American touring car championship, his 20 hp Stanley Model F matched against McCready's Rolls-Royce and G. D. W. Rose in a 30 hp Stoddard-Dayton. Each car was required to carry four passengers weighing at least 150 lbs each; Durbin won by an eighth of a mile in 55 2-5, McCready second in 1:09 2-5, Rose third. While she found this race and the others "most uninteresting," Mrs. Stanley was most impressed by the "beautiful cup...given by the Sea Board Air line" (in fact, a railway line) awarded as the prize for the Stanley touring car victory. (A. Stanley *Diary* January 22, 1907.)

The last event of the day for the Stanley team was an unscheduled five-mile match race, made up on the spot, between H. Ernest Rogers

"Old Man" Stanley in Model F Touring Car, Ormond Garage, 1907. F.E. Stanley sits in a 20 hp Model F with an early manifestation of the cowled body that later appeared on the company's 1908 production model. Frank Durbin drove this car to victory in the one-mile American touring car championship on January 22, and F.E. set a world record for steam touring cars with the Model F two days later. F.E.'s debut as an Ormond race car driver at age 57 earned him the nickname "Old Man" Stanley. Photo by Nathan Lazarnick.

Leroy Cole Collection.

driving one of the Vanderbilt cars and Blakeley driving his Mercedes. At this stage of racing history, spur-of-the-moment races such as this one were not uncommon, and the wishes of the contestants were often acceded to by officials and timers, especially if such match ups did not interfere with the regular schedule of events. Rogers this time made up for his lame showing in the first race of the day, getting off to a quick lead and never relinquishing it, winning in 3:51 4-5, Blakeley trailing by a half a mile. (*Boston Post* January 23, 1907.)

Wednesday, January 23, dawned sunny but cool with a brisk North wind. The opening event, the ten-mile open, standing-start, had five entrants: Blakeley in his 70 hp American Mercedes, L. H. Perlman with his 50 hp Welch, and the three Stanley racers equipped with 30 hp engines – the muscle cars in the Stanley stable – all entered, for the first time, together in

Stanley Vanderbilt Racer, Ormond 1907. One of the Stanley Vanderbilt cars sits on the beach between events. Due to last minute problems during the Ormond races the special cars were not able to compete in the long-distance events for which they were entered, and the only victory they recorded went to H. Ernest Rogers who defeated Ned Blakely's American Mercedes in a special five-mile match race. One of the Vanderbilts was sacrificed for its engine when Marriott's racer needed a spare.

Stanley Museum Archives.

Edward B. (Ned) Blakely in his 70 hp American Mercedes, Ormond 1907. *The absence of entries by many foreign and domestic auto manufacturers at the 1907 races left Blakely, a young Harvard tutor, practically alone as the Stanleys' chief competition. When the Stanley cars suffered a string of mechanical break-downs, Blakely was triumphant in four of the five events in which he competed, although he made no mark in the record books as his victories established no new speed records.*

Courtesy Smithsonian Institution.

one race. Marriott, the clear favorite, took the line in the "big racer." Baldwin was at the wheel of one of the two Vanderbilt cars. The other Vanderbilt was "driven by 'Old Man' Stanley," as the *New York Times* christened him. Stanley, at age 57, was not originally listed as a contestant in this race, but "was an added starter and went into the contest thinking he would do so merely for fun." (*New York Times* January 24, 1907, p.7.)

To the steam camp it would have seemed most unlikely, almost beyond belief, that with their three big cars on the line the outcome of the race "would have delighted the gasoline men who loath what they denominate as 'freaks'." (*New York Times* January 24, 1907, p.7.) But that is exactly what happened.

Blakeley's Mercedes took off from the standing start in the lead, but Marriott accelerated rapidly and "passed the fast-flying Blakeley as if the latter were anchored. Spectators held their breath as the car and its driver flew along. Then there was another sound like a muffled explosion, a burst of steam and the car left a trail along the sand where sections of its machinery were dragging. Carried by its own momentum it went along several hundred yards and then slowly began to ease up." (*Boston Globe* January 24, 1907, p.9.)

Marriott came to a halt less than two miles into the race "when splicing at the rear of the steamer broke, allowing the engine to settle, cylinders to crack" (*New York Times* January 24, 1907, p.7) – the "splicing" alluding perhaps

F.E. Stanley drives his Model F in its world record trial. F.E. sets a world record for steam touring cars on Thursday, January 24, 1907, traveling over the mile course in 45 2-5. This photo commemorating the event was presented to F.E. by D. Walter Harper, the Stanley Philadelphia agent. The woman in the foreground waving a flag might be Mrs. Mary Harper.
Stanley Museum Archives.

and for a time, looked like he might just pull the race off. It was just as well that Stanley was not a betting man, for a victory was not in the cards. Near the end of the race "Frank broke the pump rocker and could not pump water" (A. Stanley *Diary* January 23, 1907), a setback which brought the Vanderbilt car up short, Blakeley winning in 7:42 1-5, Stanley hanging on to take second in 7:52, Perlman third in 10:55.

For the Stanleys it was an ignominious day – all three of the steamers had to be towed back to the garage, "all of them...forced to lower their colors to the gasoline cars." (Kerrison 1907: p.231.) Mrs. Stanley wrote: "I came back to the hotel just sick, heart sick... I felt the cars had been disgraced." (A. Stanley *Diary* January 23, 1907.) Back at the Ormond Garage the Stanley crew labored to repair the cars, disgraced or no, by cannibalizing Baldwin's Vanderbilt with

to an earlier repair in the wake of the damage to the car received in shipment. Mrs. Stanley gives added detail: "The big racer lost the rear end of the body that was glued on – it dropped, letting the engine down – and smashing it." (A. Stanley *Diary* January 23, 1907.) John C. Kerrison reported that Marriott's engine "blew out both cylinders" and that "his car had its stern completely torn out, and it is wonderful that Marriott did not meet with personal injury." (Kerrison 1907: p.231.)

With Marriott out of the race Blakeley surged to the lead, pursued by Stanley and Perlman, Baldwin falling to the rear. Mrs. Stanley recorded that Baldwin lost a bypass valve, Kerrison that he "burned out his boiler." This left the race and the pride of the steam camp up to "Old Man" Stanley, who began to gain ground on the Mercedes,

Close-up of F.E. Stanley in the Model F during his record trial. The touring car has been stripped of its fenders (mudguards) and lights as seen in the photo on p.119. In the one-mile American touring car championship won by Frank Durbin on January 22, this car would have been raced fully-equipped and with a full complement of four passengers.
Stanley Museum Archives.

the scorched boiler and transplanting its engine into Marriott's car, ready for another day. And there was even a moment of vindication and pride for the Stanley crew. As post-race ministering to the cars wrapped up, with all the tournament's cars (and some 50 private touring cars) put away in their stalls for the night, a fuel spill on the floor suddenly ignited into a wall of flame. "Old Man" Stanley, showing remarkably quick reflexes, grabbed a tarp and cast it over the blaze, quickly bringing a near disaster under control. (*Boston Globe* January 24, 1907, p.9; *Boston Post* January 27, 1907, p.10.)

The events on Thursday, January 24, began with the 100-mile race for the Minneapolis Cup, and as anticipated, one of the Stanley Vanderbilt cars, piloted by Baldwin, was entered in the long-distance contest. Since the Vanderbilts had been specifically designed to compete in such events, there was considerable interest in seeing what the steamer would do now that it was actually entered in its first long-distance competition. The interest swiftly turned academic, as the steamer did not make the start, an undisclosed last-minute problem keeping it out of the race. The contest was won by Blakeley, his Mercedes finishing in 1:26:10.

Blakeley also won the ten-mile handicap race, triumphing over a field of eight with a time of 13:59 (45 second handicap, actual running time 8:44). Two Stanleys were entered: Rogers in his Model K and Baldwin in one of the Vanderbilt cars. The star-crossed Baldwin was left at the line when his pilot went out; Rogers' actual running time over the ten miles was 9:20 2-5, second only to Blakeley's time, but his handicap was so great he could place no higher than fourth. (*Florida Times-Union* January 25, 1907, pp.1-2.)

Marriott entered the mile record trial with the repaired racer, the new engine staying firmly in place in the car and functioning normally. The best Marriott could do on the rough course was 31 4-5, well off his record of the year before, but better than any other trial he had made on the beach in the past week. Encouraged, he knew he would have one more day, Friday, to attempt a new Land Speed Record. F.E. Stanley finished the day's events by driving his Model F touring car in the mile trial in 45 2-5, a world's record for steam touring cars, a personally satisfying achievement that "pleased him greatly." (A. Stanley *Diary* January 24, 1907.) No one would realize it for some time, but "Old Man" Stanley had just set the last world record for a Stanley steam car on Ormond Beach.

The Stanley racer on blocks, Ormond 1907. *Fred Marriott, left, and Frank Durbin, right, prepare the racer for a speed trial on the beach.*

Stanley Museum Archives.

CHAPTER TEN

"Black Friday."

"O, God, Fred's killed!"

Frank Durbin. (*Boston Globe* January 26, 1907, p.6.)

FRIDAY, JANUARY 25, the last day of the 1907 Ormond Beach Tournament had no major races scheduled. Time had been set aside for individual time trials, postponed from Monday due to poor conditions. Beach conditions had not improved significantly, but if Marriott was going to set a new world's record on the beach in 1907, it was now or never, and everyone in the Stanley camp knew it. Marriott described their preparations for the attempt in an interview in October 1955:

"The morning of the big day was on us and Stanley and me had a conference. We decided to jack the pressure up to 1300 lbs. We knew what we were doing - this time all they'd see

would be a streak. Now, in racing of this kind, you'd start out with the boiler 2/3 full, this was eight or ten miles down the beach from the starting line, you'd figure she'd be 1/3 full or more time you'd crossed the line. The first few miles you'd have your fire on full and get your fire as hot as you could and your steam as high as you wanted it. We were carryin' 200 lbs. fuel pressure and had four nozzles and four mixing tubes in that burner. Time you'd run five or six miles you'd be movin' right good and you'd be gettin' everything hot - main thing was to keep that steam up to 1300 - run as fast as you can but keep the steam up there. Then, about a mile before the startin' line, ease that throttle up to wide open and the devil with the steam pressure then – you were into the run, and speed was all that counted – it was only a mile. We were doin' fine, but the beach was **rough**…" (Marshall 1982: pp.21-22.) [*Marriott's description of driving eight or ten miles down the beach refers to the pre-race warm-ups the Stanley drivers would take in preparation for record trials. The actual flying starts would begin about a mile and a half to two miles from the starting line.*]

The races were called at 9 am, beginning with a series of special match races and a club handicap for members of the Florida East Coast Automobile Association. Then it was time for the steam car trials for Marriott in the racer, Rogers in the remaining operational Vanderbilt car, and Baldwin in the Model K "Semi-Racer." Marriott ran down the beach a few miles past the starting line and, on signal, began his first timed trial – a warm up run, actually – recording a time of 32 4-5. The other two drivers took their tentative first runs, equally unremarkable (their times lost to history), except that Rogers' car caught fire and caused some anxious moments before Rogers could stop the car and bring the flare-up under control. (*Boston Globe* January 27, 1907.) Marriott then drove back, building pressure in his boiler, and made his second attempt, more serious this time, and was clocked at 29 3-5. Still more than a second shy of his world record, it was nonetheless the first time he had officially crossed the two-mile-a-minute mark during the tournament – his best time of the week – and it caught the remaining spectators' interest.

It was nearing 1 pm and the tide was coming in as Marriott steered the racer back down the beach "to make the supreme effort" for the mile record in what he knew would be his final attempt. First Rogers drove his Vanderbilt down

the course in 35 seconds, an auspiciously fast time. Baldwin followed in the Model K, covering the mile in 42 1-2. Then the announcer called for Marriott's third attempt, and all eyes turned to track the distant red streak as it flashed towards the starting line, accelerating noticeably faster than before. "I was on the upper piazza of the clubhouse with several other people," wrote Mrs. Stanley. "Soon they said 'he's coming.' We got up to look – and saw the car go into the water as it looked [*like*] a cloud of steam. The car was dashed to atoms – and Fred inside!" (A. Stanley *Diary* January 25, 1907.)

The accident had happened so suddenly and was over so quickly it took several moments for the spectators in the stands to realize what they had just witnessed. "'God, she's gone into the ocean and blown up,' said one of the newspaper men. He realized in a moment that something had happened. There was a momentary hush, then a babel of voices. 'Get some cars down there,' said someone. 'Where is there a doctor?' asked another. 'That ends Marriott's career,' was another expression." (*Boston Globe* January 26, 1907, p.6.)

"In an instant half the crowd started for the scene, but they were not half way there when they met the Rolls-Royce car bringing Marriott back, his face covered with blood, and lying insensible across the laps of two men in the rear seat. He was taken to the clubhouse of the Florida East Coast Automobile Association, and doctors on hand immediately volunteered their services." (*New York Times* January 26, 1907, p.3.) Mrs. Stanley was there when they brought him in. "He looked so dreadfully – pale & the bloody face – I can never forget it." She anguished as the doctors began examining the Stanleys' stricken shop foreman, practically one of the family. "Oh! Why did we come down to this horrible place?" she wrote. "Truly this is Black Friday." (A. Stanley *Diary* January 25, 1907.)

Of all the contemporary accounts of Marriott's accident, one of the most detailed was compiled by James T. Sullivan, the automotive correspondent for the *Boston Globe.* Sullivan pieced together this account from his own observations and on-the-scene interviews, filing this dispatch late on the evening of the day of the accident:

"This is how the accident happened: Marriott tried his car out twice to get it tuned up. The first time it went pretty fast [*32 4-5*];

the second time it sailed along just like an arrow from a bow with never a swerve. Down past the club it went, and when the time given out as being near the record [*29 3-5*], every one felt that there was a chance for the Newton driver…

"When he got out of his car after the second trial he went to the clubhouse and had a drink and sandwich. Then he strode down across the beach.

"Meanwhile his machinist, Frank Durbin, had been working over the car. It was pounding and knocking like a hammer on a piece of steel. Marriott put on his black helmet and tied the

The racer's debris field. An early photo taken soon after the accident to the Stanley racer on the final day of the 1907 tournament. The front half of the racer lies in the foreground (right); the rear engine compartment lies further along the beach (left). The cylindrical object in the distance is the 30-inch boiler that was ejected from the wreck. Doctors later speculated that the fact that the racer broke in two and the boiler was ejected were factors that lead to Marriott's survival.

Clarence Coons Collection, courtesy Joe Green and Fred Marriott.

Augusta Stanley views the wreckage. *Mrs. Stanley grimly stands on the beach in silence and views the remains of the Stanley racer.*

flaps under his chin. Then he buttoned up his coat and stepped into his car. He gave his shoulders a shrug and said: 'Let's try again.'

"Down the beach he sped and was soon lost to view, The announcer said Marriott was going to make another try for the world's record. It was then nearly 1 o'clock…

"When Marriott went back to the starting line he said to A.L. Kull of the Wayne [*Automobile Company*], who was to give him the flag: 'I've got a strong wind behind me now, so there is a better chance to cut loose.'

"'Keep down close to the beach,' answered Kull. 'It is not so rough there.'

"'All right,' said Marriott as he went along about a mile and a half up the beach to get a flying start. When the word came back that everything was ready and the beach cleared, Marriott started. Each second found him going faster. He had a pressure of 1100 pounds in his boiler.

Down the beach he flew like a meteor streaking across the sky.

"The starting line was crossed, and Kull dropped the flag. Faster than ever the car was traveling; it was just like a speck, so quickly did it travel. Suddenly it struck a lumpy part of beach 200 yards from the starting line, and up into the air it shot. Down it came quickly, and again it bumped and rocked. Marriott tried to control it, but instantly realized it was doomed.

"The machine seemed to leap fully 50 feet before it struck the first time. The other bumps came in rapid succession, then, like something possessed with life, it suddenly headed for the ocean. Just like a log being toyed with by a wicked surf, it rolled over and over on its side.

"At least a score of times it did this. When it struck the surf the waves checked its momentum. The boiler, being heavy and having a good propulsion, flew out clear of the car and rolled

A collected pile of wreckage. Marriott requested that the pieces of the racer be collected for shipment back to the factory. Here spectators view some of the collected debris gathered together in a pile on the beach.

Stanley Museum Archives, courtesy Richard Burnham.

50 yards away into the ocean. As soon as the connection was broken between boiler and engine there was a puff of steam, and when the boiler, heated nearly to a white glow, struck the cold water a geyser of white vapor was sent 50 feet into the air.

"The fusible plug blew out, and that released the steam that had been lost. Had the boiler remained in the car Marriott would have been crushed and scalded.

"'O, God, Fred's killed!' screamed Durbin, his boon companion, as he raced for the surf, Senator Morgan, the promoter of the meet, and Kull were right behind him. All three reached the wreck together, and disentangled Marriott from the mass of iron and steel that held him a prisoner.

"It did not take long. He was unconscious, but breathing. The victim was laid on the beach, and the cars began to come up. First it was attempted to put him into a machine, but it was not possible, as there was no tonneau for the car. Another was tried with the same results. The crowd gathered about and offered suggestions.

"Then up flew Capt. Hutton's car [*the Rolls-Royce*], and into this Marriott was placed. Down the beach, being held tenderly by Dr. Stinson, one of the contestants who was at hand, and a couple of others, Marriott was speeded to the clubhouse. The blood was pouring from his cheek and he was raving.

"Into the Florida East Coast A.A. he was rushed, and more physicians worked over him. He was soon restored to consciousness. He was wrapped in blankets, placed in another car, and sent flying to the hotel here.

"Dr. J.H. White was then ready to look after him. He was taken to his room and everything possible done for him. His nerve never deserted him. When he regained consciousness he insisted on sitting, but the doctors tried to get him to lie down. They finally made him go to bed. The excitement of the race and the accident kept him up. His clothes were a mass of tangled shreds.

"After the physicians had given him another examination they stated that it was impossi-

Front section of the wrecked racer. Some of the wooden pins which held the front cover of the racer in place can be seen on close inspection of the top frame of the front of the racer. Some eyewitnesses claimed that the front cover of the racer was detached just as the car went out of control.

Stanley Museum Archives, courtesy Richard Burnham.

The racer's boiler on the beach. *The Stanley steam boiler in the racer underwent an extreme test in the accident. Running at 1,100-1,300 psi and 700 degrees F, it was ejected at high speed from a tumbling car and hurled into a cold ocean. As testimony to the safety of the Stanley design it did not explode (some exaggerated press reports to the contrary) and in fact appears in the photo to be in remarkably salvageable condition. Its eventual fate is unknown, as it does not appear in any of the assembled wreckage photos. Photo by Richard H. LeSesne.*

Courtesy Buz McKim,
International Speedway Corporation.

ble to state when he would be able to get out. It is feared that brain trouble will develop, to add to the other complications…

"This evening, when Marriott recovered from the first shock, he said: 'I feared that bump on the beach all along, and knew if I got over it all right I had a good chance at the record.'

"'When I struck the hummock the car seemed to take wings and fly like a bird up into the air. With both hands I grabbed the steering tiller, and when she struck I tried to steer her.'

"'The car seemed to go toward the sand inward, then she lifted in the air again, and

when she struck I thought I had her headed straight. The wheels must have struck at a tangent, for she headed toward the ocean, and the next thing I knew I was at the clubhouse with the doctors.'

"At a late hour Marriott was resting comfortably, and the doctors said he had a good chance to recover." (*Boston Globe* January 26, 1907, pp.1, 5.)

Sullivan was not the only detail-observant witness on the scene. Glenn Curtiss, the motorcycle and aviation pioneer, was near the starting line awaiting his chance for a speed trial when Marriott flashed by. Curtiss recorded his observations for the *Scientific American*:

"Mr. Waters (who was to ride the rear seat in our tandem trial) and myself were just back of the starting line as the 'Bug' came to the tape which began the mile. As is commonly known, these steamers come to the start with a very high pressure of steam, saving it until the line is reached, then opening wide the throttle and fairly shooting over the line. [*This is an accurate description of a **rolling** start; Marriott in this instance, however, was employing a **flying** start, in which his throttle would have been opened wide a mile before the starting line.*] This sudden spurt, together with the flat boarded surface of the bottom of the car and the fact that all the weight of the car is well back, taken in conjunction with a slight depression on the beach, formed, in my opinion, the true cause of the accident. The slight depression in the course gave the car (which was pro-

Souvenir hunters pick over the debris. A man brandishes a stick from the wreckage at another spectator, right.

Stanley Museum Archives.

vided with light springs) a toss-up. The sudden application of power assisted in raising the fore part of the car, which, as I mentioned, is very light. The floor then acted as an aeroplane – the car *glided*, with the rear wheels only on the beach. It then swerved sidewise, and when the front wheels again came in contact with the ground, it was headed toward the sea, the wheels of course went down [*collapsed*] and the car rolled over and over breaking to fragments. The boiler kept on going, and rolled several hundred feet farther than the balance of the car, the escaping steam giving the appearance of a meteor rushing through the surf.

"I have heard Marriott speak of this tendency of the car to glide, and as we actually saw

The racer's wrecked engine. Frank Durbin, right, and others examine the rear end of the wrecked racer containing the 30 hp engine. The engine drive gear is prominent in the center of the photo. This engine, which had been transplanted from one of the Vanderbilt racers, was later donated by Fred Marriott to the Smithsonian Institution's collection. The springs of the racer's suspension can be seen above each end of the axle, mounted inside the racer's lower frame.

Clarence Coons Collection,
courtesy Joe Green and Fred Marriott.

Gathering souvenirs from the wreckage of the racer. A crowd of onlookers gather as some souvenir hunters clamber over the pile.

Stanley Museum Archives.

The remains of the racer gathered together for collection. *Members of the Stanley team, including Frank Durbin, third from left, pose with the remains of the racer. Marriott had requested that the remnants be gathered up and shipped back to Newton.*

Stanley Museum Archives.

the car rise, there is no doubt about this point." (*Scientific American* February 9, 1907, p.128.)

Other eyewitnesses were reported to have seen the fore covering or nose section of the racer come loose when the car struck the ruts in the beach prior to the crash. The wood and canvas carapace or cowling was held on to the lower body of the car by a few simple wooden pins or dowels, and it was this section of the racer which had earlier sustained the most visible damage during rail shipment from the factory to Florida. Some analysts theorized that the loosened carapace, partially dislodged on impact, may have caught the wind in some fashion, causing the front of the car to sail or twist aside, sending the car tumbling and rolling out of control. (*Automobile Topics* February 2, 1907, p.1656; *New York Times* January 26, 1907, p.3.)

F.E. Stanley seems to have agreed that the accident was caused, or contributed to, by some problem with the racer - "Stanley says that had it not been for a fault of construction which was practically undiscoverable the car would have made the mark." (*New York American* January 28, 1907, p.8.) Just what he

considered the "fault of construction" to be is not recorded, but given the limited means of testing radical automotive designs prior to actual racing in Stanley's day, it is not surprising that the problem was "practically undiscoverable." Most of the observers of the accident were in agreement that "Marriott without doubt owes his life to the fact that the machine broke in two in the middle, spilling him out [*when*] the beetle-like shell broke in two sections," and if it hadn't been for the lightweight construction of the racer "his life would have been crushed during the flops of the car." (*New York Times* January 26, 1907, p.3; January 27, 1907, p.8.)

As it was Marriott's survival was quite astounding. He had suffered three broken ribs, deep cuts on his scalp, his forearm and just under his right eye, and he was a mass of bruises and contusions, but his perceived internal injuries, if any, appear to have been resolved without complications. Days later Mrs. Stanley marveled: "everything now looks as though the boy should come out with his life and limbs all right. Wonderful - wonderful. Surely his time had not yet come." (A. Stanley *Diary* January 30, 1907.)

Over the years one of the most colorful stories of Marriott's injuries and recoveries revolves around an alleged injury to his right eye. Press reports of his injuries just after his accident refer to a deep cut three quarters of an inch below his eye, beach sand inclusions, a complaint from Marriott (on regaining consciousness in the clubhouse) "that he could see nothing out of his right eye," and that the medics first thought he might lose sight in one eye. (*New York Times* January 26, 1907, p.3.) Later tests showed his vision unimpaired, but a story emerged that one of Marriott's eyes had been dislodged from its socket and miraculously replaced by a vacationing specialist, by chance on hand in the clubhouse when Marriott was brought in on a stretcher. The story persisted, and finally appeared in print in an account by F.O. Stanley, who said that Fred's accident left his "eye hanging out of its socket and had it not been for Dr. Parks from South Boston, would have been removed. But it was put back and later perfect sight was restored." (Derr 1932: p.58: F.O. Stanley 1930: p.9.) Later interviews with Marriott spawned even more colorful accounts: "Fred, unconscious, was seriously injured…his right eye had popped out of its socket and rested on his cheek. Luckily for Fred a Dr. Parks from South Boston was vacationing in the Daytona Beach area and witnessed the accident. Rather than have Fred taken to a local hospital he arranged to have him brought to a hotel room in nearby Daytona. There, using a spoon, Dr. Parks pressed the loose eyeball back into its socket with no ill effects. 'Now it's the best eye I've got,' Fred grins." (Tuscher 1952: p.75.)

Variations of this story made their way into numerous history books, even after it was pointed out that the physiology of the human eye made the story of Marriott's displaced eye-ball impossible, and its replacement even more so. (Montagu and Bird 1971: p.148.) Nevertheless, there is a plausible medical explanation for this story. Cases are known where accident victims suffering facial trauma present rescuers with an unusual situation where an injured person's eyelids are closed, or retracted, behind an eyeball (which remains fixed in its socket, just fully exposed). Should this have happened to Marriott the first rescuers on the scene would have found him unconscious, his face covered with blood, and an apparently displaced eyeball staring out at them, which would explain how the story got started.

Curiously, the medical procedure for correcting this injury, then as now, involves gently repositioning the eyelids with a spoon-shaped implement, performed when the patient is unconscious, as Marriott was when he was initially brought in from the beach. The description of a doctor pressing Fred's eyeball back in with a spoon, while not quite medically accurate, is actually close to what one would expect from an uninitiated eyewitness. Reports of the time do confirm that one of the physicians attending Fred Marriott was Dr. J. Wilson Parks, a retired specialist from Boston.

Marriott recovered quickly from his injuries, returning to the beach a month later to officiate at a race on February 22, and traveling back to Newton to resume his duties as foreman of the Stanley Repair Department on March 6. (Koopman 1962: p.68; *New York Times* March 7, 1907, p.10.) The Stanley racer, which Marriott would later refer to as the "Rocket," did not fare so well. Immediately after the accident "several thousand people gathered and began ripping away at the car for souvenirs. Every available piece that could be dislodged was taken. The fragments that had littered the course taken by the machine were soon gobbled up… The parts that were left after the souvenir hunters had got through were bundled up and taken back to the garage." (*Boston Globe* January 26, 1907, p.6.)

From his sickbed Marriott had insisted that photographs of the wreck be taken and that the remains of the racer be gathered up and shipped back to the factory. "Accordingly, a double mule team made a trip of sixteen miles carrying the debris to Ormond Station. The expense of the job far exceeded the value of the wreckage. But Stanley quickly acceded to his chief driver's wish. Following the mule team bearing the remains came the four remaining Stanley cars on their way to the station for shipment, the driver of each being at the steering post. It seemed like a funeral procession…" (*New York Times* January 27, 1907, p.8.)

Over the years questions arose as to how fast Marriott was traveling when his accident occurred, as the official timing devices on the beach did not record his time. The newsman James T. Sullivan estimated Marriott's speed at the time as 130 mph (*Boston Globe* January 26, 1907, p.1), which even if accurate would not have been the fastest unofficial time of the meet.

That distinction would fall to Glenn Curtiss, who reportedly made an unofficial time trial with his experimental 40 hp V-8-engine motorcycle on January 24, clocked at 26 2-5 at the mile, or 136.3 mph, just before his machine broke its universal joint and prevented any further, officially-recognized trials. This unsanctioned trial took place late in the day when the electronic timing device was not in operation – the *Scientific American* reported that it was "timed by stopwatches from the start by several persons who watched through field glasses a flag waved at the finish" – but all

Glenn Curtiss and his V-8 motorcycle. *Curtiss adapted this elongated motorcycle to hold one of his V-8 engines designed to power airships. Curtiss made an unofficial timed run estimated at 136.36 mph over a mile course at Ormond, but a broken universal joint prevented him from later making an official trial. Curtiss apparently never repaired or rebuilt his special motorcycle to make another attempt at the Land Speed Record.*

> *Scientific American,*
> *Stanley Museum Archives.*

the observers present believed that Curtiss had exceeded the 1906 mile record set by Marriott. (*Scientific American* February 9, 1907, p.128.) It was not clear whether this record, had it been officially timed, would have been recognized, as Curtiss's motorcycle was overweight, and there is no evidence of Curtiss making any further attempts at the Land Speed Record.

Marriott would in his later years claim that his speed had been calculated at close to three miles a minute. "Two professors from the Massachusetts Institute of Technology that I knew had set up some kind of a timing rig at the half-mile mark," said Fred, "and told me later I was traveling just a hair under 190 miles an hour." (Koopman 1962: p.66.) Marriott, coincidently, did know two MIT professors, the father-son duo of Louis and Thomas S. Derr, both avid steam car men who were familiar visitors to the Stanley factory and its repair shop. The elder Derr was an emeritus professor of Physics and one of the first registered Stanley owners; his son left MIT to found the American Steam Automobile Company, experimenting with and producing steam automotive technology into the 1940s.

The Derrs were also known by F.O. Stanley, who likewise wrote that Fred's speed at Ormond was "nearly three miles a minute, or fully 260 feet per second," drawing on a curious sports-physics analogy involving the speed of a golf ball to illustrate his point. (Derr 1932: pp.58, 60; F.O. Stanley 1930: p.9.) Whether the Derrs had anything to do with calculating the 190 mph speed figure, or were even present at Ormond Beach is unknown, and there is no evidence that there were any unofficial, experimental timing devices in use during the 1907 tournament.

Perhaps the best estimate of Marriott's speed was calculated by F.E. Stanley, according to his son Raymond. Raymond Stanley witnessed many of the events at the 1906 tournament after his parents relented and sent for him during the pre-race trials, when their son-in-law Prescott Warren was rushing a replacement engine down from the factory. During the ill-fated 1907 meet, Raymond was at home with his schoolwork, but he later published this family account in *Automobile Quarterly*. According to Raymond his father would normally position himself at a vantage point on the course where he could see the starter's flag or the smoke from the starter's pistol. When Marriott's final trial began F.E. Stanley snapped his stopwatch, then snapped it off 'the instant he saw the racer waver." He recorded a six-second run, and later measured the distance the racer traveled – a quarter of a mile – before it went out of control. Stanley's estimate, assuming that Marriott completed the mile run at the same speed at which he covered the first quarter mile, and based on his field calculations, was a projected time of 24 seconds, or about 150 mph. (R. Stanley 1963: pp.126, 128.)

The myths that arose from the racer's uncalculated speed at the time of its spectacu-

Tourists posing with the wreck. *The wreckage of the Stanley racer was fleetingly popular as a tourist attraction. Here a group of tourists gather for a photo behind an assembled pile of wreckage. The car at left, a 1906/07 Cadillac Model M, bears a sign that proclaims "Tampa to Daytona, 18 hours."*
Stanley Museum Archives.

lar crash may have helped give rise to the most celebrated Stanley myth of all: Hold the throttle of a Stanley car wide open for a full minute (or three), and Mr. Stanley would give you $1,000 (or a new car). Tales of this mythical factory offer began to circulate sometime after the races at Ormond Beach were ended, and still persist today. That the myth is connected with Marriott's crash, and that it was well-known, even gospel, to some Stanley owners is evidenced by a 1937 interview with A. A. Gilmore of Eastport, Maine, who at the time was still driving a 1924 Stanley he had purchased new at the factory in Watertown. The reporter asked him about the speed of his Stanley:

"Missus, that I can't answer. No one has ever found out. I travel at 40 or 45 steady. But that's nothing. One time the Stanley brothers offered $1000 or a new car to anyone who would drive one for a full minute with the throttle wide open. No one ever has. But Fred Marriott tried it once. Drove a Stanley in 1906 down at Daytona Beach, at 130 miles an hour. The next day he tried it again even faster but something wouldn't take it and the car split right in two. No, Fred wasn't killed but it was a miracle. Stanley Brothers withdrew their offer because they wouldn't risk human lives. Nobody ever got around to pushing a Stanley wide open after that." (*Bangor Daily News* November 6, 1937.)

When asked about the wide-open-throttle story by George Woodbury, Fred Marriott burst out laughing. "I'll tell what there is in that yarn. *Nothing*! The Stanley brothers were from the State of Maine – Kingfield, Maine – and nobody from Maine ever gave anything away to anybody for any reason." (Woodbury 1950: p.109.) That the myth should have become so convincing to so many, and to have endured for so many years is really quite remarkable, its legacy captured in the imagination of Stanley's and Marriott's quest for the speed record and the two-mile-a-minute race. S. B. Stevens once challenged Stanley to put up "$1,000 or an orange" as a wager to hold the throttle wide open for a minute over the two-mile course at Ormond Beach. How curious it would be, were that "$1,000 or an orange" to have morphed into "$1,000 or a car."

CHAPTER ELEVEN

Beaten by "Just a Trifle."

"The most valuable lesson learned by this accident was the great danger such terrific speed incurs, so we decided never again to risk the life of a courageous man for such a small return."

F.O. Stanley. (F.O. Stanley 1930: p.9.)

IT WOULD BE HARD not to characterize the 1907 Ormond-Daytona Tournament as a disaster for the Stanleys, not to mention the other steam car manufacturers they represented and the entire steam camp. That Fred Marriott had survived his horrific crash was perhaps the only bright spot of their second foray into Florida. They had very little else to show for it. The loss of the fastest race car in the world was only a small part of their overall setback.

Animosity toward the 'freak steamers', thinly veiled under the spirit of sportsmanship on the Florida sands, had been building for some time and was now fully out in the open. The day after the 1907 meet ended it was revealed that an un-named gas car manufacturer had tried to organize a boycott of the Ormond races some three months before the meet took place. Privately a letter had been circulated among all the manufacturers in the hydrocarbon branch asking them "to refrain from participating in the Ormond-Daytona meet for the reason that Stanley was permitted to enter his steamers in the same events." (*Daytona Gazette-News* January 26, 1907, p.2.) The journal *Automobile Topics* suggested that this effort was not unsuccessful, and that many of the gas car manufacturers had quietly conspired against the meet for the sole purpose "to whack F.E. Stanley over the knuckles." (*Automobile Topics* February 2, 1907, p.1658.)

At the end of the 1906 tournament it was suggested that the Stanleys never received a

Ad for the Bay State Automobile Association races at Readville, September 14, 1907. *Marriott and Baldwin headline the BSAA races at Readville. Marriott had recovered from his injuries at Ormond and returned to active racing, matched here with Baldwin in a race involving the Vanderbilt cars. Baldwin set a new steam track record after Marriott was forced to drop out with boiler trouble.*

Boston Globe, Stanley Museum Archives.

fair hearing on their challenges and grievances because "they had no friend at court." This was to become a certainty in the racing board of the AAA following the 1907 meet. The wreckage of Marriott's car had hardly been removed from the beach when the auto racing officials began to entertain suggestions for excluding the freak steamers. Some suggested a system of separate race categories, segregating the steamers off to one side with their own schedule of events. Others proposed eliminating the popular sprint events altogether, concentrating on practical, long-distance races for stock cars. A consensus of opinion (outside of the steam camp) was to require all entrants to qualify for the mile and two-mile-a-minute races by first successfully completing a long-distance event at a specified average speed. In this way, they believed, all the racers of freak construction – gas and steam – would be eliminated from the competition. (*New York Times* January 31, 1907, p.7.)

The manufacturers also urged that future Ormond meets be moved ahead to late winter, preferably in March. Meets had been held in late January to fill an opening in the calendar between the New York Auto Show in early January and the Chicago Auto Show in early February. Many of the manufacturers insisted that the schedule made it very difficult for them to prepare racing teams for the tournaments and still attend the two most important auto shows of the year. The March date they proposed would only conflict with the Boston Auto Show, of lesser importance. That the Boston Auto Show was vital to the Stanley Motor Carriage Company and might preclude them from attending future meets was to the gas car manufacturers a matter of no ill consequence.

F.E. Stanley, for his part, was determined to build another racer, more powerful than before, and to return with it to Ormond in 1908 – at least according to what was reported in the press. "Despite the accident to the machine which was driven by Marriott," wrote one

newsman, "F.E. Stanley, the maker, says he will not cease in his efforts to construct a car that will travel the mile in 25 seconds." (*New York Herald* January 28, 1907, p.8.) Another predicted that Stanley would proceed with construction of the new racer without delay, and "by March or April will have replaced the Bug with a higher-powered steamer which Marriott is to drive." (*New York Times* January 27, 1907, p.8.) Disputing this was A. G. Batchelder of *The Automobile*, who reported that "F.E. Stanley, the creator of the 'Bug,' has no idea of resurrecting his famous steam sprinter; in fact, he does not hesitate to make the definite statement that the worth of a single fast mile or two has depreciated to such an extent that it is no longer worth while to build a car for this single purpose." Batchelder further alleged that "Mr. Stanley intends to return the Dewar trophy to Sir Thomas Dewar," and that after studying Walter Christie's racer, "he states that it is his intention to bring forth a front-drive steam car in the near future." (*The Automobile* January 31, 1907, p.250.) There being no evidence of Stanley following up on either of these predictions, this last may be merely the reporter's fancy.

Mrs. Stanley's feelings on the matter were sharp and to the point: "I never want to see another automobile race and I think Frank will never race again." (A. Stanley *Diary* January 26, 1907.) To be sure, it appears that the 57-year-old Stanley would never again take a car out on a sanctioned race, although his competitive nature would reappear for impromptu 'brushes' with powerful gas cars while on tour, traveling on public roads. His competitive urge to return to Ormond and defend the Dewar Trophy was, if anything, even stronger in his chief driver. Marriott was adamant about returning. "I am going back to racing as soon as possible," he declared upon his release from the doctors' care, "and if there is a meet next Winter at Ormond the Stanley steamers will be there, for they can't bar so-called 'freaks' out of all the events by new rules, and if any one wants the Dewar trophy he will have to meet the Stanley steamer to get it." (*New York Times* March 7, 1907, p.10.)

Marriott's allusion to the Dewar Trophy indicates what the steam camp believed was their ace in the deck, for even if the AAA attempted to change the entry rules for competing cars at Ormond, the Dewar Trophy had its own rules stipulated by its deed of gift. "The deed specifically states that the trophy shall be raced for at one mile, flying start, and is open to any machine, regardless of weight, horse power or fuel. There is nothing in the deed relative to any qualifying events." (*Boston Globe* January 7, 1908, p.5.) Since the Dewar Trophy was to be contested at Ormond, and its rules ensured that it was open to all, the steam camp felt that they could prepare any vehicle to go to Ormond and defend the Dewar Trophy as they saw fit.

One steam car manufacturer who was reported building a racer for that purpose was Louis S. Ross, who had won the Dewar Trophy the first time it was offered in 1905. In early November Ross was said to be putting "the finishing touches... on a racer that should make a splendid showing at the tournament." Cognizant of the possible rule changes at Ormond, Ross had decided to hedge his bets with his new car: "It has been built to comply with any rule the racing committee may name and will enter short and long distance events. In appearance it will be totally different from its predecessors and no one may call it a freak." (*Boston Globe* November 4, 1907, p.4.)

At this time the AAA had not settled on what the new rules would be, but they had decided (on November 2) that the 1908

Ormond meet would take place in the first week in March. Some moderates on the racing committee had held out for a token qualifier, that all entrants enter a modest distance event of "at least 20 miles, probably with a turn, and finish, too, at a speed of at least 45 seconds to the mile." (*Boston Globe* November 4, 1907, p.4.)

The incoming racing board for 1908 included some hard-liners, however, including none other than Charles J. Swain of Philadelphia, one of the original dissatisfied customers for the Stanley Vanderbilt Cup racers, so sympathy for the steam camp and their 'freak racers' was decidedly lacking. By the end of the year they announced that: "In order to prevent the entrance of freak machines for the mile, two-mile-a-minute, and mile kilometer trials, all cars intending to compete in any or all of these events must compete in at least one of the long-distance contests, and will be required to maintain an average speed of 60 miles an hour for 100 miles." They also announced a closing date of February 15 for entry fees for the seven scheduled events, which included the one-mile International Championship for the Sir Thomas Dewar Trophy. (*New York Times* January 3, 1908, p.7.)

The problem was, the Dewar Trophy was in Boston, as it had been initially won by Louis S. Ross in 1905, and by Fred Marriott in 1906. Marriott had also successfully defended the trophy in 1907, as it had been uncontested, and it was still safely ensconced at the headquarters of the Bay State Automobile Association. None of the parties was willing to give it up without a fight. Senator William J. Morgan was dispatched to Boston on January 6 "to consult with Louis S. Ross and F.E. Stanley in regard to defending the Dewar Trophy," reported the *Boston Globe*.

Barney Oldfield in the "Lightning Benz," Ormond 1910. *Oldfield drove his big Mercedes to a mile record of 131.72 mph at the final Ormond/Daytona Beach tournament in 1910. In 1906, Fred Marriott's speed of 127.66 mph surpassed the previous year's land speed record by 23 mph. It took four years and a significantly larger car to exceed Marriott's record by only 4 mph. Little wonder Mrs. Stanley referred to it as "just a trifle." Photo by Richard S. LeSesne.*

Stanley Museum Archives.

"Both Mr. Ross and Mr. Stanley built racing cars this year with which to defend the trophy," the *Globe* informed its readers, and the rules and dates of the upcoming meet had been recently changed "to keep the Bostonians out of the competitions." The paper specifically pointed out that the new dates for the tournament conflicted with the Boston Auto Show, and that "Neither Mr. Ross or Mr. Stanley would enter cars for that time, because of their inability to get to Florida and be back for the more important work at the show here." (*Boston Globe* January 7, 1908, p.5.)

Senator Morgan received a chilly reception. "When Mr. Morgan saw the two men yesterday they positively declined to agree to let the trophy leave Boston, as they claim that there is nothing in the deed of gift that calls for the qualifying race at a long distance, even though their cars could easily meet the requirements." Nothing more specific is known about the Ross and Stanley racers here said to have been prepared for the 1908 races. Meeting the requirements would mean that they were able to compete in the 100-mile races. Whether Stanley had specially built a new race vehicle for 1908, or had revamped one or both of the Vanderbilt racers is unknown. What is known is that the Bostonians presented a united front in opposition to the new rules:

"As Mr. Ross and Mr. Stanley have each won a leg on it [*the Dewar Trophy*] under the deed of gift they claim that at this late day, after they have gone to the expense of building machines to defend it, no racing committee has the power to change the deed. In this they will be backed up by the Bay State A. A. officials, many of whom are angry because of the conflict of dates with the Boston show." (*Boston Globe* January 7, 1908, p.5.)

The officials at Ormond apparently refused to reconsider the matter, and when the races were held in March, the one-mile International Championship for the Dewar Trophy was not one of them. Senator Morgan tried to set up a special series of races to be held at Ormond in

late March, at which time the Dewar Trophy race could take place without conflicting with the auto shows. He tried to persuade Ross and Stanley to come down for those dates, assuring them that he had other contestants willing to meet and race on their terms.

Indeed, it was reported that the Maxwell Company had built a 12-cylinder racer specifically to compete for the Dewar Trophy, and that they were ready to engage in an open challenge "to Mr. Stanley and all others, for steam and gasoline cars, this contest to be held at the Florida Beach during or immediately following the coming tournament...and to be run strictly under the conditions nominated in the deed of gift." (*New York Times* February 2, 1908, p.S3.) It appears that all attempts to arrange a special sanctioned race for the Dewar Trophy were unsuccessful, and that the Dewar Trophy for automobile racing was retired from competi-

Fred Marriott in Model H, Dead Horse Hill, 1907. *Marriott never got the chance to race steamers in Florida again, but he continued to make his mark at New England venues. Here he sits in a Model H at the Dead Horse Hill Climb in Worcester, Mass., in 1907.*
Clarence Coons and David Berckmueller Collections.

tion. Neither Stanley nor Ross nor any other steam car manufacturer ever competed at Ormond again.

The races at Ormond-Daytona Beach continued for two more years before ending in the face of dwindling support; the Stanley Motor Carriage Company continued to produce fine cars for fifteen years longer than that. On March 16 of the final Ormond meet in 1910, Barney Oldfield drove the 120 hp 'Blitzen Benz' a mile down the beach in 27.33 seconds, or 131.72 mph. (*Boston Globe* March 17, 1910, p.1; Punnett 2004: p.90.) Word, of course, reached Newton, Mass., where Mrs. Stanley recorded it simply in her diary:

"This morning we read that the big Benz car – Barney Oldfield driving – had beaten the Stanleys record for a mile going in 27 3-5 for a mile – just a trifle better than the Stanley." (Augusta Stanley *Diary* March 17, 1910.)

There are those who would argue over whether it was, indeed, a "trifle" (motorcycle fans would point out it was barely between Marriott's record and Glenn Curtiss's unofficial time), but it is remarkable, even astonishing, that it took four long years (and an exponentially larger car) to break the Stanleys' land speed record set by Fred Marriott in 1906. Still others would raise the very real questions of what speeds Marriott might have achieved if the beach in 1907 had been in fine shape, and what speedsters F.E. Stanley might have produced had he been allowed to pursue speed records in competition on the beach as before. Rather than bow to obstructionist and discriminatory rule changes, Stanley could take solace in his long unbroken and untouchable record without compromising his standards. Although he never had the full opportunity to build and race a lightweight car that would achieve the 24-second mile he believed was its ultimate

Fred Marriott in his garage, Watertown, 1952. *Fred Marriott sits at his desk in the office of his garage at the corner of Hunt and Galen Streets, just down the street from the old Stanley factory. His hand rests on a stacked array of parts salvaged from the Stanley Rocket, including a rear brake drum, a wheel hub, the throttle, and a pressure gauge. Photo by A. O. Nicolazzo.*

Speed Age,
Stanley Museum Archives.

limit, he at least could truly rest content that with a Stanley steam car (and perhaps no other) it was ultimately possible. And as his twin brother so admirably expressed, he didn't have to risk the life of a courageous man to find out.

As for Fred Marriott, he continued to enjoy a successful racing career, and unlike so many others, did so while remaining loyal to the power of steam. Marriott drove Stanley stock cars and the Vanderbilt racers to impressive showings in local hill climbs, particularly the Dead Horse Hill contests in Worcester, Mass. He was also a frequent sight at Readville and other local tracks, where he would draw crowds to see special exhibition runs and match races, occasionally involving the other Stanley Vanderbilt driven by L. F. N. Baldwin when there

Marriott's display of Ormond Beach photos. *Fred kept a framed display of photos from the 1906 races with his own typewritten annotations on the wall of his office. Currently on loan to the Stanley Museum from the Larz Anderson Auto Museum, many of the photos in this display appear in this book. Photo by Dianne Chamberlain.*

Courtesy Larz Anderson Auto Museum.

were no gas car challengers to be found. The Land Speed Record of 1906 was the pinnacle of many achievements for Marriott. It stands out among many other speed records because it was, at the time, a near mythical speed and an exercise in daring and Yankee ingenuity, as much a human achievement as one of thermo- and aerodynamics. Photos documenting the achievement with Marriott's own annotations adorned the walls of his Watertown garage at the corner of Hunt and Galen. Marriott donated the 30 hp engine from the 1907 wreckage to the Smithsonian Institution, but he kept on his desk in the corner of his office the throttle of the most celebrated steam racer of them all.

Fred Marriott outside his garage, Watertown, Spring 1955. *Fred Marriott stands outside the Galen Street entrance to his Watertown garage in the Spring of 1955. He passed away a year later on April 28, 1956, not long after the 50th anniversary of his land speed record at Ormond Beach.*

Courtesy Frank H. Gardner.

To many of us today the 1906 Land Speed Record of the Stanley steam racer stands as distant testimony to a long-abandoned automotive technology – outmoded, old-fashioned and obsolete, yet unmatched, undeveloped and unsurpassed. To those fascinated with all things steam, and with steam cars in particular, the record perhaps means something more.

Historical retrospectives on discarded technology can be capricious, variously harsh or sentimental, and sometimes both. Defenders of old technology often try to point to past achievements to illustrate what should have been, but rarely have such striking triumphs as the Land Speed Record to make their case. Many acolytes of the steam car have dreamed

of seeing a resurgence, a modern steamer, a new champion, while others, content to work on vintage enduring steamers, carry on as a dedicated extension of Marriott's Repair Department. Perhaps for those who wait and those who toil, it is enough to look back and reflect that the Land Speed Record of the Stanley was a true achievement, and that the steam car was once the legitimate King of Speed. For those others who dare to dream, design and build a new steam racer for a new quixotic attempt at the Land Speed Record, one can only imagine F.E. Stanley and Fred Marriott, each in his own way, looking down on their efforts with an approving eye.

"Signaling all is ready for the Two Mile a Minute." Fred Marriott gives a thumbs-up signal prior to making his start in the trials for the Two-Mile-a-Minute race, January 29, 1906.

Larz Anderson Auto Museum .

BIBLIOGRAPHY

Bacon, John H. 1984. *American Steam-Car Pioneers: A Scrapbook.* Exton, Pennsylvania: The Newcomen Society of the United States.

Barrett, Walter E., Jr. 1998. *Readville: The Story of the Readville Race Track.* Dedham, Massachusetts: Walter E. Barrett, Jr.

Beeman, Joseph. 2000. *Northeast Coast of Florida.* Accessed at http://faculty.valencia.cc.fl.us/jbeeman/NE_ Coast/flne.htm.

Birchwood, Charles W. 1902. "Why Not To Florida?" *The Automobile Magazine* IV:12, pp. 985-987 (December 1902).

Chenoweth, Stanley. 198?. *A Maine Man's View of the Civil War: a Collection of Letters and Diary Excerpts from Isaac N. Stanley of Kingfield, Maine, During His 11 Months as a Union Soldier.* Typescript and facsimiles, Stanley Museum Archives.

Cooper, Carolyn C. 2003. "Myth, Rumor, and History: The Yankee Whittling Boy as Hero and Villain." *Technology and Culture* 44:1, pp. 82-96 (January 2003).

Derr, Thomas S. 1932. *The Modern Steam Car and Its Background.* Newton, Massachusetts: American Steam Automobile Company.

Dolnar, Hugh. 1898a. "American Steam Motocycles." *The Autocar,* November 12, 1898, pp. 726-729.

_____ 1898b. "Practical Motocycles at Charles River Park, Boston, November 9." *American Machinist,* December 29, 1898, pp. 969-973.

_____ 1903a. "Hill-climbing at Boston, U.S.A." *The Autocar,* May 23, 1903, p. 601.

_____ 1903b. "The Stanley Steam Car." *The Autocar,* August 8, 1903, pp. 179-181; August 15, 1903, pp. 211-212; August 22, 1903, pp. 240-242; August 29, 1903, pp. 267-268.

Edmands, B. C. 1952. "The Ross Steamer." *The Bulb Horn* XIII:2, pp. 2-4 (April 1952).

Elliott, Harmon. 1945. *The Sterling Elliott Family.* Cambridge, Massachusetts: The Elliott Addressing Machine Company.

Emmons, Chansonetta Stanley. 1916. "The Stanley Family." *Franklin Journal,* July 18, 1916, pp. 6-7. [Republished: Kingfield, Maine: Stanley Museum, c1993.]

Foster, Kit. 2004. *The Stanley Steamer: America's Legendary Steam Car.* Kingfield, Maine: The Stanley Museum.

Hallett, Blanche Stanley. circa 1954. *Memoirs.* Manuscript, Stanley Museum Archives.

Helck, Peter. 1958. "Victor Hemery." *The Bulb Horn* XIX:4, pp. 11-18 (Fall 1958).

Jerome, _____. 1898. "Along Florida Shores." *Brooklyn (NY) Daily Eagle,* January 30, 1898, p. 20ff.

Joy, Arthur F. 1956. "My Father Built the Stanley Steamer." [*Interview with Emily Stanley Warren.*] *Yankee,* pp. 32-35, 78-81 (June 1956).

Kerrison, J. C. 1907. "The Ormond Beach Races." *MoToR,* p. 231 (February 1907).

Koopman, Ted. 1962. "The Stanley Record Breaker." [*December 1955 interview with Fred Marriott.*] *Light Steam Power,* pp. 65-77 (March/April 1962).

McAvoy, George E. 1988. *And Then There Was One: a History of the Hotels on the Summit and the West Side of Mt. Washington.* Littleton, New Hampshire: Crawford Press.

McDuffee, E. A. 1955. "I Beat Them All." *Yankee,* pp. 31-37 (July 1955). [Reprinted: *Stanley Museum Quarterly* XV:3-4, pp. 16-19 (September/December 1996).]

Marriott, Fred. 1956. Interview by Frank H. Gardner, Henry Shepard and Stanley W. Ellis, Watertown, Massachusetts. Audio recording, The Stanley Museum Archives.

Marshall, Thomas C. 1982. "Interviews with the Late Fred H. Marriott." *The Steam Automobile* 23:4, pp. 14-22 (1982). [Reprinted: *Stanley Museum Quarterly* XV:3-4, pp. 20-23 (September/December 1996).]

Merrick, H. James. 2002. "The Stanleys as Educators." *Stanley Museum Quarterly* XXI:1, pp. 18-19 (Winter 2002).

_____ 2004. *"We Will Try This Hill" – The Climb to the Clouds, 1904-1905.* Kingfield, Maine: Stanley Museum.

_____ 2005. "The Stanleys' First Customer." *Stanley Museum Quarterly* XXIV:2-3, pp. 6-7 (Spring-Summer 2005).

Montagu of Beaulieu, Lord, and Anthony Bird. 1971. *Steam Cars 1770-1970*. London: Cassell & Company Ltd.

Morgan, William J. 1903. "Automobiles and Alligators." *The Automobile Magazine* V:5, pp. 424-439 (May 1903).

___ 1904. "Mainly About Men and Motors." *The Automobile Magazine* VI:9, pp. 740-741 (September 1904).

Punnett, Dick. 2004. *Racing on the Rim*. Revised edition. Ormond Beach, Florida: Tomoka Press.

Purington, George C. 1889. *History of the State Normal School, Farmington, Maine*. Farmington, Maine: Knowlton, McLeary & Company.

Richardson, Philip W. 1956. "George M. Tinker." *The Bulb Horn* XVII:2, pp. 16-19, 35 (April 1956).

Ryan, Paul M. 1934. "Early Races Served to Make Public Aware of Motor Cars." *New York Times*, January 7, 1934, p. AA2.

Sobel, Erik. 2002. "The World's Fastest Canoe." *Wooden Canoe* 25:1, pp. 6-11 (February 2002).

Stanley, Augusta M. 1904. "Tip Top Driving, Or Up Mt. Washington." *Lewiston (Me.) Evening Journal*, July 30, 1904, p. 13. [Also printed as a pamphlet entitled *The Climb to the Clouds and How It Impressed Me* (circa 1904). Reprinted: *Stanley Museum Quarterly* XXIII:1, pp. 19-22 (Winter 2004).]

___ 1919. "Biographical Sketch." In *Theories Worth Having and Other Papers by Francis Edgar Stanley*. Boston: Augusta M. Stanley.

Stanley, Carlton F. 1945. "Early History of the Stanley Company." In *Floyd Clymer's Historical Motor Scrapbook, Steam Car Edition, Vol. I*. Los Angeles: Clymer Motors. [Reprinted in several editions.]

Stanley, F.E. 1916. "The Kingfield Rebellion." Unpublished manuscript prepared for the Kingfield Centennial, Stanley Museum Archives.

Stanley, F.O. 1899. "Motor Vehicles." Paper presented at the 20th National Assembly of the League of American Wheelmen, Providence, Rhode Island, February 3, 1899. Manuscript, Stanley Museum Archives.

___ 1930. "The Stanley Steamer." Paper, "Read at the Ladies' Night of the Tuesday Club of Newton, Massachusetts, on May 20, 1930." Typescript, Stanley Museum Archives. [An edited version of this paper was published in Derr 1932: pp. 45-59.]

___ circa 1930. "Maple Syrup." Unfinished manuscript, Stanley Museum Archives. [Published: *Stanley Museum Newsletter* X:1, pp. 13-14 (March 1991).]

___ 1934. "The Kingfield Rebellion, July 1863." Typescript, May 15, 1934, Stanley Museum Archives.

___ 1936. "The Stanley Dry Plate." Typescript, May 15, 1936, Stanley Museum Archives. [Reprinted: *Stanley Museum Newsletter* VI:1, pp. 9,14,16 (March 1987); VI:2, pp. 8-9 (June 1987); VI:3, pp. 8-10 (December 1987).]

___ circa 1940. "The Stanley Twins." Unfinished manuscript, Stanley Museum Archives.

Stanley, Flora J. R. T. 1899. *The First Ascent of Mount Washington in an Automobile – made in the Summer of 1899 by Mr. and Mrs. Freelan O. Stanley*. Newton, Massachusetts: Flora J. R. T. Stanley. [Reprinted as "First Motor Carriage Ascent of Mt. Washington, August 31, 1899," in Davis, Susan S. (ed.), *1899-1999 Centennial, First Auto Up Mt. Washington: Commemorative Program*. Kingfield, Maine: The Stanley Museum, c1999.]

Stanley, Raymond W. 1932. *The Twins, including The Mink Story and Others*, "As retold by R. W. S." Boston: Raymond W. Stanley. [Portions of this work published in *Stanley Museum Quarterly* XXI:1, pp. 10-13 (Winter 2002).]

___ 1942. "Steam Lore," *The Bulb Horn* III:3, p.10 (July 1942).

___ 1945. "The Stanley Steamer." In *Floyd Clymer's Historical Motor Scrapbook, Steam Car Edition, Vol. I*. Los Angeles: Clymer Motors. [Reprinted in several editions.]

___ 1963. "Evaporating the Stanley Steamer Myth." *Automobile Quarterly* II:2, pp. 120-129 (Summer 1963).

___ 1984. Interview by Thomas C. Marshall, Jr., Brent C. Campbell, and Art Hart, Kingfield, Maine. Audio recording, Stanley Museum Archives.

Stanley Family Reunion. 1981. Transcript of conversations recorded during the Stanley family gathering June 7, 1981, Kingfield, Maine. Kingfield, Maine: Stanley Museum, c1982.

Tucker, A. B. 1906. "How an American Made World's Auto Records." *The Illustrated Outdoor News*, January 27, 1906, p. 6.

Tuscher, Vincent J. 1952. "Record-Breaking Steamer." *Speed Age*, pp. 40-41, 75 (May 1952).

Woodbury, George. 1950. *The Story of a Stanley Steamer*. New York: W. W. Norton & Company.

LIST OF ILLUSTRATIONS

Chapter 4: Mr. Stanley, His Foreman, and His Flying Canoe.

Chapter 5: Let The Races Begin.

Chapter 6: "Bravo, Stanley!"

Chapter 7: "For $1,000 or an Orange."

Chapter 8: Can Steam Go the Distance?

147

Chapter 9: "Old Man Stanley."

Chapter 10: "Black Friday."

Chapter 11: Beaten by "Just a Trifle."

INDEX